Google

®

DATE DUE

DEMCO, INC. 38-2931

Google Voice™ FOR DUMMIES®

by Bud E. Smith & Chris Dannen

Foreword by Craig Walker & Vincent Paquet
Google Voice Team

WILEY

Wiley Publishing, Inc.

Google Voice™ For Dummies®

Published by
Wiley Publishing, Inc.
111 River Street
Hoboken, NJ 07030-5774

www.wiley.com

Copyright © 2010 by Wiley Publishing, Inc., Indianapolis, Indiana

Published by Wiley Publishing, Inc., Indianapolis, Indiana

Published simultaneously in Canada

WILEY

About the Authors

Bud Smith grew up on the Left Coast and moved north — he couldn't go much further west — to Silicon Valley 20 years ago to work for a technology startup. He's an experienced technology author, computer magazine editor, product manager, and marketer. He's been writing about online communications since the early days of 14.4Kbps modems — about 1 percent of typical broadband speed today. His phones and other portable devices have included early Palms and BlackBerrys and worked for Apple when it introduced Newton, a distant ancestor of the iPhone he carries today. His books include *Creating Web Pages For Dummies,* now in its 9th Edition, and *Marketing Online For Dummies*. He holds a Master of Science degree in Information Systems from the London School of Economics.

Chris Dannen grew up and works on the Right Coast and is currently based in New York City. His technology interests include a focus on telecommunications, and Chris has used and written about iPhones, BlackBerry phones, Android phones, and many others. Chris writes for a variety of technology magazines and Web sites, including Fast Company. He was an early adopter of GrandCentral, predecessor to Google Voice, using it to fend off — uh, that is, better communicate with — the legions of PR people that magazine editors are in constant communication with. He's written two books about iPhone application development. He is completing a Master of Arts degree in journalism from Harvard University.

Dedication

We would like to dedicate this book to our families, who have been endlessly supportive as we spent equally endless hours intently studying (okay, playing with) the latest and greatest phone technology in our quest to better understand Google Voice and its place in the future of telecommunications.

Authors' Acknowledgments

Katie Mohr and Tiffany Ma, our acquisitions editors, had the vision to support us in beginning this project within days of the announcement of Google Voice and the patience to see it through many changes and new developments to launch. Beth Taylor, our project editor, patiently shepherded the manuscript through revisions and updates. Lynne Johnson, our technical editor, brought both depth and breadth of experience as well as a long-time Android fan's perspective to our work. Mary Bednarek, executive acquisitions editor, lent help and encouragement at important junctures.

Publisher's Acknowledgments

We're proud of this book; please send us your comments through our online registration form located at `http://dummies.custhelp.com`. For other comments, please contact our Customer Care Department within the U.S. at 877-762-2974, outside the U.S. at 317-572-3993, or fax 317-572-4002.

Some of the people who helped bring this book to market include the following:

Acquisitions, Editorial, and Media Development

Project Editor: Beth Taylor

Acquisitions Editor: Katie Mohr, Tiffany Ma

Copy Editor: Beth Taylor

Technical Editor: Lynne d. James

Editorial Manager: Jodi Jensen

Editorial Assistant: Amanda Graham

Sr. Editorial Assistant: Cherie Case

Cartoons: Rich Tennant
   (`www.the5thwave.com`)

Composition Services

Project Coordinator: Kristie Rees

Layout and Graphics: Ana Carrillo, Christine Williams

Proofreader: Christopher M. Jones

Indexer: Potomac Indexing, LLC

Publishing and Editorial for Technology Dummies

   Richard Swadley, Vice President and Executive Group Publisher

   Andy Cummings, Vice President and Publisher

   Mary Bednarek, Executive Acquisitions Director

   Mary C. Corder, Editorial Director

Publishing for Consumer Dummies

   Diane Graves Steele, Vice President and Publisher

Composition Services

   Debbie Stailey, Director of Composition Services

Contents at a Glance

Table of Contents

Foreword

···

A few years ago, we looked at all the phones in our own lives and discovered things had become quite complicated: one for the office, another at home, a cell phone (maybe even two) for taking calls on the run. We had to remember a different number for each device, and so did our friends, family, and co-workers. We missed important calls whenever we stepped away from the desk or forgot a cell phone at home, and checking voicemail on all those phones proved more trouble than it was worth. We rarely listened to voice messages, and when we did, it was only to delete them.

The idea for GrandCentral, which later became Google Voice, was born out of our own frustrations. We worked on web-based technologies before and quickly realized the Internet could help everyone gain more control over their phones and communications. We eventually organized the product around a single phone number that links all of your phones together, a single voicemail box that is accessible from any of those phones with all of your messages saved online, and many features we all wished for, like voicemail transcription and a phone spam filter to keep unwanted callers away.

Today, the Google Voice team remains focused on making your communications better and we will continue developing new features that give you more control over how you communicate. We hope you enjoy exploring Google Voice through this book and thank you for using the service

Craig Walker and Vincent Paquet

Google Voice

Introduction

· ·

*G*oogle Voice may be one of those rare trifectas — a product that's truly new, truly important, and immediately recognized as such from the time it first appears. Why might this be?

Google Voice combines three of the most important trends of our time: the increasing power of our computers; the even faster-growing power of cell phones and smartphones; and the meteoric rise of Google to become the world's leading Internet innovator.

Google Voice brings all this energy together in a product that's free, easy to use, and available to anyone in the United States. If you have at least one phone and at least occasional access to a computer, then you can find immediate benefit in Google Voice. People with multiple phones and a lot of contacts — journalists, bloggers, salespeople, and savvy PR pros — are among the first to adopt it. Hundreds of thousands more are expected to follow.

Google Voice is simply a layer on top of the tools you already use, yet allows these tools to do much more than they did before. It's still unknown, of course, just how much of a difference it will make over time, but its status as one of the most important new offerings of recent years has been acclaimed by newspapers, magazines, and the technorati alike.

But what about you, the new Google Voice user? Although it's easy to get some superficial use out of Google Voice, it's a deep product. To really take advantage of it means changing some existing habits and reorganizing the way you communicate. It also requires you to learn a few other new tools, such as dialer apps that run on smartphones. Luckily, all this work is likely to pay off handsomely. Effort you put into Google Voice today will pay off for a long time to come.

So enjoy the time you spend learning your way around Google Voice, and use this book to guide your experimentation with it. Google Voice is exciting and will change the world, at least a bit. You should have some fun as you learn to use it to its utmost capabilities.

About This Book

It's *about* one of the most exciting products around — and it's *about* 360 pages long.

What do you find in these pages? The best and most in-depth guide to using Google Voice around. You learn how to thoroughly integrate Google Voice into your daily life and work. We show you how to use Google Voice along with the cell phones, land line phones, and computer(s) you already have and use every day, and how to shop for new gear that works best with your new Google Voice communication style.

We go beyond Google Voice itself to show you how it can best be used in organizations large and small, and how to get the most out of dialers that run on the leading smartphones from Apple, RIM BlackBerry, and manufacturers who use Google's Android mobile operating system. We even discuss etiquette for the best use of Google Voice in your work and personal life.

Foolish Assumptions

We've done our best to cram this book with information and insights, but almost no one will read it all the way through save our long-suffering editors. That's because you are likely to discover some of the functionality of Google Voice on your own or from friends and colleagues before, during and after the time you spend reading this book.

You're likely to need the chapter on one smartphone, but not all the chapters on all the smartphones we discuss. You may decide that you need to start with the chapter on Google Voice etiquette or that you never need it, and could have written a better guide to the topic yourself.

What do you need to use this book? A smartphone is enough, or a phone of any type and access to a computer. The more phones you're responsible for — whether that's just your own phones or also those of friends, family or coworkers — the more widely you'll use what you learn here. Even a single phone, though, can be used better if you know how to get the most out of Google Voice in managing it.

You do need to be an experienced user of the Web and an experienced user of your phone so you can change settings. If you're not super Web-savvy, don't worry — we talk you through everything. This book can save you time and prevent common mistakes, but Google Voice isn't rocket science.

The figures in this book show up-to-date Windows screen shots for a consistent appearance. Being Web-based, though, the instructions and steps in this book work equally well for Windows, the Macintosh, a netbook, or a smartphone — almost any device that can run a Web browser.

Conventions Used in This Book

The _conventions_ in this book are standard ways of communicating specific types of information, such as instructions and steps. (One example of a convention is the use of italics for newly introduced words that are then defined — as with the word "conventions" in the first sentence of this paragraph.)

Here are the conventions for this book:

- New terms are printed in _italics_, and then defined shortly afterward.

- Information used in specific ways is formatted in a specific typeface. In this book, one of the most common kinds of information displayed this way is Web addresses; that is, text you enter into the address bar of a Web browser to visit a specific Web site or Web page. Web addresses appear in special text like this: `www.dummies.com`.

- Google Voice is fast-paced and evolving, as are the Web sites that support it and describe it, and the products, such as dialers, that work with it. By the time you read this book, some of the product names and URLs listed in it may have changed. For updates, please visit our blog at `www.gvdaily.com`.

- Representative browser versions appear among the figures.

- Related, brief pieces of information are displayed in bulleted lists, such as the bulleted list that you're reading right now.

- Numbered lists are used for instructions that you must follow in a particular sequence. This book has many sequential steps that tell you just how to perform the different tasks that, when taken together, can make you a successful Web author.

How This Book Is Organized

We began this book very soon after Google Voice was announced, before it was available to anyone outside Google and a few ladies and gentlemen of the press and early adopters. We finished it just a few months later, which is breakneck speed for a major book project about such a new product. During that time some things in the real world and our understanding of how to get the most out of Google Voice both evolved.

So things changed along the way. And we began, and will continue to maintain, a blog at `www.gvDaily.com` to help describe and help you with any changes that occur after this book goes to print.

Part I: Setting up Google Voice

If you set up a mousetrap correctly, you end up minus a bit of cheese and plus a trapped mouse. It's the same with Google Voice. If you make a strong beginning with it, you get results without a lot of additional effort. We devote Part I to showing you all the things that people who don't have this book may trip over in setting up Google Voice.

Part II: Maximizing Your Voice

Google Voice has four layers of settings — for your phones, for individual callers, for groups of callers and for all callers as a whole. It can be controlled live from a phone before or during a call, from any Web-enabled phone, from a smartphone and from a Web browser. Getting the most out of all these settings takes some doing, but don't be intimidated. We make it easy for you to get the most out of Google Voice, and to save time and money as you do so.

Part III: Maximizing Your Handset

If you have a cell phone, no matter what kind it is, Google Voice will help you get the most out of it. We plumb the mysteries of the Google Voice Mobile site and Google Voice dialer apps for iPhone, Android phones, and BlackBerry phones to help you become a savvy, capable power user in very little time.

Part IV: Playing Well with Others

Google Voice works well with Gmail, other Google Apps offerings and even a third party tool, Gizmo5. It also "plays well" in small business and the enterprise. We show you how to get all these players operating as a team.

Part V: The Part of Tens

You only get one chance to make a first impression, and that's as true in your use of Google Voice as it is anywhere else in life. Our Part of Tens chapters show you how to use the emerging etiquette for Google Voice to make it a positive for all those you come into contact with.

Icons Used in This Book

 Marks information that you need to keep in mind as you work.

 Points to things you may want to know but don't necessarily need to know. You can skip these and read the text, skip the text and read these, or go ahead and read both.

 Flags specific information that may not fit in a step or description but that helps you create better Web pages.

 Points out anything that may cause a problem.

 Using Google Voice can save you a great deal of time. This icon highlights information that will help you save time.

 Using Google Voice can also save you a great deal of money. This icon highlights information that will help you save money.

Part I

Setting Up Google Voice

The 5th Wave   By Rich Tennant

"For 30 years I've put a hat and coat on to make sales calls and I'm not changing now just because I'm doing it on the Web in my living room."

In this part . . .

Google Voice changes and improves the way your phones work for you. Here we show you how to get it set up right the first time, including how to save time and money with Google Voice.

Chapter 1

A Day in Your Google Voice Life

Google Voice is a marvelous mashup — all the power and control we associate with computers at their best, combined with the warmth, spontaneity, and flexibility of talking to other people. Although you need to spend some time figuring out how to get the most out of Google Voice, the service can ultimately simplify your life.

Google Voice is not only powerful and capable in its own right, but it works alongside other Google services. You can get a lot out of it for personal use, and take it even further in a business context.

Google Voice is not to be confused with Google's Voice Search, which allows you to search the Internet by speaking words out loud; nor with Google Talk, a service for using a computer directly for text messaging and computer-to-computer voice conversations. Both of these are valuable services, but they don't overlap with Google Voice, which allows you to fuse all your telephone lines into one central, Web-accessible hub.

Google Voice helps you manage real live phones, with all the voice quality and convenience that only a telephone has, along with voicemail for all of them. Unlike Voice over Internet Protocol (VOIP) services, Google Voice lets you add the convenience of the Web while preserving the voice quality and convenience that only a telephone can offer.

And Google Voice saves you time, money, and hassle. Anyone can improve their life with Google Voice — while businesses can do even more, by cutting costs and adding services in a way that can not only reduce expenses, but really move the needle on what a business can offer customers.

Discovering Google Voice

Google Voice reduces the cost of calls, making national calls free and international ones much cheaper — perhaps a tenth the cost of a direct-dialed cell phone call. And Google Voice notifies you of voicemail messages and allows you to record phone calls, so that you can manage conversations as well as the phones themselves.

Here's how it works: Google Voice gives you a single, virtual phone number, from almost any area code in the U.S. that you'd like. That number, in turn, can ring any or all of your other phone lines — your work phone, cell phone, and so on, meaning that you can be reached with just one number.

Google Voice also changes the way you can handle calls. Like any phone service, it records voicemail messages. And it sends you notification that a voicemail message is waiting.

You can also screen callers and listen in on voicemail messages before deciding whether to pick up the call, just like an old-fashioned answering machine. And it lets you block callers, send certain numbers straight to voicemail, and set up custom mailbox greetings for discrete callers. You can record calls on the fly, send and receive SMS text messages, and keep your entire call history online.

All of these capabilities were part of GrandCentral, the service that Google bought in 2007 and made the foundation for Google Voice. Google Voice adds several new capabilities.

One is support for text messaging, or SMS, from your GrandCentral phone number. This feature was missing in GrandCentral but is added in Google Voice, making the service much more seamless to use. Figure 1-1 shows the SMS interface, new with Google Voice.

A wonderful bonus, though, is very inexpensive international calls — a few cents a minute to most countries, instead of ten or more cents, or even the better part of a dollar, per minute from different land line and cell phone plans.

But it also allows you to access your voicemail messages and listen to them online. You can forward a message to a friend or embed it in a Web site. Most amazingly, Google Voice transcribes your voicemail messages instantly — not perfectly, but surprisingly well, in most cases — so that you can read them on-screen, in your e-mail inbox, or as a text message. So if you're staying in touch by e-mail, as more and more people do these days, you don't have to leave *text mode* to stay in touch with, manage, and respond to your voice messages.

Google Voice also supports conference calls and call merging, so you can easily (and cheaply) plan a conference call. You can also spontaneously expand a typical two-person call to include more people. This is a major improvement for all of us who have not been able to make a conference call happen when we badly needed one. Google Voice also lets you switch an incoming call from one phone to another without hanging up and redialing and to record part or all of an incoming call.

Figure 1-1:
Google
Voice keeps
you from
making an
SMS of
things.

Google Voice is potentially useful for anyone, but it offers an additional level of ease and utility when used with a smartphone. Google Voice-specific applications are also already available for iPhone and Google Android.

There's much more, as we describe throughout this book. But you can already see that Google Voice can make a big difference in how — and how effectively — you can use your phones.

Waking Up with Google Voice

Let's begin with a typical workday as it might unfold for you using Google Voice. Google Voice makes you more capable and accessible with regard to work, yet at the same time better able to protect your personal life and personal time.

Even if you don't work, much of the following applies to attending school, volunteering, keeping up with friends — anything that you do in groups. (And all things that you have more time for if you're not working.)

It's 6:20 a.m., and 10 minutes before your alarm goes off, your cell phone rings. Normally you would have no choice but to answer — what if it's important?

But with Google Voice in place, you know that the person must be important if the phone is even ringing, because you've sent all nonessential callers straight to voicemail for the night. Still, you let the call ring through to voicemail. It gets picked up by Google Voice, and you listen in to the message as it is being left. You hear that it's a message from a work colleague about the commute being crowded — something you need to know, but not a call you absolutely have to answer.

You're in control. In this case, you pick up the call as the message is finishing up so that you can thank your friend. But you could have just let it go if you wanted. You have the information you needed, and your blood pressure stayed low throughout.

You get up and get ready for work quickly. As you shower and eat your breakfast, you turn off the ringer on your cell phone, but both e-mail and voicemail messages show up onscreen in your e-mail inbox. (Figure 1-2 shows a transcribed voicemail message in Google Voice.) So you can glance at any messages shortly after they come in and respond to anything urgent.

You've planned a quick call to an overseas colleague before you leave for work, catching them at the end of their workday. In the past, you might have had to get to the office extra early to place the call, because it would be cheaper to make and appear on your employer's bill, not yours. But with Google Voice, the call is so cheap that you can make a quick call without worrying about the cost.

What were they thinking?

The Google Voice story starts with a company called Dialpad. Dialpad was a voice-over-IP (VOIP) pioneer, offering free phone calls over PCs. After crashing in the dot-com bust in 2001, Dialpad got new management — including Craig Walker and Vincent Paquet, later the co-founders of GrandCentral. The new management team made the company profitable and helped sell it off to Yahoo!, who used it as the core of their Yahoo! Voice offering, launched in 2005.

The key inspiration behind GrandCentral was the realization that the same technology that could help in making cheap calls could be used for call services as well. The key technical innovation in Google Voice is a *soft switch* — a telephone call switch, like an old-fashioned switchboard but built in software. The services offered first by GrandCentral, and now by Google Voice, are largely applications running on the soft switch.

Yet the "secret sauce" of GrandCentral, and now of Google Voice, is only partly capability. The other part is simplicity. As first implemented by the GrandCentral team, and cleaned up and improved with help from Google, Google Voice has one of the cleanest, simplest, most attractive, and easiest to use interfaces one could imagine for such powerful software. It took considerable self-discipline on the part of the development teams to make Google Voice so easy to use.

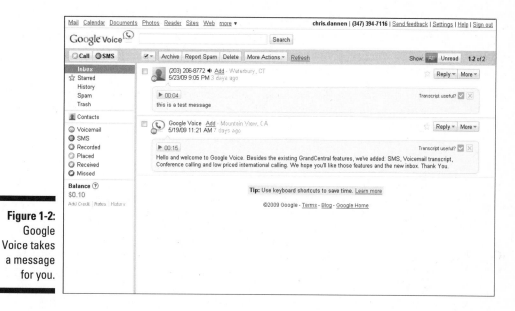

Figure 1-2:
Google
Voice takes
a message
for you.

You call into Google Voice from your home phone instead of your cell phone, because the cellular connection can get a bit weak where you live. Then you dial through to your colleagues, at just a few cents a minute, and get through your business. But the call goes a bit long and you switch it to your cell phone, without interruption, to say your goodbyes as you grab your coat and head out the door toward work.

At Work with Google Voice

On the drive to work, you dutifully wear your hands-free headset and listen as a couple of calls come in, but you don't answer; you just listen to the messages being left, knowing you can cut in if you have to, but otherwise deferring most of your responses until you get to the office. You're less tense than usual, because the ringing of the phone doesn't compel an immediate response on your part.

You get to the office on time. At work, you open the two e-mailed voice message transcriptions from Google Voice and send e-mails in response. Before a meeting, you open up Google Voice on your computer and block your personal contacts, sending their calls to voicemail (supported, of course, by e-mail transcriptions, so you can respond if anything urgent comes up).

At work, you receive an important call on your Google Voice number and then use Google Voice to record part of it. Google Voice automatically notifies the other party with a verbal message. You're able to concentrate fully on the call, with no need to take notes as a record. At the end of the call, you easily conference in your boss, despite that she is on the road, to add a few final words.

After the call is over, you forward the recording to the other party by e-mail (a practice that takes any possible tinge of rudeness out of recording someone on the phone). You then embed the recording in a blog post in your company's internal blog, so others can listen to and learn from it.

Throughout the day, you and your colleagues use Google Voice to flexibly manage calling groups for calls to individuals who are away from their desks or to the department as a whole. Many routine calls from vendors are automatically routed to voicemail or to other associates.

With Google Voice, it's much less important to be at your desk. Calls to your Google Voice number can go to both your desk phone and your cell phone, so you can use whichever one is handier. When you are away from your desk, a smartphone interface allows you to make and manage calls easily through the company's Google Voice account, saving you hassle and the company a lot of money while keeping control. Figure 1-3 shows an Android interface for Google Voice of a type that many organizations are likely to be using.

Figure 1-3: Use Google Voice to put home on the back burner for a while.

Whether at your desk or on the move, using the phone in a conference room or your cell phone, you no longer need to worry over the cost of long calls to faraway colleagues. For international calls, you only pay a few cents per minute. And you pay the same rates on your cell phone — which is more convenient, but uses minutes from your plan — or from a desk phone. You can even use any handy land line without worrying that you're putting charges on someone else's bill.

Relaxing at Home with Google Voice

At home, the most exciting thing that Google Voice makes possible is what *doesn't* happen.

You don't get any nasty surprises on your home phone voicemail that you missed a package delivery, or missed a plumber's appointment, or missed your last chance to pay your credit card bill without a penalty. You've received any such voicemail messages during the day, as both e-mail transcripts and as actual voice messages you can pick up from any Web browser or phone. And you've been able to deal with any occasional mini-crisis before it becomes a real one.

You don't get any calls during dinner, whether by yourself or with your family, because you can block all calls and leave a message that you'd be available later that evening. Figure 1-4 shows the Google Voice screen you use to make this happen quickly.

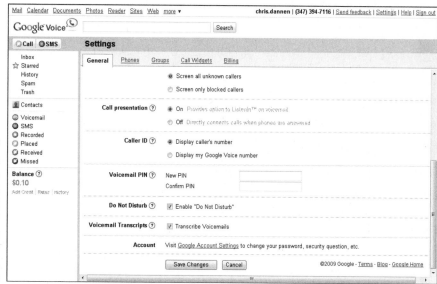

Figure 1-4: Use Google Voice to protect "home" from "phone" for a while.

And you don't get any sales calls, ever, because numbers from unknown callers don't ring your home phone anymore. They get sent straight to Google Voice's voicemail-with-e-mail-notification, so you can respond to any calls you actually want within a reasonable time and never have to bother with the rest. (Or, leave your phone open to calls but rely on Google Voice's telemarketer database to screen out the vast majority of sales calls.)

By using Google Voice, you can go to bed early without the phone ringing, watch a movie without interruption, or stay up late making cheap, Google Voice-enabled calls to friends, family members or work colleagues in various time zones around the world.

Grasping the Bottom Line

In the next few chapters, we show you how to get the most out of Google Voice. Managing phones from a computer interface is new to everyone, so there's going to be some cogitation involved, and it may take some practice.

So it's worth reflecting a bit on the benefits that Google Voice brings as inspiration for the effort you need to put in to really master it and make it your friend.

Saving time and reducing stress

With Google Voice, your phones ring less. Until Google Voice, your phones owned you — the very first ring of a phone was something you had to deal with right then and there. But Google Voice gives you so much control: allowing you to block calls, let a call roll through to voicemail — then answer it if needed — and more. Your phone rings less, and you're in control when it does.

Most of the early adopters of Google Voice are likely to be people with lots of phones to worry about. Google Voice cuts down on the relay game you play with friends and family. But its stress-reducing qualities shine through even if you only have a single landline phone plopped in the middle of your living room (or, as more and more people do, a single cell phone always near you).

How does it really save time, though? It's a question of attention. Before, each call and voicemail message commanded the same amount of attention, because you never knew the content of the call in advance. Now you can prioritize calls and voicemails the same way you do other forms of communication, such as e-mail and printed mail, which you can judge by a brief glance. That's why people have switched so much of their communications to e-mail from the phone; it's easier for our brains to filter by reading than by listening. Google Voice allows the achievement of a happy medium between e-mail-centric and voice-centric communication, each of which has its advantages.

Saving money

Today, overseas calls can cost several dollars even for a few minutes, especially from your cell phone. Even long-distance U.S. calls can add up. You either have to force a call to be shorter than it should be, or grin and bear the cost.

Conference calls are hard to set up, subject to hard and fast trunk line availability and time limits, and often very expensive indeed.

Calls home to loved ones while on a business trip can be very expensive, either burning a hole in your pocket or prompting quizzical questions from your boss — or his or her boss. And juggling time zones against access to cheaper calling opportunities is a nightmare.

Skype, Google Talk, and similar computer-supported calling services have made a dent in phone costs. But they lack the call quality and reliability of landline phones and the flexibility of mobile phones. Privacy is harder as well. (How many intensely private phone calls get made in Internet cafes and other public places to save money?)

Google Voice really gives you the best of the computer and the phone. You can make calls where you want to, when you want to, with exponentially less worry about cost. This aspect of Google Voice will improve many people's lives.

Gaining control

"Power to the people" was a popular theme of the flower children back in the 1960s. Google Voice, like a lot of other Internet-based technology, makes it a reality.

Although getting a grasp on all of the features takes some work, it's also really cool to be able to control what happens with your phones. And, beyond the personal level, it's even cooler to be able to control how groups of phones interact with groups of people. A few years ago, there was a lot of talk about PDAs — Personal Digital Assistants. Google Voice makes not only your own phones, but all the phones around you into little helpers that can accept some calls and push off the rest to another phone or voicemail (with e-mail accompaniment).

It may take years for the practice of phone management through Google Voice to catch up with so much that's new — the possibilities that Google Voice itself, smart phone interfaces, other add-on products and future improvements in all of the above will make possible. Some of Google Voice's capabilities and cost savings are likely to work their way into competing products as well, so the environment will change for everyone, Google Voice users or not. But the end result will be phones that do what people want them to do, rather than phones that make people do unneeded work.

Google Voice is going to change the way you and everyone else uses phones. So you've made a smart choice by adopting Google Voice, and by investing in this book to get the most out of it. You can start getting the benefits right away — you can save hassle, time, and money, while gaining control and getting out in front of a technology that may change all our lives.

Chapter 2

Getting Ready for Google Voice

· ·

· ·

Google Voice can change how you live. But that's only if you let it, by integrating Google Voice with the phone numbers and phones you already have.

When you first sign up for Google Voice, you select a new phone number with an area code originating in the state and area of your choosing. Then you can give out your new number and try to get people to start calling you on that one instead of your cell phone number and your other numbers.

However, getting people to change their habits is really hard. People tend to keep using your other numbers, evading your fancy new Google Voice setup (At least, not without some tricks, which we describe later in this chapter.)

Another reason why making this happen is difficult is that people — especially cell phone users — tend to call you back on the number you called them from. So even if they have your Google Voice number in their phone list, when you call them from, say, your home phone, they call you back on the same number — bypassing Google Voice.

But the whole secret of Google Voice is to have one number (your Google Voice number) that you control from a PC or smartphone, so in this book we let you in on how to use it most extensively. You don't really get much out of Google Voice unless people call you on your Google Voice number, or unless you forward various phones to Google Voice.

We also tell you how to arrange things so that you save a ton of money on your calls and get all the features and convenience of Google Voice, all the time — even if you already started using Google Voice the easy-seeming way. The key trick is to assign your cell phone number to Google Voice.

Assigning Your Cell Phone Number to Google Voice

So here's a change in your life: assign your cell phone number to Google Voice. Doing so removes the existing number from your cell phone, so you then have to get a new SIM and a new number for the phone itself.

Unfortunately, at the time of this writing, this capability is being hinted at and not yet offered. If it is on offer, seriously consider taking advantage of it, as described here. If not, see the steps in the next section for adding a new Google Voice number.

The No. 1 complaint people had about GrandCentral, the precursor to Google Voice, was that they couldn't assign their cell phone number as their GrandCentral number.

If you are able to assign your cell phone number to Google Voice, you pull a rather neat bait and switch. People think they're calling you on your cell phone, which means direct access to you wherever you happen to be. But really, they're calling Google Voice, which you can use to shield yourself from and manage incoming calls.

Figure 2-1 shows the before and after of how your cell phone works, before and after you assign your cell phone number to Google Voice.

Cell phone number =
Google Voice number
Secret cell phone number
Publicly known cell phone number

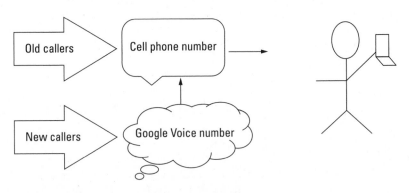

Figure 2-1:
Let your cell phone number (and Google Voice) be your umbrella.

Old callers → Cell phone number

New callers → Google Voice number

ADDING A NEW GOOGLE VOICE NUMBER

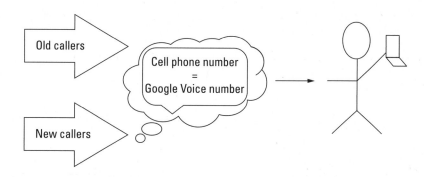

USING YOUR CELL PHONE NUMBER AS YOUR GOOGLE VOICE NUMBER

 You can assign your cell phone number to Google Voice even if you already have a GrandCentral or Google Voice account with its own phone number. Just create a new Google Voice account and assign your cell phone number to it. Then change the voicemail message on your old account to give your new number. You'll still get voicemail notifications e-mailed to you from the old account. You'll need to check for SMS text messages in the old account during any transition period.

 Don't keep too many Google Voice accounts over time, as the unused *ghost* account is potentially confusing to you and your callers. You should only keep an account if you're getting real value out of it. So if you stop using a Google Voice account, don't just permanently forward to a new account and forget. Create a plan to migrate people off the unused number and then delete it within a month or two.

If you get a new Google Voice number (it will cost $10 to change your Google Voice numbers, unless you are starting a new account) instead of assigning your cell phone number to Google Voice, a lot of people will still have (and call you on) your cell phone number. It will be tempting to return calls and texts to them directly from your cell phone, without dialing through Google Voice, perpetuating the problem. You can only fully move onto Google Voice with a determined effort.

Getting a New Number from Google Voice

You may decide to do things the easy way (easy at first, anyway) and get a new phone number from Google Voice. Or, if the ability to move your cell phone number to Google Voice has not yet become available, you may have no choice. The following sections go over a few tips for handling a brand new Google Voice phone number.

Choosing an area code

If you choose a number from Google Voice, you have a choice of area codes to use. People sometimes end up regretting the choice they make.

(You may face the same decision as to what area code you want if you buy a new cell phone or SIM. Don't think people won't drive a few miles or use mail order or online order to get a more desirable area code for their "cell"!)

Area codes were stable for a long time, and your area code used to give people a good idea of where you were from. As population, and the number of phone numbers per person grew, the U.S. split into more and more different area codes. San Diego County, for example, had one area code as recently as 25 years ago; now it has four. Los Angeles, which had three, now has 15! (See Figure 2-2 for a map.)

/www.nanpa.com/area_code_maps/display.html?cainset2

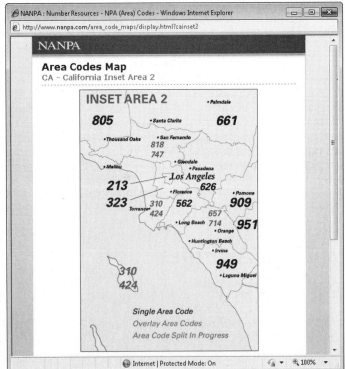

Figure 2-2:
Los Angeles
is up to 15
area codes.

Mobile phones have complicated the picture further, because many people keep the same mobile phone number even when they move (or after area code boundaries shift, moving their home and/or office phone into a new area code). And some areas have *overlays*, where older phone lines have one area code and newer phone lines have another.

So now, if you choose a Google Voice number when signing up, you have a difficult choice to make, if you live and work in different area codes. (With your mobile phone having either or perhaps yet a different one.) Which area code should you use for your Google Voice number?

Three issues are involved:

- ✔ **Ease of dialing from a landline:** People outside your chosen area code have to dial the extra digits for a different area code. (Your mobile phone callers will presumably use some kind of contacts list or speed dialing capability.)

- ✔ **The potential cost to your callers:** The cost issue is getting smaller because more and more people have free statewide or even, as with Google Voice, free national calling.

- ✔ **The coolness factor:** You might live in La Jolla, with the *cool* 858 area code that encompasses some desirable beach areas, but work in San Diego, with the blobby 619 area code that covers most of the rest of the city. Or you might even work in Escondido, part of the immense 760 code that includes most of California's inland desert. Which area code do you choose?

We can help you simplify the ease of dialing and cost issues. Who most often calls you from a landline phone? That's where ease of dialing matters, and often cost too, as landline phones don't have as many plan options and are less likely to dial through Google Voice.

And, who most often calls you on their own dime? (As the saying goes, even though pay phone calls now cost a lot more than a dime.)

These callers are likely to be your family and close friends. So you might want to consider using the same Google Voice area code as they do, if they're somewhere near your home and/or work.

Consider your own needs as well. If you'll be using landlines to dial into Google Voice (which gets you better call quality and more comfort and avoids using cell phone minutes), you'll want a number that's likely to be free from whatever land lines you're most frequently near.

In this case you may want to use the area code for where you work, rather than where you live, especially if the vast majority of your calls are going to be from work or from people calling in the area code where your work is located.

And for business purposes, you may want to get a Google Voice number in an area code that covers an area you want to expand to.

Using your new Google Voice number

Some of your friends and family may have several numbers for you, and call you at work some of the time, *and* on your mobile or at home — basically guessing where you are and leaving redundant voicemails.

This can be a hassle for you, especially if you're deliberately not picking up the call. Many of us have had the experience of having the desk phone ring at our job, ignored it, and then heard our cell phone ring with the same person trying again. This is especially annoying if you're having a conversation at the time.

So you want to get people to use your Google Voice number so that you can take full advantage of it. The best way is to leave messages on all your *real* phones asking people to call you on your new number instead. Then, be tough and only pick up on calls to your *real* phones that are coming to you through Google Voice.

The alternative is to use your Google Voice number as an additional number, a shield for less-wanted calls, and for cheap long-distance, international, and conference calling, as discussed in Chapter 7.

Using the new number as a secondary number was popular for GrandCentral numbers, back before Google Voice took over, because GrandCentral didn't have as many features. Also, the GrandCentral Web site was Flash-based, meaning it didn't work on many cell phones. GrandCentral also lacked dialers for mobile phones.

Most people found it too hard to fully convert people to the new number. Also, GrandCentral simply discarded SMS messages to a GrandCentral number, so people kept using their cell phones, with the GrandCentral number as an alternative.

Part of the reason GrandCentral got such great reviews, and Google Voice got such good early reviews as well, is that this kind of usage for Google Voice was perfect for media people — reporters and reviewers. Such people have a lot of casual contacts that they need to be in touch with some of the time, and to shield themselves from most of the time. GrandCentral kept users' real phone numbers private, and the e-mail alerts for voicemails were convenient, too. All this helped GrandCentral get strong early reviews and laid a good foundation for Google Voice with the journalistic community as well.

Saving Money on Your Cell Phone Bill

You can save money on your cell phone bill two ways: by switching to a less robust plan and by reducing the extras on your bill.

Here are the two main things you pay for on your cell phone plan and how to cut them with Google Voice:

- ✔ **Minutes:** You're paying for minutes of using your cell phone each month. With Google Voice, you can switch an incoming call to a nearby land line handset that's one of your verified Google Voice phones — as explained in the next chapter — by pressing * at any point during the call. All your Google Voice phones will ring; pick up the nearby landline hand set and continue the call.

  For outgoing calls, you can still use a land line hand set, but you have to dial Google Voice from the handset, and then dial the destination number as well. You can use your cell phone for looking up the number you need, but you still have to dial a bunch of digits.

- ✔ **Texts:** You can send texts from Google Voice using the Web interface or using a dialer program on your cell phone with no impact on your bill. You still pay for texts you receive because they'll be forwarded through to your cell phone.

The extras, both planned and unplanned, can multiply your bill several times over. Trim your bills by trying out the following tips with Google Voice:

- ✔ **Making phone calls to other countries:** Google Voice cuts the cost of these calls to pennies a minute — 2¢a minute to China or landlines in France, for example. If you make the call from your cell phone, you're still using cell phone minutes, but you can avoid calls that can total hundreds of dollars in a month with this feature. You can also cut out *bolt-ons* on your bill, where you pay a set fee up front for cheaper access to specific countries.

- ✔ **Making phone calls while in another country:** Google Voice will not make your cell phone ring while you're in another country. Much of the time, this is a good thing, because it avoids all sorts of costs and time zone hassles; you control costs by always initiating the call. When you call Google Voice to initiate or manage calls from your cell, it's a roaming call back to a U.S. number, so you want to keep your minutes down.

  You may find that you need to give out your *real* cell phone number to some people so they can reach you immediately, which undermines your use of your Google Voice number. Alternatively, you can pick up a cheap, pay as you go SIM or cell phone while you're in-country. (These are common in other countries, though rare in America.) Doing this saves you money on in-country calls and gives you a number that can be rung from anywhere.

One if by land

Landline phones have several advantages when used with Google Voice:

✔ The landline phone is likely to have unlimited free local calling minutes, even on low-cost plans, so your calls to a local Google Voice number are free.

✔ No problems with getting a signal.

✔ No running down your cell phone battery.

✔ Usually, better voice quality.

✔ Often, more comfortable handsets.

The combination of these features makes long calls in particular much easier and worry-free.

Brief your U.S. friends and colleagues about the time zone difference before you travel to avoid those painful middle-of-the-night phone calls.

We describe how to use Google Voice with VOIP services that can save you more money on top of what Google Voice saves you, in Chapter 15.

You may well be on a 12-month or 18-month cell phone plan, perhaps as part of the deal that got you a free phone. You have to keep paying the minimum you agreed to, even though you may not be using all of your included allowances. When the time period of the plan runs out, you can switch to a lower-use or pay as you go plan.

The only problem here is that lots of people get their phones for free, or highly discounted, along with a robust cell phone plan with a lot of minutes and text messages included. The package of a free or discounted phone and a relatively expensive plan does cost you money; however, the cost is well hidden. To use Google Voice, you want a robust smartphone so that you can run the best dialers and Google Voice's mobile Web interface, but you must pay for it directly if it's not built into a plan.

If you consistently underuse your cell phone minutes and text allowance once you switch to Google Voice, consider a pay-as-you-go-plan. Look for one that auto-recharges from your credit card or bank account, so you never run out of minutes (which is unacceptably embarrassing on a business call).

At least one major provider now offers free Wi-Fi calling; calls are free if your phone can get a Wi-Fi connection. (Wi-Fi calling is good in many homes and offices; not so good in places where you have to pay by the hour for Wi-Fi, then may not reach the party you're dialing!)

If you use Wi-Fi calling, it will almost certainly cut your use of minutes and text, but perhaps in unpredictable ways. Consider a pay as you go plan with the Wi-Fi calling feature, if the combination is available.

Keep an eye open for good deals on cell phones with pay-as-you-go deals. Special deals with pay-as-you-go will be how you get phones going forward. This new dispensation should boost Google Android phones, which may be able to offer the ultimate in integration with Google Voice.

Getting a New Cell Phone for Google Voice

Sooner or later, you may want to get a new cell phone that can help you get the most out of Google Voice.

To use Google Voice, you probably want a smartphone — a phone with a big screen that can do a lot, including surfing the Web, getting e-mail, and playing back your Google Voice voicemail messages.

Web capability allows you to use the special mobile version of the Google Voice Web page to manage Google Voice. (There's still some work to do for Google here – it's not as cool as the Gmail mobile Web page or Gmail application on various smartphones.) And e-mail capability allows you to conveniently view the voicemail transcriptions that Google Voice sends you.

You can also use a non-smart cell phone and do all your Google Voice and e-mail management from your computer, in which case just about any phone will do.

But if you do go the smartphone route, what do you want in a cell phone to use with Google Voice? Look for a few key items:

- ✔ **Big screen:** The Google Voice Web page works best, and you can see more of your e-mail call transcriptions on a big, high-resolution screen.

- ✔ **Good keyboard:** Google Voice now fully supports text messaging, and you also want to receive and possibly reply to voicemail transcriptions on your mobile phone. So you should feel comfortable typing entire sentences on your new phone.

- ✔ **A strong Google Voice dialer application**: You can just use one dialer program, but the more there are for your phone, the more likely you are to find a really good one.

- ✔ **Touch screen**: Maybe. For some people, doing more with a cell phone means that a touch screen, especially a multi-touch screen that recognizes gestures, is all the more valuable. For others, it's an unneeded extra. Try it and decide for yourself.

Table 2-1 lists major types of mobile phones and the screen size and resolution, keyboard type and number of dialer apps for Google Voice. We ordered the list by the area of the screen, which is the most important stat for how good a Web browsing or e-mail reading experience you will have. (Using Web pages on a smartphone has been compared to looking into a room through a keyhole. It helps to have the biggest keyhole you can get!)

As mentioned, the list of phones is ordered by the area of the screen. (The resolution, in dots per inch, is important too but is similar for all these screens, about 160dpi.) Note that the diagonal measurement of a screen is a bit deceptive; a cut of only about 10 percent in the diagonal measurement, from 3.5 inches on the iPhone 3G to 3.2 inches on the BlackBerry Storm, results in a drop of nearly 20 percent in the screen area, from 6 square inches on the iPhone to 4.9 square inches on the BlackBerry Storm.

For a competing phone — or, perhaps, a possible future offering from Apple — to offer something comparable to an iPhone-type experience, it needs to have a screen with a diagonal measurement not very much less than 3.5 inches.

Of course, this list will quickly go out of date, but it gives you an idea of the options that were out there around the time that Google Voice was introduced, in mid-2009.

Table 2-1	Phones and Specs for Google Voice			
Phone type	**Screen size/ resolution**	**Keyboard type**	**Dialer apps**	**Notes**
iPhone 3G	3.5" diagonal 6 sq. in. 480 x 320	Onscreen keys	0*	Huge early target for GC and GV adoption
BlackBerry Storm	3.2" diagonal 4.9 sq. in. 480 x 360	Onscreen keys	2	Google has a very good app for BlackBerry
Google Android myTouch	3.2" diagonal 4.7 sq. in. 480 x 320	Onscreen keys	1	Google has an excellent app for Android
BlackBerry Bold	2.6" diagonal 3.1 sq. in. 480 x 320	Full keyboard	2	Google has a very good app for BlackBerry
BlackBerry Curve	2.4" diagonal 2.8 sq. in. 320 x 240	Full keyboard	2	Google has a very good app for BlackBerry
BlackBerry Pearl	2.2" diagonal 2 sq. in. 240 x 260	Dual-use keyboard	2	Google has a very good app for BlackBerry

See the sidebar "Apple and Google Voice dialers" for details.

We haven't seen any statistics yet, but our anecdotal impression is that the iPhone has the lead as a Google Voice tool in the early running. It seems that iPhone had the most share among GrandCentral users and among people who got an early Google Voice account as well. iPhone users are also big users of Google search, Google Voice Search, and other Google apps.

Many of these people have multiple cell phones, such as a BlackBerry for work and an iPhone for personal use, but the iPhone is what they pull out to impress people. And the iPhone has the key feature needed to get the most out of Google Voice: a big screen. In fact, the biggest screen, by a good margin, of any leading phone. Unfortunately, the only choice iPhone users have at this writing is the Google Voice mobile Web site. (See the sidebar "Apple and Google Voice dialers" for details.)

BlackBerry smartphones tend to have smaller screens, although the Blackberry Storm has an only slightly smaller (about 20 percent less area), and slightly higher-resolution screen than the iPhone. It also, like the iPhone but unlike other BlackBerry smartphones, lacks a physical keyboard.

BlackBerry phones are more often issued by big organizations, and as such are less likely to have their numbers assigned to Google Voice. As mentioned above, it's not uncommon for people to have both an iPhone, for personal use, and a BlackBerry that gets used more for e-mail than anything. It will be interesting to see how these two-phone users integrate Google Voice into their lives.

The most potential for Google Voice seems to be with the Google Android phones, with the parent company is the same as for Google Voice. These phones meet the key needs any Google Voice user has: a great smartphone with a fully integrated dialer, so no extra steps at all for calling, receiving, or managing calls or SMS text messages.

We look into how to use major Google Voice dialers in Part III. But if you're thinking about a new cell phone, think about how you're going to use it with Google Voice as you make the call (uh, the decision, that is).

Apple and Google Voice dialers

In a controversial move, Apple pulled existing Google Voice apps from the App Store and denied Google's application for a new app in August 2009. The Federal Communications Commission has officially inquired into the reasons.

It's unknown what will happen going forward: whether the existing apps may be restored or whether Google's free dialer, which would pretty much put the existing apps out of business, will be approved. We have coverage of Google's free dialer in Chapter 12 and Chapter 13, and have retained coverage of the other apps in Chapter 11.

Handling Your Home Phone

With people so often out of the house during the day, managing one's home phone is one of the toughest tasks in modern life. In some homes, the landline doesn't get used much, except for those sales calls that still sneak through. Yet in other phones the land line is used frequently. Many young people don't have land line phones at all.

Those of us who do have a landline phone can sympathize. Having the phone ring in the middle of the night is one of the small nightmares of modern life. Having dinners, baths, conversations, and naps interrupted by the phone is one of the great hassles — a source of both humor and frustration.

If you are among the majority who still do have a home phone number, here's a suggestion: forward it to Google Voice, much or all of the time. That way you can manage calls, get voicemail transcriptions, screen out sales calls and on and on.

Forwarding your landline may require you to pay for forwarding capability through your phone company or by buying a new landline phone. Once you do this, though, you get a lot of control. And a lot of power. With a landline phone used with Google Voice, you can pay very little for phone service that includes free local calls and not much else. This gives you a phone with excellent reception and call quality, no worries about keeping the phone charged, and, often, more comfortable handsets. Google Voice gives you everything else you need.

If you forward a phone, such as a landline phone, to Google Voice, as we suggest, you can't then forward calls from Google Voice to that phone. You can still call Google Voice from it for outgoing calls, though.

Instead of forwarding your home phone number, there's a similar method for accomplishing the same goal, especially useful for homes with several people in them: turn off the ringer on your home phone (a hammer may help) and leave a message on your answering machine or answering service giving an individual number for each person in your home. This will quickly train people away from using your home phone number, without disabling it completely. (Except for whatever part you've hit with a hammer.)

Handling Work Phones

If you work for someone else, you're likely to have a desk phone with a direct dial number, an internal extension number, or both. You may or may not have someone to answer the phone for you if you're not there, but even if you do, they're unlikely to be on duty all the times that you're at work.

In many organizations, you may also have a work-issued cell phone. Your work-issued cell phone may be *locked down* (intended to be used in a prescribed way, no changes desired, or perhaps not even allowed). Or you may be expected to use your personal cell phone for work purposes when required.

In these cases, the only way you can use Google Voice is to forward your work phone number(s) to your personal Google Voice account when you're away from your desk or don't wish to be disturbed and want the voicemail messages to go someplace where they're easier to manage. (This is different from assigning your work phone number to Google Voice, which may not be possible: Google Voice doesn't work with extension phones.) Check policies at your office; organizations can be expected to try to get on top of this quickly. Also, experiment to see whether you can assign your work phone number to Google Voice if you so desire (and if your employer's policies allow it; see the next paragraph).

If you're employed by someone else, forwarding your phone to Google Voice may be okay, but you really shouldn't give out your Google Voice number as your work phone number without explicit permission. Doing so can interfere with your employer's procedures for managing phones and phone calls — and will interfere with you, too, when you change jobs. Finding out that you've used a Google Voice account as your work phone number could cause the head of your CIO (Chief Information Officer) to implode!

Here's an example of the problems such a step could cause: Using your Google Voice number as a work number may help you poach clients from your old employer. Even this specific example doesn't sum up the whole problem; large organizations spend a good deal of time on issues of governance and control that specifically exclude things like an individual (such as you) routing business calls through an outside company (such as Google).

Creating a Google Account

Before you set up Google Voice, you need to have a Google account. This section shows you how to sign up for a Google account if you don't already have one. This section has some tips that may be useful if you decide to create a new Google account for your Google Voice use.

The most basic reason for creating a Google account first is that Google won't let you do it any other way. But Google Voice is expected to have cool integration features with other Google applications that also require a Google account, so your effort may pay off in any event.

If you already have a Google Apps account — especially if you're paying for it, as larger organizations have to do — you might think that you already have an account you can use for Google Voice. But, while sensible, you'd be wrong. If you already have a Google Apps account, create a new Google account just for use with Google Voice, using the steps later in this chapter. (Unfortunately, your contacts from your Google Apps account won't be imported into Google Voice either.)

One key expected feature for Google Voice is enhanced integration with Gmail. And Gmail is already pretty cool, with some of its advantages being particularly pronounced when used with Google Voice:

- **Huge storage:** Gmail launched with 2GB of storage per user, which was huge at the time and the allocation is constantly growing, for both new and existing users. At this writing, it's grown past 7GB and shows no sign of stopping. When you start getting your voicemails as e-mail attachments and wanting to access and store them flexibly, huge storage will be of, well, huge importance!

- **Great flexibility:** Gmail is fully flexible in terms of forwarding and copying e-mails to other accounts. (Some other free e-mail Web services have less flexibility.) This is great for students (who use their school accounts more or less at different times of year), young professionals (who tend to change jobs a lot) and so on. And it's great for use with Google Voice.

- **Integration with other e-mail applications and phones:** Gmail has both POP3 and, lacking from many providers, IMAP support. This makes it easy and flexible to fully integrate with Outlook, Apple Mail, and other e-mail applications.

- **Special phone applications:** Google creates special applications for Gmail or Google access on various cell phones. The BlackBerry Gmail app is one of the coolest around, as is Gmail support on the iPhone. Android has excellent Gmail integration.

- **Integration with Google Apps:** Google has a whole set of applications called Google Apps, including word processing, a spreadsheet, a calendar, support for your own domain name and more. Integration with Gmail, and for each app with the others, varies. You can ignore these other Google offerings or run a small or medium-sized business off them, at very low cost. Google Voice is separate from Google Apps, so how to get them working together is up to you. See Chapter 16 for more information.

- **Integration of contacts lists:** Gmail is great for importing contacts from all sorts of sources, as we describe in Chapter 4. The contacts are automatically synched with your computer. And Gmail's contacts are shared seamlessly with Google Voice.

✔ **Offline mode:** Gmail is the only Web-based e-mail that also works offline for reading and creating messages, a critically important feature for any kind of serious e-mail use on cell phones.

✔ **Translation:** Gmail can translate your message to and from many languages with a single click, yet another rare capability.

If you already have a Google account and, in particular, if you're already a Gmail user, you're in good hands. If you're not, look at the list of features above and see if there are any key things on it that Gmail does, and your current e-mail doesn't. If so, consider using Gmail after you set up your Google Account.

Follow these steps to create a Google account:

1. **Go to** www.Google.com.

   The famous Google Search page appears.

2. **Click the Sign in link in the upper-right corner.**

   The Google Accounts page appears, as shown in Figure 2-3.

Consider scrolling down to check the captcha (word verification graphic) near the bottom of the page to make sure you can read it before entering anything. If you think the captcha might trip you up, click the Refresh button on your browser to get a new one before you fill out the page.

3. **Click the Create an account now link in the lower-right corner.**

   The Create a Google Account page appears, as shown in Figure 2-4.

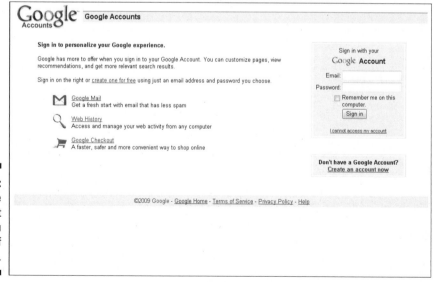

Figure 2-3: A Google Account gives you lots of options.

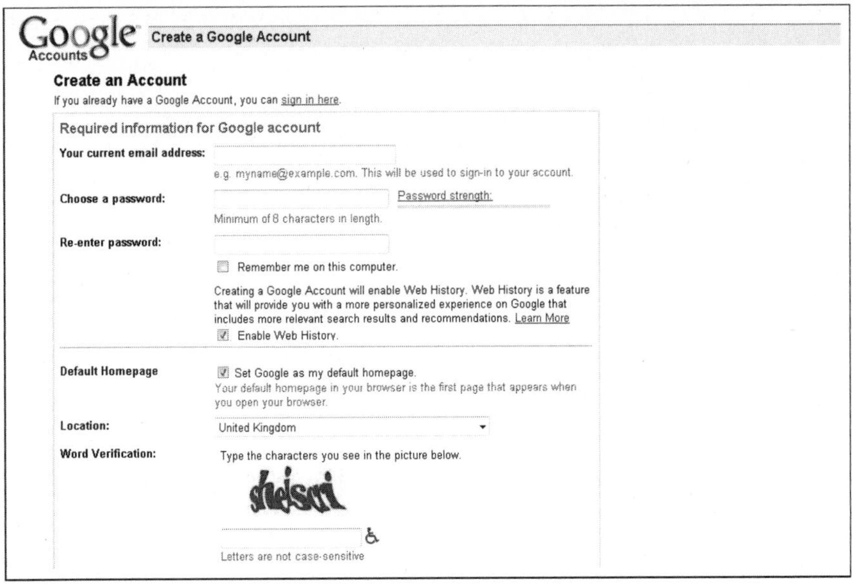

Figure 2-4:
Creating
a Google
Account is
simple.

4. **Enter your current e-mail address.**

   You need an existing e-mail account to "bootstrap" the creation of a Gmail account. If you ever have trouble accessing your Gmail account, this other account will be your way back in, so choose carefully.

5. **Choose a password.**

   You need a password of at least 8 characters. Google displays a bar to show the relative strength of your password. (A stronger password is harder to algorithmically guess.) Mixing letters and numbers and adding special characters makes your password stronger.

6. **Click the checkbox to remember you on the current computer.**

   This option is very convenient — but risks letting others easily access your e-mail when they use your computer. Our experience is that Google never fully logs you into a computer, but always asks for your password before showing your e-mail.

7. **Click the checkbox to enable Web history.**

   Web history gradually shifts your search results and recommendations based on your history. For instance, a water skier who has Web history enabled will gradually get different results for searches about "skiing" than a snow skier will.

8. **Click the checkbox to set Google as your default homepage.**

   Google is as good a homepage as any, especially because searching is the first thing you want to do when you open a new Web page. (Though Gmail may be even better, you won't miss voicemail notifications that arrive via e-mail, and the Gmail home page has a Google search box on it.)

   If you get used to having Google as your default homepage, searching is as easy as opening a new browser window. If you then use a different computer that's set up differently, so you need an extra step to start a search, the other computer will seem broken!

9. **Choose the country you're in, or want Google to treat you as if you're in, from the pull-down menu.**

   The country you choose gives you options specific for that country in Google Search, Google News, and possibly other Google offerings.

10. **Type the captcha, the word verification characters, that Google displays.**

    The captcha verifies that you're not a machine creating an e-mail account to send spam from.

    Google's captchas tend to be hard to read, so this may take you a couple of tries. Don't think it will be any easier if you click on the wheelchair icon to use the disabled option; a voice reads off a series of digits, which you're supposed to enter, while another voice talks in the background, but just as loudly, making it hard to follow the *main* voice.

11. **Review the Terms of Service in the scrolling box, or click the Printable version link, to open them up on a new page and review them.**

12. **Review your entries and make sure you're happy with them. If you are, click the button: I accept. Create my account.**

    Google begins the process of creating your account by sending a verification e-mail to the e-mail account you indicated.

13. **Visit your other e-mail program and open the e-mail Google sent you.**

    The e-mail includes a link to click for verification.

14. **Click on the verification link.**

    The Web page shown in Figure 2-5 appears to confirm that your account has been created.

For the user name, type `yourusername@yourgoogleappsdomain.com`. For instance, if you have a Google Apps domain called gvdaily.com, and your username is heyuser, then enter `heyuser@gvdaily.com` as the user name.

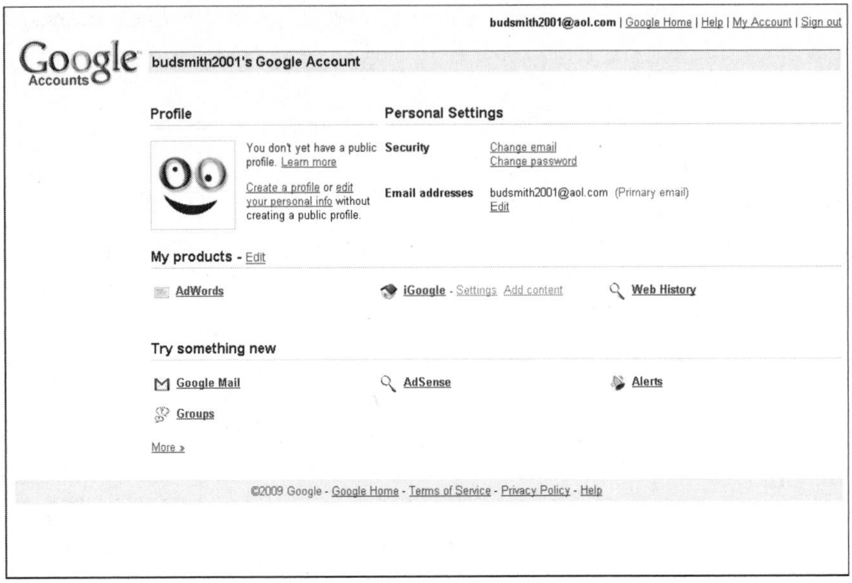
budsmith2001@aol.com | Google Home | Help | My Account | Sign out
Google Accounts
budsmith2001's Google Account
Profile
Personal Settings
You don't yet have a public profile. Learn more
Create a profile or edit your personal info without creating a public profile.
Security
Change email
Change password
Email addresses
budsmith2001@aol.com (Primary email)
Edit
My products - Edit
AdWords
iGoogle - Settings Add content
Web History
Try something new
Google Mail
AdSense
Alerts
Groups
More »
©2009 Google - Google Home - Terms of Service - Privacy Policy - Help

Figure 2-5: You're confirmed! Welcome to your Google account.

Setting Up a Google Profile

A Google Profile is a lot like a Facebook page. Once set up properly, it has your picture, your name, and a brief description. It can even allow people to contact you without showing your e-mail address.

It might seem like a lot of extra bother to set up a Google Profile, especially if you already have a Facebook page, a MySpace page or something similar. But Google Profiles will become ever more important as more and more people use Google services.

For example, a Google Profile makes you much easier to find by people using search engines, including the leader, Google. Create the profile; then make it public.

For anyone who begins using Google Voice, the service will probably become a "tipping point" that causes you to spend a lot more time interacting with Google. As you do so, and as friends, family members, and work colleagues do so as well, the value of having a Google Profile will grow.

A Profile can serve a similar function to a Facebook page; if you already have a Facebook page, you might want to crib some of the content from it to use on your Profile!

As with Facebook and other social networking tools, having an online record like this one can cause problems as well as benefits. For example, if you're making a career change and have a new CV carefully calling attention to what is actually your rather limited sales experience, your Google Profile page identifying you in your current role as a nuclear physicist may cause confusion for potential employers. (Or vice versa.) Consider keeping the careers information in your Profile a bit vague if needed to give you flexibility.

Always "Google" yourself before applying for a new role and specifically check resources like your Facebook page, MySpace page, Google Profile and so on. Make sure you're ready to discuss all the results.

Follow these steps to set up a Google Profile:

1. **Go to the Google home page at www.google.com and sign in.**

   Your account information appears. The information includes part of your (empty) Profile, your personal settings, and a list of the products you use.

2. **Click the Create a profile link.**

   The Create your profile page appears, as shown in Figure 2-6.

3. **Fill in the fields with your information: your name, where you grew up, where you live, and so on.**

Figure 2-6:
Time to
profile
yourself.

Mail Calendar Documents Photos Reader Sites Web more ▾   budsmith2001@aol.com | Help | My Account | Sign out

Google Create your profile
The more information you provide, the easier it will be for friends to find you. Learn more

About me   Photos   Contact info

First name   Last name   Change photo

Changing your name here will change it in all Google products. Learn more

Other names   ☑ Allow people to contact me (without
                                       showing my email address)
Maiden name, alternate spelling

Where I grew up   Where I live now   Places I've lived

What I do   Current company   Companies I've worked for

Examples: Actor, Engineer, Scientist

                                    Current school   Schools I've attended

A little personality

Short bio   B I U ≔ ≔ ☞   Something I can't find using Google

                                            Examples: paradise, love, Atlantis, Oceanic 815, spam
                                            My superpower

                                            Examples: flying, teleportation, time travel, eating chips and salsa

4. **Click Change Picture to upload a picture of yourself.**

   Nothing livens up Google Voice and other Google applications like photos. Make life a little more interesting for your online friends by uploading a photo — and ask them to do the same for you.

5. **Create a short bio.**

   Try to gracefully split the difference between the lively, fun, caring person your friends and family know and the, for instance, ruthlessly efficient, profitability-obsessed, power-hungry automaton you appear to be to your work colleagues.

6. **Link to other online information resources about yourself. Click Add after each link.**

   It might look like you can only create one link, but actually you can create as many as you like.

7. **Keep the default URL (which uses your Google e-mail user name) or choose a random one that Google will generate for you. Click the link See other options to display the alternative URL you can use for your profile.**

   A random URL appears as a choice next to the one which uses your Google e-mail user name.

   The URL is exposing your Google e-mail user name. This could expose you to spam. (As can any other online information that includes your e-mail address.) Though Gmail has excellent spam control tools, you may not want to add a possible entry point for spammers. If so, use the random URL.

8. **Click the Create a Google profile button to create your profile.**

   Your new profile appears onscreen.

Chapter 3

Setting Up Google Voice

. . . .

In This Chapter

▶ Getting a Google Voice account

▶ Choosing an area code and phone number

▶ Getting your General settings right

▶ Verifying your phones

▶ Creating a ring schedule

. . . .

How wonderful is the human voice!

— Henry Wadsworth Longfellow

*I*n one sense, setting up Google Voice is something you do once, when you create your account and make your initial setup choices. But it's also something you do over and over again as you use Google Voice and your phones. And something which you will redo, at least to some extent, if you move or change jobs or just get a new mobile phone.

How you set up Google Voice also changes how people reach you. (See the previous chapter.) So there are some really interesting decisions involved.

If you're new to Google Voice, you might find it a bit overwhelming. But don't worry; you're onto a winner. It seems, at the time of this writing, that Google Voice, or something very much like it, will become a normal part of using telephones for many years to come.

As you set up Google Voice, just remember that the goal is to make your life simpler and more enjoyable. For most of us, that means the goal is to "set it and forget it," to first get Google Voice configured with your phones in a way that works well, then not have to change things much. This chapter can help you do things right the first time.

Some people, though, enjoy endlessly experimenting with Google Voice, their phones, Google Voice applications for smartphones, other third-party applications and devices, and all the options available on each. Because each individual situation is different, we can only hope to get you experimenters off to a good start with Google Voice. We then leave it to you to make it work exactly how you want it to as that changes each day.

Getting Invited

If you haven't received a Google Voice invitation yet, visit `voice.google.com` and sign up to get one. You just need to enter your name and e-mail address. Google e-mails you when they're ready to invite you to Google Voice. Or, you may be required to get an invitation from a current user, as was the case with Gmail for many months. Google uses these delays to smooth out peaks in signups for, and usage of, the service.

Speaking of which, you may want to prepare by creating a Google account now, while you're waiting. See the steps at the end of Chapter 2 for specific instructions. And read the rest of Chapter 2 so you can think about how you want to use your phones with Google Voice.

A Google Apps account allows you to use options such as Google Docs, a set of online applications, similar to Microsoft Office. While individual accounts are free, large organizations that use Google Docs pay a small annual fee per user. If you already have a Google Apps account, you might think that you already have an account you can use for Google Voice. But, while sensible, you'd be wrong.

If you already have a Google Apps account, create a new Google account just for use with Google Voice, using the steps at the end of Chapter 2. For the user name, type `yourusername@yourgoogleappsdomain.com`. For example, if you have a Google Apps domain called `gvdaily.com`, and your username is heyuser, then enter `heyuser@gvdaily.com` as the user name.

Choosing an Area Code and Phone Number

It's finally appeared. What you may have been awaiting for months, or perhaps even, if you were trying to get into GrandCentral, for years: the e-mail from Google inviting you to sign up for your Google Voice account!

Your first job is to follow the link in the e-mail and choose your Google Voice number. After you do this, your Google Voice account is activated. Although you need to perform a lot of other steps to get much use out of your account, choosing your Google Voice number is the crucial step that establishes your account.

Going in, choosing a Google Voice number has a lot of limitations, including:

✔ If the area code you want is not available, you have to choose a nearby area code, preferably in the same state. (Again, to increase the odds of free or cheap calls to your Google Voice number from various phones.)

✔ You can't choose an international number, nor can you forward calls from Google Voice to an international number.

✔ Vanity numbers and 800 numbers are not available.

✔ You can't choose an extension as your Google Voice number.

✔ You can't even forward Google Voice calls to an extension, which is a major problem for many people with regards to their jobs.

✔ You can't port another number to Google Voice, though Google says, in Google Voice Help, "we hope to offer this option in the near future."

Setting up your phone number

The first step is to choose an area code. In the previous chapter, we described how to choose the area code you want to have for your Google Voice number. Now it's time to actually choose it. Follow these steps:

1. Open the e-mail from Google.

The e-mail appears, as shown in Figure 3-1.

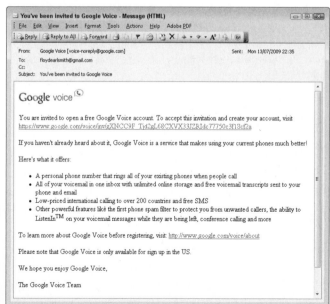

Figure 3-1:
The long-awaited invite arrives.

2. **Click the Click here to sign into Google Voice link. If you're asked to sign into your Google account, do so. If you don't yet have a Google account, use the steps at the end of Chapter 2 to sign up for one.**

Your Web browser opens and the Choose an Area Code screen appears, as shown in Figure 3-2.

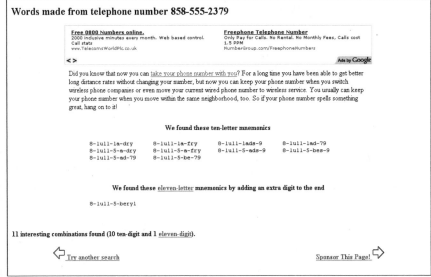

Words made from telephone number 858-555-2379

Free 0800 Numbers online.
2000 inclusive minutes every month. Web based control.
Call stats
www.TelecomsWorldPlc.co.uk

Freephone Telephone Number
Only Pay for Calls. No Rental. No Monthly Fees, Calls cost
1.5 PPM
NumberGroup.com/FreephoneNumbers

Ads by Google

< >

Did you know that now you can take your phone number with you? For a long time you have been able to get better long distance rates without changing your number, but now you can keep your phone number when you switch wireless phone companies or even move your current wired phone number to wireless service. You usually can keep your phone number when you move within the same neighborhood, too. So if your phone number spells something great, hang on to it!

We found these ten-letter mnemonics

8-1ull-1a-dry	8-1ull-1a-fry	8-1ull-1ads-9	8-1ull-1ad-79
8-1ull-5-a-dry	8-1ull-5-a-fry	8-1ull-5-ads-9	8-1ull-5-bes-9
8-1ull-5-ad-79	8-1ull-5-be-79		

We found these eleven-letter mnemonics by adding an extra digit to the end

8-1ull-5-beryl

11 interesting combinations found (10 ten-digit and 1 eleven-digit).

⇐ Try another search

Sponsor This Page! ⇒

Figure 3-2: Choose an area code for your Google Voice number.

3. **Inspect the available area codes and choose the one you want.**

In most cases, you want the same area code as your home phone, work phone, or cell phone, so you can conveniently make calls to your Google Voice number and be sure that the call is free.

If your cell phone number is different from your home or work phones, consider tilting toward the area code used by one of your landlines in choosing your Google Voice area code. Calls from a landline to Google Voice won't incur any charges if the call is local.

4. **Click Accept to finalize choosing the number.**

5. **Dial the number to test it.**

Try calling the number. You should get Google Voice voicemail message, because you have not yet set up Google Voice to ring any actual phones. We explain how in the following sections.

To find an up-to-date map of North American area codes, visit the North American Numbering Plan Administration site at www.nanpa.com. Choose the tab, Area Code Maps, in the left-hand navigation.

Want to find out if a number you're considering spells something great — or something awful? Visit www.phonespell.org, shown in the figure, and enter the phone number you're considering. A family member of one of the authors is "lucre wary" — being distrustful of money is something to avoid if you're in business!

Disseminating your new phone number

Excuse the fancy word, but you now have a task ahead of you — to get your new Google Voice number out to all the friends, family, and colleagues and suppliers of goods and services who have your cell phone number or home phone number. (Perhaps those who have your work number as well, if you want your work calls to go through Google Voice.)

We hope that your effort isn't reminiscent of the voice-over for the introduction of the Star Trek television series: a "five-year mission" that requires you "to boldly go where no one has gone before." But it might feel like that sometimes!

We describe how to manage all your phones in relation to Google Voice in Chapter 2. Here's a quick list of ideas to help you get your new number out:

- **Send out new business cards.** Your new business cards can list your Google Voice number in place of your cell phone number. Include a cover note describing why you're making the change, and how responsive you'll be able to be with the new services afforded by Google Voice. (Don't mention that you'll now be able to take a bath without fear of interruption for the first time in years!)

- **E-mail and call all your contacts.** Send out an update to everyone you know with your new Google Voice number. Again, explain how you'll now be more accessible.

- **Ignore calls that don't come through Google Voice.** Calls from Google Voice can be set up to announce the caller and let you listen in on them as they leave a message. If a call comes to you that isn't through Google Voice, ignore it.

- **Change your greeting on your cell phone message.** When someone calls your cell phone directly, not through Google Voice, let them go through to voicemail. They get a message that gives your new Google Voice number and doesn't ask them to leave a message on your cell phone.

- **Debark your home phone.** Turn off (or, more brutally, disable) the ringer on your home phone. Record a message on your home phone number giving the Google Voice or other number(s) for everyone in your family or group of housemates.

✔ **Give people your Google Voice e-mail address.** You can give people your Google e-mail address, which is just the ten digits of your Google Voice number, plus @googlevoice.com. This gets the number in their hands, and the messages forward to the *real* e-mail account you have set up to use with Google Voice.

After you've let everyone you can think of know your new number, some of them might still use the old one(s) — and there might be some people you missed.

Google Voice makes it much easier to deal with cell phone calls, especially from people you don't want to deal with urgently. Because you can limit your immediate accessibility to the people you care about most, there's a temptation to give your cell phone number out more widely.

Giving your number out too widely is a big problem. If you give your new number out too widely, you trigger a flood of phone calls; if you don't answer them, the phone calls are followed by e-mails with transcribed voicemail messages.

Keep your Google Voice number close. Even think twice about sending it to each and every one of your current contacts. No sense in triggering a flood of "how you doing?" responses that you then have to deal with. Maybe you can wait and let some people know along with sending out holiday cards.

If you really want to be ruthless about it and force a changeover by everyone you know to your new Google Voice number, here's how to go the extra mile — and save money in the process:

✔ **Change your home phone number.** Get a new home phone number. (Tell the phone company you've been getting annoying calls on the old number, which is true enough.) Don't give it out to anyone. Just use it for Google Voice.

✔ **Get rid of your home phone.** Simplify your life and save big bucks: be like so many young people today and get rid of your landline. With Google Voice, you can manage calls to your cell phone by who is calling you, not by which of your phones rings.

✔ **Change your cell phone number.** This one is the "dark side of the force" approach to stopping people from calling you on your cell phone. Drop your old cell phone number. (You may have to add a second phone to your plan and then drop or just stop using the SIM card of the first one. It's worth it.) Then, set up Google Voice to display the Google Voice number when it's calling, as described in the next chapter rather than the caller's number and only answer when you see that number.

✔ **Get rid of your cell phone.** Here's the real Zen guru approach to using Google Voice! Make your life more peaceful. Receive all your calls as voicemail messages through Google Voice on your computer or, if you're traveling, a laptop, netbook, or the nearest Internet café. Reply only by e-mail or SMS text messages sent through Google Voice.

Does anybody really know what time it is?

When you select a time zone from the pull-down menu, you see that Google Voice has a rather idiosyncratic list of time zones. You might expect a list of 24 options — one per time zone. Instead, there are dozens more with variations on the main ones. The list is alphabetized oddly, too.

Actually, the list is capturing some of the many exceptions to standardized time zones found in specific states and cities. For example, Arizona is in the Mountain time zone, but it doesn't observe Daylight Savings Time. And the list is alphabetized according to the locality name, ignoring the name of the overall time zone where that's included.

The default time zone in the scrolling list is Eastern Time, which is GMT-5 hours. (This zone, like the others, takes daylight savings time into account.) Atlantic Time (Halifax), the part of Canada east of the U.S. Eastern Seaboard, is GMT-6 hours. It's a bit below Eastern Time in the list. The other choices for North America, moving west, are progressively further above Eastern Time in the list.

When choosing from the scrolling list, you should look for the specific city or locality you're in, and choose it if it's reflected. Otherwise, use the major time zone that covers everyplace else. For convenience, the major time zones for North America, as given in the scrolling list, are:

✔ (GMT-10:00) Hawaii Time

✔ (GMT-09:00) Alaska Time

✔ (GMT-08:00) Pacific Time

✔ (GMT-07:00) Mountain Time (America/Denver)

✔ (GMT-07:00) Mountain Time (Arizona)

✔ (GMT-06:00) Central Time

✔ (GMT-05:00) Eastern Time*

✔ (GMT-04:00) Atlantic Time (Halifax)

✔ Eastern Time is the default setting for Google Voice.

Getting General Settings Correct

Many of the cool features of Google Voice are controlled by the General tab in the Settings area. Before you use Google Voice, you need to do a bit of work to make some features work properly, in the same way you would set up a new voicemail system.

The General settings can be divided into two groups. The first few settings are truly general; they affect the handling of all calls to your Google Voice number. The remaining settings affect what happens when you're actually interacting with a call as it rings the phone(s) that you have nearby.

Choosing General settings 1: Overall settings

These steps tell you how to handle the initial group of General settings for Google Voice, which affect your overall account: the language used, the time zone you're in, the general voicemail greeting, and you're recorded name.

Follow these steps to set the first group of General settings for Google Voice:

1. **Go to the Google Voice page at voice.google.com, or by choosing Voice from the My products list shown after you sign into the home page of your Google account at www.google.com.**

   The Google Voice page appears.

2. **Click the Settings link at the top right of the page.**

   The Settings section appears, with the General tab highlighted, as shown in Figure 3-3.

Figure 3-3:
To get ready, get Settings right.

3. **Verify the Language and Time Zone.**

   Verify the language choice. At this writing, the only choice is English (U.S.). For the Time Zone, choose your time zone; the default is (GMT-05:00) Eastern Time. See the "Does anybody really know what time it is?" sidebar for details.

The Time Zone setting determines the voicemail and call time settings that show up on the Google Voice Web site and the time stamp on voicemail notifications. It also affects ring schedules for specific phones; see the "Ring schedules and time zones" sidebar, and the following section for details.

4. **Look to see which Voicemail Greeting is selected; play it back if needed. Add additional greetings if you wish.**

   The standard greeting for Google Voice is a woman with a neutral American accent saying, "The Google Voice subscriber you have called is not available. Please leave a message after the tone." This greeting may be appropriate for all situations, or you may want to leave a personalized greeting. You can record additional greetings and use them instead of the System Standard.

   See the next section, "Get Your Name or Greeting on Record," for instructions.

   Google Voice has a general greeting, plus separate greetings for groups of users: Friends, Family, and Coworkers. You can even have specific greetings for specific people! If you do create a greeting at this level, it will be available in your greetings menu to use with other callers as well.

5. **Click Play to hear the Recorded Name. Change it if you want, as shown in Step 6.**

   The pre-existing recorded name is "The subscriber," spoken in a mechanical-sounding voice. You probably want to change this. See the next section, "Sharing Your Greetings," for instructions.

6. **Click Record New to change the greeting.**

   Google Voice will try to open a dialog. Your browser may block this and display an error message instead. Look in your browser window and clear the error message that is probably at the top of your browser window and proceed. (You may need to click Record New again.)

   A dialog box appears like the one in Figure 3-4.

7. **Use the pull-down menu to choose a phone for Google Voice to call you on — or, enter a number directly, including the area code. If you want to remember the choice, click the checkbox to set it. Click the Connect button.**

   Watch carefully: A response briefly appears, "Calling. . . " and the destination.

   The designated phone will ring, and Google Voice will know that this is the first time you've called into your own voicemail, and prompt you to record your name, so callers know who they've reached.

8. **Click Play to hear the recording of your name and check that you're happy with it. Press the pound (#) key to save it.**

   You're then prompted to go on and record a greeting.

9. **Record your greeting. Press the pound key to save it.**

10. **To be notified of new voicemails by e-mail, select the Email message to checkbox. From the pull-down menu, select any of the e-mail addresses you have already associated with your Google account, which will already be listed; or click the Add a new email address link to add another e-mail address.**

    If you click the link, your Google Account page with your personal information appears. Use this page to add additional e-mail addresses to your account.

11. **To be notified of new voicemails by text (SMS), click the Send a text (SMS) message to: checkbox in the Notifications section. Use the pull-down menu to choose one (and only one) of the cell phones associated with your account.**

Having the two Notifications options right next to each other can be a bit confusing, because you can turn them on and off independently of each other. A new voicemail message can cause you to get an e-mail message *and* a text (SMS) message; just an e-mail; just an SMS; or neither.

Only phones that have been verified for your account and designated as mobile phones can be selected for notification. (You can have several phones designated as mobiles verified for your account, but each such phone can only be associated with one Google Voice account at a time.)

If the phone you need is not available in the pull-down list, use the steps in the section below "Verifying Your Phones" section to add it. Google Voice displays an on-screen code, then calls your phone and prompts you to enter it. Then return to this tab and select it for text messaging.

12. **Test your settings work so far. Call your Google Voice number from a friend's phone and leave a message; listen to the voicemail greeting and the recorded name. Then return to the Google Voice Web site and look at the time stamp on the voicemail message to make sure the time zone is correct. Verify that you got an e-mail alert (if you asked for one) and a text (SMS) message (if you asked for one).**

    Change any settings that are incorrect.

Sharing your greetings

One of the most fun and highly valued things people do with Google Voice is to have different voicemail greetings for business colleagues, friends, and family — even for different individual callers.

When you add a voicemail greeting to Google Voice, it goes into a scrolling list of recorded greetings. You can use any greeting from this list as your General (default) greeting; specifically for Friends, Family or Coworkers; or, even more specifically, for individual callers.

We recommend that you begin by recording a new greeting to use as your new Voicemail Greeting in the General section, as described in Step 4 of the earlier Global Settings section. The System Standard greeting is pretty bad.

Follow these steps to record a new greeting for Google Voice and switch greetings:

1. **Go to any of the Web pages that accept greetings settings: The General tab under Settings; the Friends, Family or Co-workers Edit pages under Groups; or the Google Voice settings page (not the generic Edit page) for a specific contact under Contacts.**

2. **Click Add to add a new greeting.**

   Google Voice tries to open a dialog box. Your browser may alert you that you have pop-ups blocked for this site. You should allow Google Voice to open pop-ups. Then proceed. (You may need to click Add again.)

   A dialog box appears, such as the one shown in Figure 3-4.

3. **Type the name of the greeting and press Enter.**

   The Record Greeting dialog box appears, as also shown in Figure 3-4.

   Give specific and memorable names for your greetings, or it will be all too easy to forget what they are — and then, in a hurry, to assign the message where you burp out the first few bars of "Jingle Bells" to your boss! (For example, name such a greeting "Burped Jingle Bells," rather than just "Jingle Bells," to remind yourself of how to use it appropriately in the future.)

   You can arrange with a friend to record a greeting for you. Call the friend directly first to set it up, then choose or enter their number in the next step.

Figure 3-4:
An error
message,
the Greeting
Name
dialog and
the Record
Greeting
dialog.

4. **Use the pull-down menu to choose a phone for Google Voice to call you on, or enter a number directly, including the area code. If you wish to remember the choice, click the checkbox to set it. Click the Connect button.**

   Watch carefully: A response briefly appears, "Calling…" and the destination.

5. **The designated phone will ring, and Google Voice will prompt you — or your friend — to record the greeting. When you're done, press the pound key.**

   The recording is played back to you.

6. **Press 1 to accept the greeting or 2 to re-record it.**

   If you re-record the greeting, it will be played back to you. Repeat this step until you're happy. (The greeting may be played back hundreds of times, so you want to have it right. No pressure then!)

7. **Record additional greetings if you care to.**

   Consider a general greeting for all callers, group-specific greetings for friends, family members, and co-workers, and individual greetings for the people who call you most. Use the links to re-record, rename or delete any greetings as needed.

When it comes to creating a set of greetings, there's no time like the present! You get more out of Google Voice by taking a bit of time for setup steps like this one.

8. **Call your Google Voice number and check that the voicemail message you have selected works correctly.**

   Consider changing the voicemail greeting in the General tab so you can hear all the greetings you plan to use before others do, then return it to the voicemail greeting you want to have in the General tab.

   Re-record any greetings that aren't up to snuff.

Choosing General settings 2: Handling live calls

After you have your truly global settings in hand, it's time to specify how Google Voice will handle specific calls that actually get through and make one or more of your phones ring. Figure 3-5 shows the options in question.

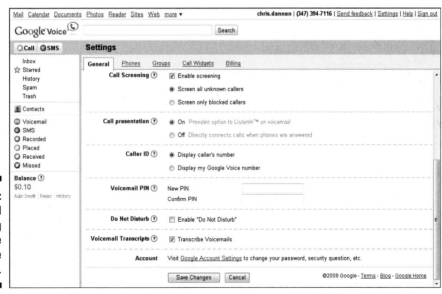

Figure 3-5: How should you ring me? Let me count the ways. . . .

Some of the settings don't mean quite what you would think, so fasten your seat belts — it's going to be a bumpy ride!

You'll be interacting with the voice of Google Voice, a generic female voice which we refer to as Genevieve.

Follow these steps to set up how Google Voice handles specific calls and voicemails:

1. **Click the checkbox to Enable screening of your calls.**

   The language here is a bit confusing. You might think screening is what you do when *you* decide whether to answer a call depending on who's calling. But Google Voice uses screening to mean the step before that. To Google Voice, screening means "asking the caller to state their name, and then playing it back to the Google Voice user."

   Google Voice shows either the Google Voice number or any Caller ID phone number on your Caller ID display, depending on the option setting you choose. (We describe this in Chapter 4.) If the phone number is in your Contacts, The voice of Google Voice (Genevieve) also speaks the contact's name out loud.

   This option is about what to do if the phone number is blocked, or is not blocked but is not in your Contact list. If you enable screening, Google Voice can ask the caller to state their name; Google Voice records what they say and plays it back to you so you can screen your non-Contacts calls.

   When Google Voice gets a call from a number that's not in your Contacts, Genevieve asks the caller for their name and stores it. Your next call from the same number causes the same recording to play, even if it's a different person calling from the same phone number. This can be confusing!

2. **If you enabled screening, select the first radio button to Screen all unknown callers, or select the second radio button to Screen only blocked callers.**

   The wording here is confusing. The first option, Screen all unknown callers, really means "Get and play back a name if the caller's number is blocked, or if the number is unblocked, but not associated with a Contact." The second option, Screen only blocked callers, really means "Get and play back a name only if the caller's number is blocked."

   If you want to screen calls, we suggest you use the first option, Screen all unknown callers, unless you have a good reason to use the other option. It's hard to think of when you'd want to screen only blocked callers. For unblocked callers, you do have their phone number which can (often, not always) be displayed to you via your phone's Caller ID display, but if you knew the number well enough to recognize it, you probably would have associated it with a contact and not have this issue.

One of the great joys of using Google Voice is being able to screen out unknown callers; only the Screen all unknown callers option really helps you do that.

3. **Choose a Call presentation option — On to have Genevieve speak your phone options on each call, including the option to ListenIn™ on voicemail, or Off to directly connect the call when the phone is answered.**

After Genevieve announces the caller, if call presentation is on, she states four ways to handle the call:

- 1 to accept it,

- 2 to send it to voicemail,

- 3 to ListenIn™ on the voicemail, or

- 4 to accept the call and record it.

(The recording is announced so the caller knows it's happening.) If call presentation is off, you just connect straight to the call (option 1).

Google likes the ListenIn name so much they've trademarked it. Google Voice users like the ListenIn option so much they consistently name it as one of their favorite features of Google Voice. So we suggest that you begin with this option On and only turn it off if you find it to be a waste of your time.

Forcing the call to voicemail by using Call presentation has another advantage — it makes sure the voicemail message is left in Google Voice, with centralization, access from multiple points, optional alerting and transcription and so on. If you just let the call ring through, and a voicemail system associated with one of the ringing phones gets it first, the voicemail message will be on that system instead, which defeats part of the purpose of Google Voice. In use, Google Voice does seem to take the voicemail message most of the time.

4. **Choose a Caller ID option — Display the caller's number or display the Google Voice number.**

You can have the caller's number displayed or you can have your own Google Voice number displayed. You really need to see both so you can guess who's calling (from having the caller's number displayed) and so you know what your options are (from having the Google Voice number displayed if the call is from Google Voice).

We recommend that you have the caller's number display and quickly get everyone using your Google Voice number so you can safely assume that you have Google Voice capabilities on all your calls.

5. **Add a Voicemail PIN if you want. After the New PIN prompt, type a four-digit PIN code. After the prompt, Confirm PIN, type the same code.**

If you don't use a PIN, you can only check your voicemail from a Web browser or from a phone that you've directly connected to Google Voice voicemail, typically your cell phone. (See the "Verifying Your Phones" section for how to set this up.)

If you do use a PIN, you can optionally be required to enter it when you call from a directly connected phone. But the real magic is when you call your Google Voice number from any non-directly connected phone and press the * key during the greeting. If you've set up a PIN, but only if you've set up a PIN, Google Voice prompts you for the PIN, then allows you access to voicemail.

Enter your PIN carefully both times, as differing entries won't be flagged until you press Save Changes (see Step 10 below). Worse, if you carelessly make the same mistake twice, you'll set a PIN code that you don't know; you'll have to contact Google to somehow get it cleared or delete your account and start over.

6. **Click the checkbox to set it and enable the Do Not Disturb option. This sends all calls made to your Google Voice number straight to voicemail.**

You can also turn Do Not Disturb on and off by dialing into your Google Voicemail. It's too bad this option is somewhat buried in the Google Voice site and also takes several key presses to turn on and off in Google Voice voicemail, as it's an important option you're likely to use frequently.

Consider bookmarking this page on your computer and, if you have this capability, smartphone's Web browsers. Then you can change the setting quickly.

7. **Click the checkbox to enable voicemail transcripts. Clear the checkbox to disable them.**

This is a key feature of Google Voice. We recommend that you turn it on at first and only turn it off again if it proves to be more annoying than helpful.

8. **Click the link to change your Google Account Settings, such as your e-mail addresses, security options, shipping address, payment method, and so on.**

See Figure 3-6 to see an example of a Google Account and to get an idea of the options you can change.

Figure 3-6:
Google
helps you
account for
yourself.

9. **Click Save Changes to store the changes you've made or Cancel to clear them.**

10. **Test the settings you changed. See if your calls are screened, and if you get options when calls are made to you. Leave and pick up voice-mail messages.**

    Make any changes you need to in the settings to get them working the way you want them to.

That's it, the end of a long journey, from the top of the settings under the General tab to the bottom.

We recommend that you test each of the option settings you've just chosen to make sure it works the way you expect. Doing this might require the help of a friend, or some juggling by you as you hold a phone in each hand! The best time to check is now — not to have your new system fail, or work in some wondrously unexpected way, just when you need it.

Ring schedules and time zones

If you use the Ring Schedules feature for specific phones that you've verified for use with Google Voice, the Time Zone settings determine when the phone is prevented from ringing. If you change the time zone because you're travelling, this changes the on and off times for phones that may not be on the move with you.

You may need to change the ring schedule for one or more of your phones to reflect this; see the following section for how to do this.

This is a good reason to think carefully before using ring schedules, or to manage them carefully if you do.

Verifying Your Phones

Your Google Voice number is your new input for phone calls. It can output them in three ways:

- ✔ Voicemail link.
- ✔ Voicemail message transcripts.
- ✔ Phone calls to one or more of your numbers.

It's the third of these that we're concerned about: phone calls to your numbers.

The key word there is *your,* as in your numbers. Google Voice doesn't let you forward calls to your Google Voice number to just any old phone numbers. You have to prove you have access to the numbers so that you can verify them first.

You will need to do this at one or more times when you have access to your home phone, work phone, and of course your cell phone — even to the phone of a friend or family member who you might hang out with sometimes, and want to forward your calls to.

You can't use an extension as a target for forwarding calls. If you have an extension phone near you, you have to use your cell phone instead or go without.

Though Google Voice isn't very smart about extensions, it's quite specific about how it uses and shares other phones. It allows up to two people to enter the same home phone or office phone number.

But that's only two, so if you have two adults and two kids, all with your own cell phones, you can't all have Google Voice accounts pointing to the same home phone. So if you have crowds at work or home, plan in advance which two people get to claim a given phone number in Google Voice.

Only one person can associate their Google Voice account with any one cell phone number.

Being there

Being There is a 1979 film in which Peter Sellers plays a gardener who becomes an adviser to business leaders and presidents. (It's worth seeing or seeing again.) Being there is also what you'll have to do when you verify each of the phones you want to use with Google Voice.

To complete the verification steps described in this section for a specific phone, you have to have access to it. For example, to verify your work phone as a phone you can control via Google Voice, you have to be near it or have it forwarded to a phone you are near. That's because, after you enter the details of a phone into the Google Voice Web site, Google Voice shows you a confirmation code and then calls the phone in question.

You have to answer the phone and enter the confirmation code. Only then is the phone verified as a phone you can use with Google Voice.

Getting your Gizmo number

You can use Gizmo5, also known as the Gizmo Project, for voice calls, video calls, and text messaging from your PC. PC to PC calls are free; other calls are available at low cost. Gizmo runs on cell phones, where it uses mobile phone plan minutes (and may incur data transfer charges) but does not incur long distance charges. To learn more, go to www.gizmo5.com.

If you're a Gizmo user, and want to use your Gizmo phone with Google Voice, you need the phone number for it. To get your Gizmo phone number, go to my.gizmo5.com. Your phone number is displayed below your name and most likely has the area code 747.

If you're interested, 747 is, like, totally the code for the San Fernando Valley section of Los Angeles (made sort of famous in the Moon Unit Zappa song *Valley Girl* and the movie based on the song).

For more about Gizmo, see Chapter 15.

This is true for a business phone, your home phone, your cell phone (that one should be easy), a phone at a friend or family member's house, and any other phone that you want to forward calls to through Google Voice.

So you may need to complete the process of verifying all the phones you want to control via Google Voice over time, and with a bit of travelling around; and you may need to repeat these steps when you're on a trip, for instance, and want to use a nearby phone through Google Voice.

Stepping through verification

Follow these steps to verify a phone number:

1. **Go to the Google Voice page at `voice.google.com`, or by choosing Voice from the My products list shown on your account home page.**

   The Google Voice page appears.

2. **Click the Settings link at the top of the page.**

   The Settings section appears, with the General tab highlighted.

3. **Click the Phones link.**

   The Phones tab appears, as shown in Figure 3-7.

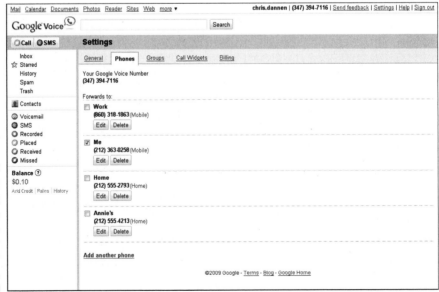

Figure 3-7: Make it easy to phone home or your other numbers.

4. Click the Add another phone link.

The Add a new phone page appears, as shown in Figure 3-8.

5. Enter the name of the phone.

Enter a name that clearly identifies the phone. You'll probably be setting up your call forwarding in a hurry at some point — perhaps through a mobile phone interface in the moments before your plane takes off, for example. You want to make it easy to do things right.

6. Enter the phone's number.

Enter the number of the phone. Use the format (XXX) YYY-ZZZZ for consistency with Google Voice. (For a Gizmo phone, the number is on your my.gizmo.com page. For details, see the "Getting Your Gizmo Number" sidebar.)

7. Enter the type of phone.

Enter the type of phone: Mobile (SMS messages will only go to phones designated as mobiles), Work, Home, or Gizmo. Only one Google Voice account can claim a given mobile number; two Google Voice accounts can claim the same work or home number. Gizmo is a phone-to-phone Voice over IP service; see the sidebar for information on how to get the phone number to use for your Gizmo account.

Figure 3-8: Put a phone under the control of Google Voice.

8. **For phones designated as Mobile only, click the check box if you want to receive SMS messages on this phone.**

   The next steps are tricky. They're both somewhat hidden behind an Advanced Settings tab. The first one is pretty much a one-time set and forget kind of setting, while the other is something you do want to get right at the beginning but may want to alter in the future.

9. **Click Show Advanced Settings.**

   The Voicemail Access and Ring Schedule fields appear. We describe the Voicemail Access setting, which is included in Figure 3-4, here, and the Ring Schedule setting in the next section.

10. **Set Voicemail Access to Yes for phones that you usually use exclusively and No for shared phones.**

    This step usually means setting Voicemail Access to Yes for your cell phone and No for your other phones.

    The Voicemail Access setting is a bit misnamed. It should really be called "Go Directly to Voicemail" or something similar.

    You always have *access* to your Google Voice voicemail when calling one of your phones; just press the * button on your phone after the other phone has started ringing. But if you choose Yes for this setting, calling your Google Voice number from this number will go directly to your Google Voice voicemail, without the opportunity to let the call ring through.

    So if you set this setting to Yes for your home phone, and someone tries to call you on your mobile from your home, they'll go straight to your voicemail. To avoid confusion, you should do what Google says in a help message to try to clarify things: "Only select this option if you do not share this phone with anyone else." Ever.

11. **If you set Voicemail Access to Yes, then click the radio button for PIN required, if you want to protect your voicemail, or PIN not required, if you want to get straight to it.**

    The PIN is set in the Settings tab.

    We describe how to set the ring schedule separately, in the next section, as the fields described here are long-term settings; you may change the ring schedule more frequently (for example, each time you have a day off work). For now, you can leave the ring schedule set to the default, which is that calls set to ring through on this phone always do so.

12. **If you want to set the ring schedule for the phone now, refer to the steps in the next section.**

    You can proceed to verify the phone now. You can then change the ring schedule, and other settings for a specific phone, without re-verifying it.

13. **Click Save.**

    The Verify your Phone dialog box appears, with a phone verification code, as shown in Figure 3-9.

Figure 3-9:
Now it's time to verify the phone number.

14. **In the pop-up dialog box, click Connect.**

    The phone you're verifying rings.

15. **Pick up the phone. Google Voice prompts you, verbally, to enter the verification code you see in the Verify your Phone pop-up. Enter it using the phone's keypad.**

    Google Voice hangs up the phone, and the on-screen process is complete. You are returned to the Phones tab onscreen, with the new phone added to your list of verified phones.

16. **Repeat this process for all the phones you want to use with your Google Voice number.**

   This may involve travelling to a friend's house or waiting until the next time you're at work, for example. Focus on getting this done, because you won't be able to set and forget many of your Google Voice settings until you do.

17. **Test the results.**

   Test all the settings from the General tab and all the phones listed here. Better that you find out any problems than that your callers do.

Setting Which Phones Ring

The key to using Google Voice is having control over which phones ring when. So, by using the Ring Schedule setting, Google Voice allows you to control whether one of your, which sounds simple. But it doesn't allow you to control whether the phone rings when someone calls it directly, which is something you might want but Google Voice can't do. Google Voice can only manage calls that people make to your Google Voice number.

The Ring Schedule setting allows you to control "only" whether one of your phones rings *when Google Voice routes a call through to it at a specific time.*

Until you've actually used Google Voice, this takes a little imagination. So imagine that you've set up Google Voice so that calls from some callers only go to your work phone, and further imagine that your work phone is in your study. You don't want your work phone ringing during non-working hours. (So your contacts in, say, Singapore don't get confused about time zone differences and make the phone in your study ring in the middle of the night.)

In a sense, you're turning off that phone — for calls routed to it through Google Voice — on some days or times of day. If that phone is completely controlled through Google Voice — which you may have achieved, using some of the more radical steps described earlier in this chapter — it will only ring on calls that first go to Google Voice, are routed to that phone, and are within times set by the ring schedule.

Calls routed to that phone that arrive outside the hours specified in the ring schedule go through to your Google Voice voicemail. Which, if you've chosen your settings to allow it, sends you an e-mail or even an SMS alert that you have a voicemail and sends you a transcription of the voicemail message, with the actual message attached as an MP3 file.

This feature is useful less often than you might think but is intensely useful when you need it. It's useful less often than you might think because it doesn't directly control the phone in question; it only controls calls routed to that phone through Google Voice. But it can be intensely useful for phones that are in shared-access areas or whose ringing might disturb people with the "wrong" calls if allowed to ring through at the "wrong" times.

However, we assert that this setting should be used carefully. It's confusing to have calls to your Google Voice number ring a specific phone some of the time — and not others. It's even more confusing that the controls for this are in a semi-hidden setting in your Google Voice Settings Web site.

Not only is it confusing; there's a lot of potential for extra work here. You don't always work the same days and hours. So the more carefully you set the ring schedule, the more likely you are to have to mess with it for even small changes in your actual schedule. For instance, the Ring Schedule settings differentiate between weekdays and weekends, which fits most of us, until a national holiday, vacation day, or sick day comes along. And being early or late to work can play havoc with a custom schedule.

So we suggest you not set up a ring schedule for a phone at all unless you're quite sure that you need one. Also be ready to tweak the schedule as your schedule, inevitably, shifts.

The reason this level of control might be important is for a phone that has its own voicemail. If you let calls to that phone ring through when you're not around, they will be picked up by the phone's voicemail, not in your Google Voice voicemail, with its centralization and cool features.

Follow these steps to set a ring schedule:

1. **If you're not already on the Add a new phone page in the Phones tab under settings, then do the following: from your Google Voice page, click the Settings link on the left-hand side and the Phones tab. Click Edit for the phone whose schedule you want to change.**

   The description you've created for the phone appears.

2. **Click the Show advanced settings link further down on the page.**

   The Ring Schedule section appears, as shown in Figure 3-10.

3. **For the Weekdays area, choose Always ring on weekdays, Never ring on weekdays, or Use custom schedule.**

   If you click Use custom schedule, the Do not ring phone from *start time* to *end time* option appears.

4. **If you've chosen Use custom schedule, set the time range in which the phone is not to ring.** Use the Remove link and the Add time range link to set and manage multiple periods of blocking — for instance, to accommodate lunchtime.

   This option gives you a lot of control but also a lot to remember. Consider writing down the settings you've entered someplace more visible and accessible than in this sub-sub-sub-menu of your Google Voice screen.

Figure 3-10:
Manage
the timing
of "ringie-
dingies"
from Google
Voice to a
phone.

5. **Repeat Steps 3 and 4 for the Weekends area of the Ring Schedule.**

   Figure 3-11 shows a complex schedule typical for a business: calls allowed during working hours on weekdays and not at all on weekends.

   If you're open Saturday, for instance, you'll need to change the settings in the Weekends area each Saturday to allow calls through on Saturday working hours but prevent all calls on Sunday. Similarly, you'll need to make changes in the Weekdays area if you take a day off during the week.

6. **Click Save.**

   If you're editing a phone that was already one of your verified Google Voice phones, you'll be returned to the Settings area of your Google Voice Web page. If you're setting up a phone that hasn't yet been verified, you'll be returned to Step 12 in the previous section to verify your phone.

7. **Test the ring schedule.**

Try some calls within and outside of your ring schedule hours to make sure it works as intended.

Figure 3-11: You can fine-tune the ringing of your phone.

The Ring Schedule option gives you a lot of control but also a lot to remember. Consider writing down the settings you've entered someplace more visible and accessible than in this sub-sub-sub-menu of your Google Voice screen.

Focusing On General/Default Settings

Some of the settings that you first set in this chapter can be purposefully used or overwritten for specific groups or contacts. (When you get calls from phone numbers that aren't in your contacts, the settings you set here are used.)

Here's how the settings you establish here interact with settings for specific groups and contacts:

✔ **Which phones to ring.** Which phones ring when someone calls you? Set it on the Phones tab of the Settings area for all incoming calls. This is called the Default for this setting by Google Voice. For a group, you can use the Default settings established here at the General level — meaning, the behavior for that group changes when you change the General setting — or use specific settings for the Group. For a contact, you can use the Group setting, which could be the Default setting or establish specific settings for the contact.

✔ **Which voicemail greeting to use.** This option is always selected from a pull-down list that you can edit wherever you see it at the overall level, for a group or a contact. You can add to the list, delete entries and so on. However, you can only specify the default greeting — the one used when a contact doesn't have a setting specified for themselves or a group they belong to — from the General tab of the Settings area. You can set specific greetings for groups or individual contacts at those levels of setup.

✔ **Whether to use call presentation.** This option includes the ability for you to control specific calls based on the Caller ID and the caller's name, which Google will speak for you, and to listen in on a voicemail message to decide whether to pick up the call. You can turn call presentation on or off in the General tab of the Settings area, as described here. For a group, Google Voice will then allow you to pick up this overall setting or override it for the group. For a specific contact, Google Voice will allow you to pick up the group setting or override it for that contact.

In choosing which phones to ring and whether to use call presentation, there are two main strategies you can use. If you use the Default setting for most or all of your groups, and the group setting for most, probably not all, of your contacts, the top-level setting established here has a lot of power. If you use a lot of specific group and individual contact settings, the top-level setting only reliably applies to calls that aren't from phones that belong to your contacts.

As for voicemail greetings, the same applies; you can focus more on specific greetings per group and per contact, or on one overall greeting that's easily changed.

The way settings cascade varies by setting and by the level you try to control it at. So take your time and think through how you want the global settings you choose here to work. If you set up your groups and contacts with specific, low-level settings, then want to make a quick change that applies right across Google Voice, you may have to do a fair amount of work to make the changes stick for all your contacts.

With greetings, there's a twist. You can create a voicemail greeting called, say, "Current" that you intend to use flexibly, and point to it from as many as possible of your groups and individual contacts. This greeting can include changing information such as your availability as you travel. By re-recording it, you will be giving callers the most recent information.

If you do this enough, it will be like an audio Twitter triggered (twigged?) by calling you. If you keep the messages up to date and use a bit of humor, people may be calling to hear your messages, not to speak to you!

Chapter 4

Upgrading to Google Voice from GrandCentral

In This Chapter

▶ What's Google doing with my GrandCentral account?

▶ Going over the differences

▶ Preparing to upgrade: Wait!

▶ Feeling the power

▶ Exploring Google Voice

---

*I*f you're a GrandCentral beta user, you're one of the lucky few who have gotten to learn firsthand the power of managing your phones from one centralized tool. If you're new to Google Voice and have no idea what GrandCentral is, don't panic: you can skip this chapter altogether. (Or read it anyway, just to get a sense of the history of Google Voice.)

Still reading, GrandCentral folks? As early as March 2008, you may have noticed that you had the option to "upgrade" to Google Voice when you logged on to your GrandCentral account. What's that all about? If you've already upgraded, you may have been wondering: that was quick; did I miss anything?

This chapter explains where GrandCentral came from, and what has changed since it was purchased and rebranded by Google as Google Voice. You find out the numerous benefits of upgrading as well as a few drawbacks.

Before you make the transition, there are a few things you should know, but don't worry; if you're savvy enough to use GrandCentral in the first place, the upgrade is a cinch. After the process is all said and done, this chapter delineates all the new things you can do with your Google-fied account.

When you transition to Google Voice, you may lose access to GrandCentral; different people's experiences seem to vary. Neither your contacts nor your voicemails and recordings are transferred, but you can move them over with the steps we recommend. But to be careful, you need to do this before you upgrade; steps for doing this are given below.

Making Special Considerations for Alaska, Hawaii, and Canada

Google Voice comes with a few geographical caveats. If you call Alaska, Hawaii, and/or Canada a lot, you've enjoyed the fact that GrandCentral made these calls for free; with Google Voice, they initially cost 4¢ a minute for Alaska, 2¢ a minute for Hawaii, and 1¢ a minute for Canada. However, the charge for calls to Canada was removed in summer 2009.

So for making calls to Alaska and Hawaii, you save money by sticking with GrandCentral as long as you can. (Missing out on Google Voice's cool new features is a tough tradeoff!) This consideration is especially important if you live in either state. The hassle of adding money to your account to be ready to make such calls may be a bigger worry than the actual cost, but it's a new hassle and expense with Google Voice compared to GrandCentral.

GrandCentral didn't give out GrandCentral phone numbers with area codes for Alaska, Hawaii, or Canada. But GrandCentral does allow calls placed to an area code in the lower 48 states to be forwarded through to phones with Alaska, Hawaii, and Canada area codes, and at no cost as well.

Google Voice does not allow phones with Alaska, Hawaii or Canada area codes to be added to the phones that can receive calls. In the upgrade, your existing phones are "grandfathered in," but you can't add new ones. This is the same treatment as people outside the U.S. receive, and not very welcome. Google has discussed extending the free call area to Alaska, Hawaii, and Canada, and offering area codes from these areas as well.

If you're based in Alaska, Hawaii, or Canada, add all the phones you can think of from these areas to your GrandCentral account *before* you upgrade. Then you can continue using them to receive calls placed to your Google Voice number.

What about the maple leaf crew?

Canadians share the same international calling code designation as Americans — 1— () and are thoroughly integrated into a unified North American calling scheme. But some new services "leaf" out Canadians.

GrandCentral was a partial exception. It didn't give out phone numbers with Canadian area codes, only U.S. ones. So Canadian users were reluctant to give out their Google Voice numbers (with the U.S. area codes) to Canadian business colleagues, friends, and family because calling it cost extra. The numbers were great to give to U.S. contacts though.

GrandCentral did allow phones with Canadian area codes to be added to a GrandCentral account. So calls to your GrandCentral number would ring your Canadian phones, at no charge.

At the time of this writing, Google Voice is not as flexible. Canadian phone numbers that are already in a GrandCentral account are grandfathered into the upgrade; they can still be used with Google Voice. But you can't add more phones with Canadian (or any other non-U.S.) number to the service.

So for Canadians, sticking with GrandCentral is the more flexible option at the time of this writing — though it means missing out on all the great Google Voice features. Check Google Voice Help online at `www.google.com/support/voice/` to see if the situation has changed.

Baked Alaska – and boiling Hawaiians

In 2008, in an historic first, America finally elected a president from a group of Americans that had long battled for proper recognition, that had sometimes felt slighted, left out, or ignored in America's ever-evolving story.

Yes, in 2008, America finally elected its first Hawaii-born President.

But Alaska and Hawaii are still left out from full and free participation in an important new American experience: the use of Google Voice.

With GrandCentral, calls to Alaska and Hawaii were free. Now they're 2¢ a minute to Hawaii and 4¢ a minute to Alaska.

No Alaska or Hawaii area codes are available as phone numbers from Google Voice, just as there weren't with GrandCentral. That means that if you're from one of those states, you have to live with a phone number that has an out-of-state area code. But you also can't have calls made to Google Voice ring through to your Alaskan or Hawaiian phones.

As long as Google Voice continues to charge extra for Hawaii and Alaska calls, and GrandCentral is still available and doesn't charge extra, people who call to and from Hawaii and Alaska will have lower costs with GrandCentral, but more features with Google Voice. A tough choice!

Discovering How Google Got Your GrandCentral Account?

GrandCentral was founded in 2005 by Craig Walker and Vincent Paquet, a couple of seasoned geeks with a great idea for controlling phone lines using an Internet-based tool. They had previously started a service called DialPad and sold it to Yahoo! DialPad became Yahoo! Voice, a service that allows users to make calls over the Internet from computer to computer.

After DialPad, Walker and Paquet had a fabulous new idea. They realized that making phone calls over the Internet wasn't so great if you had to use a computer to do it. They envisioned a Web service that let you centralize all the phone lines in your life, and control them all from anywhere using a Web interface but still let you make calls from your phones instead of the computer. That idea became GrandCentral.

Sometime between 2005 and 2008, you probably heard about GrandCentral and decided to give it the old college try; after all, it was free. Like a few thousand other early adopters, you got an e-mail invitation once you signed up, and away you went.

And you were lucky. GrandCentral had a lot of breakthrough features, making it amazingly useful for a free, 1.0 product. And the interface was robust and well-executed; nearly everything it did, it did well.

Google bought GrandCentral in July of 2007 for a cool $95 million. Great, you thought: GrandCentral is now backed by one of the wealthiest and most innovative tech companies on the planet. And you waited for terrific new Google-y features to pop up. And then you waited more.

Gradually, your waiting turned into despair. Was Google ignoring their acquisition? Maybe you read the howls of abandonment from GrandCentral users in the site's support forums. Maybe you noticed that GrandCentral's staff stopped responding. Woe became you.

Then that gleeful day arrived: March 11, 2009, when Google finally re-launched GrandCentral as Google Voice. They had been secretly working on the project all along. You instantly forgave their inconsideration.

Better yet, Google Voice was only open to a select few press and other insiders plus existing GrandCentral users like you, who were allowed to upgrade for months before Google Voice was opened to the public. Google Voice numbers were selling on eBay for hundreds of dollars. You went from being a technology orphan to being part of a small, envied elite overnight.

You can find many forums for discussing GrandCentral and Google Voice. Here are a few highlights that might be interesting to you before you upgrade:

- Export your GrandCentral phonebook before upgrading; import it first thing after upgrading.

- Google says you can still access your GrandCentral account to get old voicemails, but some people have found that not to be the case.

- A few people like the old interface better, at least on first exposure to the new one. Most like the new one better.

In pain? Information is the answer

A few former GrandCentral users have had more brickbats than bouquets for Google Voice. Here are some concerns that were raised — and the answers:

✔ **Where are all 100 names, addresses, phone numbers that I had in my GrandCentral Account?**

It's pretty easy to export your GrandCentral contacts and import them into Google Voice, as described in this chapter. The trick is that Google says you can do this before or after the upgrade, but some users report not being able to get back into GrandCentral after upgrading. So export before you upgrade to make sure you don't have problems.

✔ **Why are all my friends and family now being asked to "say your name" on every single phone call? (GrandCentral let me turn that "bad feature" off.)**

You can turn this off in Google Voice, too, by disabling Call Screening in the Settings menu: for all callers, for groups of callers and for specific callers one at a time; see the next chapter.

✔ **I have to pay for every text message Google Voice is now sending me. (How do I turn that off?)**

This person is now seeing the text messages that were simply lost when they were on GrandCentral; losing them is worse than getting them, we think! But there is cost and interruption involved if the texts come through to your phone.

You can turn off text message forwarding in Google Voice so the messages only show up in your Google Voice Inbox and not on your phone. But you can only do this for all text messages on one phone at a time, by turning off the "receive SMS on this phone" feature for each of your cell phones. Or you can block all input from a given user. You can't turn text message forwarding on and off by group or by individual caller, which would be a good thing.

A very few have even asked to be converted back to GrandCentral! But if the upgrade makes you nervous, just be patient — the only real "gotcha"s in the upgrade are the potential loss of contacts and messages, which we show you how to work around in this chapter; and the loss of RingShare, which is sad for some but not likely to be a stopper for anyone.

And, in case you were wondering, there's no way to get back to GrandCentral after you've upgraded to Google Voice.

And that's most of it. Much less static than usual for any kind of big upgrade.

Understanding the Differences

Even before you upgrade, there's good news. With Google behind the service, you may feel a lot more confident in using it. And GrandCentral's revenue plans are kicked into touch; whatever Google eventually does to make money from the service, it's likely to cost you less than the $14.99 a month that GrandCentral planned to charge.

As for the upgrade itself, there isn't much bad news. Almost everything that GrandCentral offered is still there in Google Voice: one number, a unified voice mailbox, control from the Web, the ability to manage incoming calls including blocking spam, and listening in on incoming calls.

You still get free domestic long distance calls and e-mail notifications of voicemails, with a link to the audio file attached. You can customize voice-mail messages and divert calls temporarily.

There's really only one missing feature: RingShare. That's the ability to link a custom MP3 file to replace the normal ringing phone sound. (Like a custom ringtone but for your callers to hear, not you.)

RingShare is just gone, and there's no sign it will ever return.

Web call buttons are still available in Google Voice, but your GrandCentral ones won't survive the transition; you need to replace them with new, Google Voice buttons. And that's about it on the minus side.

The first change you notice after you upgrade is the look. The interface has changed considerably, and for the better. Gone are the clumsy menus and antiquated tools of GrandCentral, replaced by Google's lightweight and quick-loading interface.

Figure 4-1 shows the opening screen of GrandCentral. Figure 4-2 shows the opening screen of Google Voice. You can see from a quick look that there's more going on in Google Voice — yet it looks cleaner.

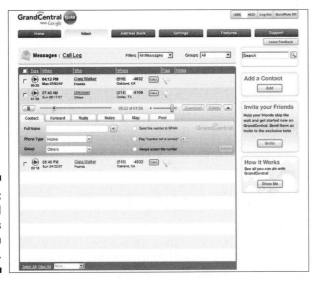

Figure 4-1:
Grand
Central was
the nexus in
its day.

Figure 4-2:
Google
Voice is
all about
screening
callers and
managing
your
voicemail
Inbox.

The new interface puts the voicemail Inbox at center stage, and everything else in a pane on the left-hand side.

If you use other services such as Gmail or Google Docs, Google Voice will feel like home. (In fact, better than home; the Google Voice interface is easier and cleaner than, say, Gmail.) If you're not an experienced Google account user, you can quickly get used to the new way of things.

And the transition is not purely cosmetic. Google has added a handful of fantastic new features (what you can do) and functionality (the way you do it). We count ten new features that can save you time and money and make your telephone life more convenient:

✔ **Cheap international calls:** All the money-saving potential of Skype and its competitors, such as Google Talk, and then some — France and China, for two examples, are just 2¢ a minute. And it's available where you really need it: on your phones. More on this in Chapter 7.

✔ **SMS text messaging:** This was the biggest missing feature in GrandCentral and the biggest "Yes!" in Google Voice for GrandCentral users. You can receive texts to your Google Voice number and have them forwarded to your cell phone — rather than having them disappear into the ether, as happened with GrandCentral. You can send texts from your Google Voice number, too. Unfortunately, you can't send international texts.

✔ **SMS message logging:** Text messages are saved in your Web account forever, where you can review them, search them — it is a Google service, after all — forward them, and so on.

✔ **Voicemail transcription:** This is shown in Figure 4-3. You're used to GrandCentral's Inbox list of calls and e-mail alerts for voicemails. Now, every e-mail alert has a transcription attached to it, so long as the caller said something more than a grunt. It's automated and a bit rough — there is rarely any punctuation — but especially useful for picking out phone numbers that are contained in a voicemail, since Google's transcription engine seems to identify those very accurately. However, transcription makes rambling voicemails look even sillier than they sound. Still, voicemail transcripts make it easier to know how urgent it is that you respond and help you to handle many of your voicemails via e-mail.

✔ **Free and easy conference calling:** Conference calling for most people is expensive and difficult, sometimes even impossible to do when you need it. Not with Google Voice, especially when you add the advantage of free domestic and cheap international calls to reach your conferees.

Figure 4-3:
Google
Voice
transcribes
each
voicemail
automati-
cally.

✔ **Easy call recording:** You can record calls at any point; your caller gets a warning message and then you're off and running. A link to the recording is e-mailed to you after the call. Especially useful for conference calls.

✔ **GOOG-411 integration:** Now you can call Google's information line directly from Google Voice to make a verbal request for the locations and phone numbers of local businesses.

✔ **Calls from the Inbox:** You can now make calls directly from your voice-mail inbox, making call-backs easier. You can also embed voicemails or recorded calls in your blog or Web site for all the world to listen to, though you may want to get permission first.

✔ **GoogleVoice Mobile:** A much better looking and more robust mobile site for Google Voice control. Works on any Web-enabled phone.

✔ **Dialers:** A dialer is a cell phone software application, or *app*, that runs directly on the phone rather than through a Web site. Google is actively developing dialers of its own and supporting developers in creating dialers as well. The result is a richer array of choices than was available for GrandCentral.

The Google in Google Voice is a gift that will keep on giving. Not just in the service itself, with its cleaner interface and new features, but in integration.

Google Voice is already especially easy to use with Gmail, as we describe in Chapter 11. And the dialer for Google Android is particularly nice, as we describe in Chapter 8. But the key point is that with Google behind it, Google Voice is likely to be integrated with many more Google and non-Google products.

More subtly, Google Voice will also be much more acceptable to businesses than a minor-league product from an independent startup like GrandCentral ever was, because of the assurance that the behemoth search company will always be around to stand behind its products.

Barriers to entry

The biggest barrier to entry for Google Voice, as for GrandCentral, still has to do with dealing with a new number. This is really two problems: training people to use your new number and the fact that they keep seeing your old number after you've moved.

The second problem is much easier to manage now. GrandCentral lacked SMS support, so texts had to go to and from your "real" cell phone number. Google Voice has SMS support, which is a big plus in any event. And if you're dutiful about dialing in to Google Voice before calling or texting out, you can maintain the impression that your GV number is your "real" number.

But dealing with a new number is still a hassle. What's needed is the ability to port an existing cell phone number to Google Voice. Google is actually promising this capability for the near future — but you can't be certain it will happen until it does.

When people can move their cell phone numbers to Google Voice, expect a surge of adoption. Google Voice will become a great way to save money with and manage the cell phone-based relationships people already have.

Et tu, iPhone?

If you've been using a GrandCentral dialer on your smartphone, it will still work after you upgrade to Google Voice. Better yet, you'll be able to take advantage of some of the more full-featured dialers that Google and other third party-developers are developing specifically for Google Voice.

You can find out more about how to integrate your smartphone into your Google Voice life in Part III of this book.

Before You Hurry Up, Wait

You probably want to upgrade from GrandCentral to Google Voice sooner rather than later. You may well be forced to do it eventually, if Google closes off GrandCentral. And in any event, it makes sense to start getting the advantages sooner rather than later.

But before you upgrade, consider the following issues:

✔ Moving your GrandCentral contacts to Google Voice.

✔ Keeping your GrandCentral voicemails available after the move to Google Voice.

✔ Creating a Gmail account, if you don't already have one, as a preferred home for the flurry of e-mails and transcripts that Google Voice will produce.

Both GrandCentral and Google Voice are quite different from your previous way of using your phone. It's best to stop investing in optimizing a deprecated platform, as the HTML people put it, and start putting your efforts into the one that has a long and bright future in front of it.

And, given that you're going to move, you don't want to spend a lot of time after the changeover reassembling contact information and worrying about old voicemails.

We take each issue — contacts, voicemails, and Gmail — in turn, telling you what to do before you upgrade, as well as what to do if you've already upgraded and are having problems.

Creating a Gmail account

If you're preparing to upgrade from GrandCentral to Google Voice, now is a really good time to create a Gmail account. You may even want to create a specific Gmail account just for your Google Voice messages and voicemails.

We go through the reasons for this in Chapter 11. What we can address here is, why now?

When you start using Google Voice, you're going to associate it with an e-mail account. You want all your notifications and transcripts from Google Voice over time to be in the same e-mail account where you can find them easily.

And you want that e-mail account to be flexible, easy to use for forwarding, and easy to integrate with tools such as Outlook and Apple Mail. You also want it to be well integrated with Google Voice — now and in the future — easy to search and free. Gmail is the natural choice.

So seriously consider taking the time now to create a Gmail account, learn a bit about Gmail — the high points are covered in Chapter 11 — and use it as your Google Voice e-mail account right from the start.

Keeping contact(s) with GrandCentral

Managing contacts seems trivial, but it's actually one of the great issues in computing today. People expect to sign on once to their computer, if at all, and have access to all their programs, files, and Web sites. Similarly, they expect to have one set of contact information for each person important to them.

Microsoft Outlook, which is a bit of a dinosaur, keeps a fan base of many millions largely because of its solid base of contact management capability across e-mail, meetings, and phone number and address information. Apple and Google are each trying to pull off the same thing.

So getting your contacts from GrandCentral into Google Voice (where you can integrate them with other Google services, with Outlook, or Apple services as well) is a big deal.

When you export your GrandCentral contacts, group information is lost. So you either have to deal with all your contacts in one big blob or use the Tip in Step 3 below to work around the problem.

If you are about to upgrade, or you've already upgraded and still have access to your GrandCentral account, follow these steps to export your contacts:

1. **Sign into GrandCentral.**

2. **Click the Inbox tab.**

   Your GrandCentral Inbox appears, perhaps the last time you'll see it!

3. **Click the Address Book tab.**

   Your Address Book appears, as shown in Figure 4-4.

   Consider going into each group and exporting your contacts one group at a time, so you can import them that way, too.

4. **Click the Export link.**

   A dialog appears asking what file format the exported addresses should be stored in.

Figure 4-4:
Say good-
bye to your
grand, cen-
tral address
book.

5. **Click the Import mail and contacts button.**

   A dialog box requesting the e-mail address appears, as shown in Figure 4-1.

6. **Click the CSV File button.**

   A dialog box appears to allow you to choose where to save the file.

   Choosing CSV File exports your file as a Comma-Separated Value (CSV) file, which you can import into Google Voice. You can also make changes to it in a word processor or spreadsheet program such as Microsoft Word or Excel, or their Google Apps counterparts.

7. **Save the file in a location in which you can readily find it for importing.**

   We recommend that you save it to your desktop so you can easily find it.

If you've already upgraded, but can still get into GrandCentral, you can follow the steps above at any time. However, the longer you wait, adding contacts to Google Voice as you go, the more risk you have of duplicate contacts.

If you've already upgraded, and can't get into GrandCentral, you're probably stuck recreating contacts in Google Voice, unless you have your contacts stored in Outlook, Apple Address Book, or another program. One quick work-around is to e-mail your key contacts and ask them to either e-mail you their contact information or call you. Doing either makes it easy for you to create a new contact for them in Google Voice.

Saving your GrandCentral voicemails and recordings

Part of the advantage of using GrandCentral was to centralize your voice-mail messages and to get them onto your computer where you could deal with them more easily. Another part was the ability to record a call during the call. And part of the advantage of Google Voice is that it continues the GrandCentral capabilities and adds voicemail transcripts. (We're still waiting for transcripts of call recordings!)

If you haven't upgraded to Google Voice yet — or if you have done so and still have access to GrandCentral — you can take full advantage of Google Voice's new capabilities. First, you have to arrange to export links to your key voice-mail messages from GrandCentral. Then upgrade to Google Voice.

We've incorporated this trick into the steps for getting your GrandCentral voicemails into Google Voice:

1. **Sign into GrandCentral.**

2. **Click the Inbox tab.**

3. **Click the Messages link.**

   A list of your messages appears, as shown in Figure 4-1.

   Next is the most important step, and it has to do with destroying infor-mation rather than saving it!

4. **Delete all your unnecessary voicemails. Capture any needed To Do items and contact information first. Leave only voicemails that have important information contained inside them.**

   As shown by the transcript feature in Google Voice, sound files are a terrible place to lock up important information. Liberate yourself from them!

5. **Now only your critical messages remain. Click a message, then click the Forward tab. Fill in your own e-mail address in the To Email field. Fill in the note with pertinent information about the call as you can. Then click Send.**

   An e-mail message is sent with a link back to the voicemail message. The link works even if you are unable to access your GrandCentral account after you upgrade.

   Nothing is forever — don't count on your GrandCentral voicemails always being there. Deal with them one way or another, including bring-ing them into Google Voice as described below.

6. **Repeat for your remaining messages.**

What if you have already upgraded to Google Voice and can't get into your GrandCentral account? If you can find the e-mail notification that GrandCentral sent you, the link in that will still work.

But if you do have access, it's easier to use the systematic method in the steps above — getting rid of the chaff first and tipping yourself off to what's in the remaining messages — than to go through potentially hundreds of noti-fications to find the few voicemails that you want to keep.

Making the Move

Actually upgrading from GrandCentral to Google Voice is simple.

First, you need to receive an invitation to upgrade. That invitation appears in a box at the top of your GC account when you log in. An announcement of Google Voice is shown in Figure 4-5. At the time of this writing, the vast majority of GrandCentral users have received their invitation — but a few haven't.

If you have an invitation — and you've exported your contacts, forwarded a link to any old voicemails, and (optionally) opened a Gmail account, as described above — you're ready!

Follow these steps to move from GrandCentral to Google Voice:

1. **If you don't have a Google Account, use the instructions in Chapter 11 to create one.**

    All you need is an e-mail address of some sort. We recommend that you also create a Gmail account, as described in Chapter 11, as it's very useful for handling Google Voice e-mail messages, even if you don't use it for anything else.

Figure 4-5:
The invite can be an annoyance, especially if you don't get one.

2. **Sign into your Google account at Google.com.**

   Sign in to your Google Account using the e-mail address you want to use with Google Voice. This is important; you can't change it later.

3. **In a new browser window, sign into GrandCentral.**

   The message inviting you to upgrade appears, as shown in Figure 4-5.

4. **Click the link in the invitation message labeled Yes, Upgrade me.**

   You are asked to enter your password.

5. **Type your password.**

   After a brief pause, you'll be upgraded. The Google Voice screen will appear.

   Congratulations! You're now a Google Voice user.

6. **Bookmark your Google Voice page in your browser. You can get to Google Voice directly by going to http://google.com/voice.**

7. **Check whether you can still access your GrandCentral account.**

   Try signing into GrandCentral and see if you can still access your account. If you can, that's good news, in case there's anything you still want to retrieve. But it may not be there forever, so get any data you need out sooner rather than later.

Rerecording your name and greeting

You have to rerecord your name and greeting after you move to Google Voice. Do this quickly, before someone calls you!

Chapter 3 describes how to do this, if it's not enough like GrandCentral to be easy. You may also want to look through the rest of Chapter 3 to be reminded of other settings that are the same between the two systems, but whose details may have faded for you since you first set up Google Voice.

You also have to change any custom settings and recreate any WebCall buttons.

Importing your GrandCentral contacts

After you're in Google Voice, the next step to take — before you even take a look around — is to import your contacts. Having your contacts in Google Voice bring it to life and make it useful right away.

You want to import your contacts from GrandCentral first because they're phone number-centric. You may well have other contacts that you can import later, which are e-mail-centric or balanced among different contact methods. You want the phone number-centric ones first as a base in Google Voice.

Google Voice allows you to integrate different contact records for the same person fairly easily. After you do this, the combined information becomes part of your Google Contacts. You can use these across various Google services such as Gmail and combine them with other programs, such as Microsoft Outlook or Apple's Address Book.

Follow these steps to import contacts you exported from GrandCentral:

1. **Open the Google Voice Web site and click Contacts in the left-hand menu.**

   The Contacts page appears.

2. **Click the Import link in the upper-right corner of the page.**

3. **Click the Browse button to find the CSV file from GrandCentral to import.**

   The Choose File to Import dialog appears.

4. **Find the file you exported from GrandCentral and click Open.**

   The file path appears before the Browse button, as shown in Figure 4-6.

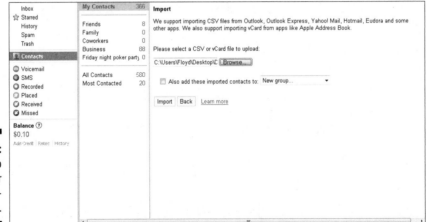

Figure 4-6:
Time to bring in your not-so-long-lost data.

5. **To also add the contacts to a specific group, click the checkbox and chose the group name from the pull-down menu, or specify that they'll be placed in a new group.**

   The contacts are placed in the All Contacts list in any event, from which you can place them into specific groups relevant to Google Voice. They will only all be placed directly into a specific group if you click the checkbox here.

6. **Click Import to import the contacts.**

   The contacts are brought into Google. Some contacts may not be brought in; if so, one or more error messages will appear to describe the problem(s).

For instructions on how to export and import other contacts, see Chapter 5.

If you have more than 3,000 contacts in a CSV file, the additional contacts won't import. Open the CSV file in a word processor or spreadsheet and save it as two or more separate CSV files, each with fewer than 3,000 contacts.

Importing your voicemails and recordings

Now you may have taken our advice and dealt with your old voicemails and recordings in GrandCentral, then deleted them. But perhaps you had a precious few you just had to forward to yourself, or perhaps you had so many that you had to export them all so you could deal with the lot of them later.

So now you have a few, or a lot of, e-mails with links to GrandCentral voicemail messages and recordings. And now that you've upgraded to Google Voice, you may or may not be able to get back into GrandCentral to access them.

At some point, GrandCentral may become permanently unavailable. And perhaps at the same time, or perhaps at a different time, your GrandCentral voicemail and recording files may become permanently unavailable. And dealing with old voicemails that aren't in your one and only, unified Google Voice voicemail inbox is a pain in any event.

So the sooner you deal with your voicemail and recording files, the better. You can either deal with them as e-mails or, through an admittedly slow, clumsy and error-prone process, bring them all the way into Google Voice.

To deal with them as e-mails, create a folder, or, in Google Voice, a label, and store all the emails with links to voicemails and recordings there. But remember, they're never safe from the original GrandCentral file being deleted.

But you may want to get the voicemail message or recording fully into Google Voice. This may especially be true if it has sentimental value or needs to be shared, as a recording, with others. So follow these steps to bring the message fully into Google Voice:

1. **Open the e-mail with the voicemail or recording linked to it.**

2. **For a voicemail message, use a nearby phone to call your Google Voice (was GrandCentral) number. Let the call go through to voicemail.**

3. **For longer recordings, you need two phones (as recording a call only works on incoming calls). Call from one phone to Google Voice. Pick up from a phone that the call rings through to. Press 4 to start recording the call.**

4. **When Google Voice starts recording, click the link in the e-mail to play the voicemail or recording back. Turn the volume up loud.**

5. **Play the message or recording through. Hang up.**

   Google Voice stores the voicemail or recording and sends you an e-mail with a link to the voicemail or recording.

   For a voicemail, Google Voice also includes a transcript. (The audio quality of the audio file and the accuracy of the transcript may not be very good because of the convoluted playback and recording process.)

You've now imported the voicemail message or recording fully into Google Voice. You can manage it just as you would have in GrandCentral, but with the added benefit (for voicemails) of a transcript.

Touring Google Voice

Much is the same in Google Voice as in GrandCentral, and you may not want to wade through this whole book trying to figure out what's different. Here are a few highlights.

In keeping with those priorities, logging into your shiny new Google Voice account presents you with the voicemail Inbox at center stage, and the rest of your stuff in a pane on the left-hand side. Go ahead and feel your way around. The first thing you notice: it takes fewer clicks to get to the features you want, because almost everything is laid out in one of the two new nav bars at the top and left of the screen.

As you can see every time you open Google Voice, Google has re-structured the interface to give real primacy to voicemail messages. They've assumed (and probably rightly) that your favorite things about GrandCentral included its ability to screen callers, send certain callers straight to voicemail, and record calls into your voicemail inbox.

Not only is getting around within your account easier, but getting around Google's suite of services is easier, too. Just like Gmail, Calendar, Reader, and all of Google's other tools, Voice has been blessed by Google's application nav bar at the very top of the window, letting you breezily switch between, say, your e-mail and your Voice account with one simple click.

Like Gmail, Google Voice relies on the "axis" style interface: two perpendicular toolbars on the top and left of the screen. Google has stuck all of the action-verb buttons — Call, SMS, Archive, Report Spam, Delete, and so on — in a bar atop the screen. The pane on the left is reserved for various folders such as your voice and text message inboxes and your call logs.

Also notice a little balance-counter for the money you have in the account. Don't freak out—Google Voice is still free, and so are domestic calls. The balance counter is just for international calling, which requires you to pay.

If you're familiar with Gmail, the blue action bar across the top of the inbox works basically the same way. And just like Gmail, you can now bumble around Voice with more than 20 keyboard commands.

The important ones all start with typing the letter *g,* (as in "go to"). They let you navigate around the folders in the left-hand pane. Just type g and the first letter of the folder you want (v for voicemail, s for starred, and so on) and Voice will switch to that screen. For more on these shortcuts, see Chapter 7.

Finding the new stuff

Where are the cool new features? Many of them "just happen"; the rest are seamlessly integrated into the Google Voice interface, as they should be. There are no flashing signs saying "New feature here." You can see some of the new features in Figure 4-7.

So here's where the new features show up:

- ✔ **Discounts on international calls is something that "just happens"; you place the call and get the cheaper rate.** For a list of rates, click the Rates link at the bottom of the pane on the left.

- ✔ **You no longer add credit to your account by using PayPal — you use Google Checkout.** Each of which, for one reason or another, has passionate fans and detractors. (Don't worry; they both work fine.) To add credit to your account, click the Add Credit link right next to the Rates link on the bottom left of the pane on the left of your screen and follow the instructions, as described in Chapter 7.

- ✔ **Conference calling is done by pressing keys during a call.** Same with recording an incoming call. Check the Cheat Sheet at the front of the book for details. Recordings are e-mailed to you automatically at the end of the call.

- ✔ **Voicemail transcription is automatic.** Google Voice gives you its best shot at a transcription with every voicemail message alert.

Figure 4-7:
Can you find
the key
features?

✔ **SMS text messaging — it is easier to receive than to give on this one.** SMS text messages you receive just show up in your Inbox, and you can deal with them just like e-mail messages now. And you can send SMS text messages from within Google Voice Web site without using up your cell allowance.

However, SMSing from your mobile phone requires you to use a dialer and dial into Google Voice before sending the text. (So it's your Google Voice number that the recipient responds to.) A dialer application helps (see Part III), but it's still extra work.

✔ **Contact management is just better.** It's easier to create, edit, and merge contacts, and your contacts are automatically part of your Google contacts.

✔ **GOOG-411 integration is automatic.** You can easily call Goog411 to get phone numbers and locations of businesses from within Google Voice.

✔ **Making calls from your voicemail Inbox makes callbacks easier.** Just call the number while in your Inbox. Both your main phone and the number you're calling will ring.

✔ **Embedding voicemails or recorded calls in your blog or Web site takes just a couple of steps.** See Chapter 6 for more information.

✔ **Using the GoogleVoice Mobile Web site on your Web-enabled cell phone is a snap.** Gp to the Web site `voice.google.com/m`. Details on how to use it for different phones are given in Part III. Choosing and using dialers for different phones is in Part III as well.

Finding more

After you've identified the "nuggets" of brand new features, there is also some news about the way things are organized.

Head over to your Contacts menu on the left. The new three-pane view does away with GrandCentral's cumbersome list format, and lets you create and manage groups of contacts (friends, family, coworkers) more easily. Note that Google has also automatically imported your Gmail contacts into the All Contacts heading, so that you can add the people you e-mail most into your Google Voice list.

Google has also taken the liberty of grouping the people you talk to most via e-mail and Voice into a handy Most Contacted list. If you care to cut down that list to a useful size, try the Suggested Contacts button in the right-most pane. It creates a new group of people you talk to frequently via e-mail, but who aren't in your Voice contacts list yet. Find duplicates? Check the boxes next to them, and notice that the right-most pane allows you to combine them into a single contact, with all the information from both. See Chapter 3 for more about working with Contacts.

Note that calling and texting new numbers is easier than before, too. Just click Call or SMS at the top left of the blue action bar, or type *c* or *s* from the keyboard, and enter the number you want to contact.

Another great little feature: the blue Tip bar at the bottom of your voicemail inbox. We cover everything you need to know about using Voice throughout this book, but the tip bar serves as a good reminder.

After you've gotten a good feel for the new layout, head up to the top right-hand corner of your screen and click the Settings tab, as shown in Figure 4-8. Go over all your preferences — a couple of them will be new — and make sure you've got things set the way you like.

The Settings tab is also the place you can change the way GV treats groups of contacts — specifically, which voicemail message they hear, and how their call is presented to you.

In Settings, you also notice the Call Widgets tab. If you had a Call Me button from GrandCentral embedded in your blog or Web site and you'd like to upgrade it to a Google Voice-branded button, you can do that here.

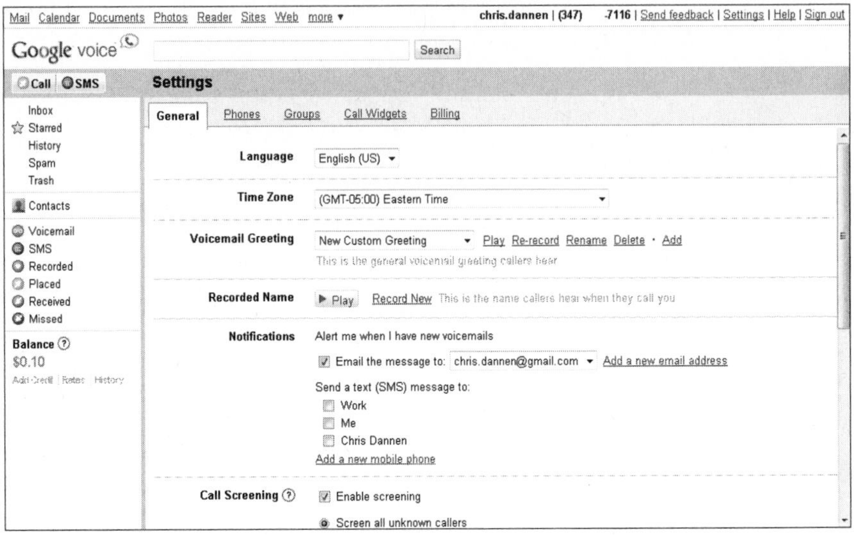

Figure 4-8:
Check your
settings, old
and new.

Finally, Settings is also the place to add money to your Google Voice account for international calling.

Like something about the new interface? Hate something? Use the Feedback link at the top-right corner of your screen (next to Settings) to tell Google just what you like or dislike about the upgrade. Do it now, while the differences are still fresh in your mind. Google is known for listening to its users, and as a GrandCentral upgrader, you have a special perspective that can help them improve the service.

Now get out there and do some calling!

Part II
Maximizing Your Voice

The 5th Wave · By Rich Tennant

"His name is D'Marco D'Magician. He's helping us tap into the power of Google Voice."

In this part . . .

You want to get the most out of Google Voice while spending the least money. We show you how to do that across the many settings and options that you can adjust and take advantage of while using Google Voice.

Chapter 5

Managing People in Google Voice

Communications is all about people — and Google Voice is all about giving you more ways to be in touch. It fills in the gaps between e-mail, your computer, and your phones.

But getting the full advantage of all this integration means importing contacts into Google Voice and managing them. Indeed, some of the power of Google Voice comes from putting people into groups, then managing those groups as a whole. But the groups only make sense in Google Voice, so managing them has to be done there as well.

This chapter spells out the easiest ways to get the most power out of Google Voice with the least work. As with the settings in the last chapter, you must do a small chunk of work up front, plus minor ongoing efforts, with the right up-front steps making maintenance easier. In this chapter, we show you how to do things right the first time and give you an easy-to-use reference source when you need to make changes in the future.

 When you import data into Google, the imported information overwrites any existing contacts that have the same e-mail address. So, we recommend that you import early to avoid the frustration of putting new information directly into a Google contact, then overwriting it with older, imported information.

Importing Contacts into Google

People have long used PCs to bridge the gap between business and calling cards, paper address books, printed phone books, scraps of paper, and their phones. For example, one of the authors (Smith) used an early Macintosh to keep a very tightly formatted list of key contacts that he could easily print out, fold up, and put in his wallet. (Where it rapidly became dog-eared from frequent use.)

Now PCs and mobile phones are so useful for capturing and storing data that people tend to have a proliferation of contact information. Beginning to use Google Voice gives you a good opportunity to bring a lot of it together.

Google Voice erodes the barrier between e-mail and telephone communication, so your Google Voice contact information should be quite robust, including at least a person's name, e-mail addresses) and all of a person's phone numbers.

Your Google Voice contacts are actually contacts that work right across Google — in Gmail, in Google Calendar, and more. If you only use Google Voice, that's fine, but if you use other Google tools as well, you leverage the work you do in each one across all of them.

The idea is for Google to be able to suck in all the contact information you already have online and also make it easy for you to enter offline information as well. You can then share the result with all your other programs.

Using more Google tools also help you if you're a smartphone user, as Google's Mail mobile Web sites and client apps for various smartphones are, at least at this writing, the best in the business.

However, Gmail's contact management capability is still not as strong as Microsoft Outlook (known as Entourage on the Mac), which is still used by most people in a way that works on one machine at a time. It's even common for people to have distinct Outlook setups on their home and work computers, with very different but overlapping data, and to have to spend time managing them separately and reconciling contacts that are shared between them.

People spend time wondering how to get separate clients like a cell phone or Google Voice updated with both their work and personal electronic contact information files. This hassle is part of the reason it's popular for people to have separate cell phones for personal and work purposes. (Which kind of misses the whole point of going digital and even of having what are intended to be "all in one," not "all in two," mobile devices, but is still the best approach for a lot of people.)

This argues for making Gmail your main online e-mail program, importing as much information as you can into Google, then using Gmail for all your data or at least all your personal data. You may need to maintain your work information separately, though of course you'll have overlap between the two.

In this section, we describe how to get contact information into Google from three of the main sources: online e-mail programs; Outlook on Windows or its counterparts, Entourage and Address Book on the Mac; and paper-based records, such as a diary or business cards.

If you have a Gmail account, Google Voice will be pre-populated with those contacts. However, you may still want to use the steps in this chapter to get additional information into Google Voice, from where it will be available in Gmail and other Google services.

Avoid having Google Voice become an isolated piece added to a welter of personal information across various digital and paper-based forms. Use Google to centralize as much of your personal information as possible.

If you use GrandCentral, see Chapter 5 for information on how to move your GrandCentral contacts into Google. It's not automatic, but it's not difficult. Do it before you start entering information into Google Voice, though, to avoid duplicating effort.

Gmail has a major problem, said to be due to errors in its trademark registration in the U.K. While Google calls the service "Gmail" and allows people to use e-mail addresses ending in "gmail.com," the legally correct name of the service in the UK is "Google Mail," and the proper ending for Google's e-mail addresses in the UK is the off-putting "@googlemail.com." U.K. users sometimes have trouble verifying their identity on services where they've registered with a "gmail" account and the service has recorded them as having a "googlemail" account; let's hope this problem doesn't become global.

Export and importing Webmail contacts and e-mail

Google has introduced a new tool to help import contact information and even e-mails from other Webmail services into Gmail. It combines exporting information from the source and importing it into Google Voice.

Some other programs have had such tools in the past with good results. For example, Microsoft has had a tool based on TrueSwitch, which also underlies the Google offering, since mid-2007.

The intent is to get users like you to switch from your old e-mail provider to Gmail. For Google Voice users, this is generally a good idea. And the timing is good, too, because you're going to be contacting people to get them to use Google Voice, so you might as well take the opportunity to give them a new e-mail address for you as well.

Google's tool supports most major online e-mail providers, including AOL, EarthLink, Hotmail, and Yahoo! All you need is access to the account — the user name and password — and a bit of time to go through the steps, plus up to a day or two for e-mails to transfer over if you've so requested.

For a complete list of supported Webmail providers, check the list at this URL:

```
http://mail.google.com/support/bin/answer.py?answer=117173
```

For unsupported providers, and e-mail readers such as Outlook, Entourage, and Apple's Address Book, use a CSV file for interchange, as described in the next section.

But Google's import tool for contact information and e-mail messages is the best way to do this, if it's available for your account. Follow these steps to use the tool:

1. **If you don't already have a Gmail account, create one. Go to gmail. com and follow the steps shown to create your account.**

   The import tool was initially available only for new Gmail accounts, but is, at this writing, steadily being rolled out to existing Gmail accounts as well.

2. **Open your Gmail inbox.**

3. **Click the Settings link in the upper-right corner.**

4. **Click the Accounts and Import link.**

   The Accounts and Import options appear.

5. **Click the Import mail and contacts button.**

   A dialog box requesting the e-mail address appears, as shown in Figure 5-1.

Figure 5-1: Enter the e-mail address to import from.

6. **Type the e-mail address of the account you want to import from.**

   A dialog box requesting the relevant password appears.

7. **Type the password of the account you want to import from.**

   A dialog box requesting you to set the import options appears, as shown in Figure 5-2.

8. **Select import options; check or clear checkboxes to import contacts; import mail; continue importing mail for 30 days; and to add a label to all imported mail.**

   For our purposes here, you definitely want to import contacts. Only import mail if it has things you want to keep and if you intend to shut down, or at least mostly stop using, the account; otherwise you can just leave the existing e-mail in the other account.

   If you do import the other account's mail, we suggest that you create a label shorter than your full e-mail address, such as just the name of the provider: "Hotmail" or some such.

   E-mail importing may take several hours or even a few days to complete.

9. **Click Start import.**

   Although timing might vary depending on a number of factors, the contacts information should be imported in a matter of minutes. E-mail importing may take many hours or even a few days. If you've chosen to import newly arriving e-mail messages over the next 30 days, these may take a day or two to show up as well.

Figure 5-2:
Enter the
e-settings
for
importing
contacts
and/or
e-mail.

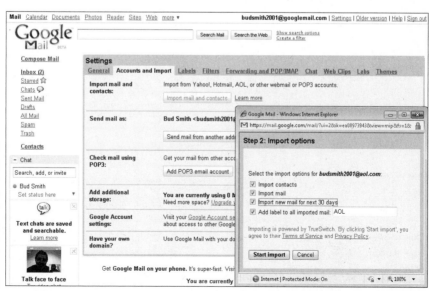

The Accounts and Import tab displays a message showing that importing is in progress. It will also give you the option of whether to send out all messages using the Gmail account as the reply-to address, or whether to use the account the e-mail message was sent to — whether that's the Gmail account or the account(s) being imported — as the reply-to address.

You can change the From address on specific e-mail messages by clicking the Change link in the From address area of the e-mail message.

You can use Gmail as a kind of control panel for several e-mail accounts, either on a transitional basis as a step toward getting rid of some of them or as an easier way to manage accounts you intend to maintain.

10. **Return to the Accounts and Import tab of your Gmail account to check on progress, as shown in Figure 5-3.**

Keep checking this page to follow the progress of the importing process. When the process is complete, you'll receive a notification via e-mail.

Exporting a CSV file from your mail reader

Most programs that store address book information, such as Microsoft Outlook, Microsoft Entourage for Mac, and Lotus Notes, can export address data in a standard file type called a CSV file. The CSV, or comma-separated values, format is a text file with commas, as the name suggests, separating the values.

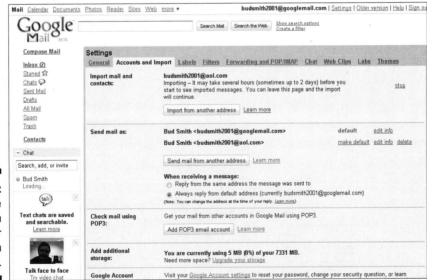

Figure 5-3: Change the From address or check in on progress.

The great thing about CSV files is that you can easily create, read, and modify them yourself. You can edit the file most easily in a spreadsheet program — Google has a free one — being sure to export it again as a CSV file.

Apple's Address Book exports contacts in vCard format, which Google can also import.

To get address book information from such programs, you export it as a CSV file (or in vCard format), then import the file into Google. (Thus the "free trade" pun in the title of this section.)

Follow these steps to export address book information from Outlook 2003; the process is similar for other programs:

1. **Open Outlook or the other program or online service.**

2. **Choose File⇨Import and Export.**

   The Import and Export Wizard appears, as shown in Figure 5-4.

3. **Choose Export to a file from the scrolling list and click Next.**

   The Wizard prompts you for the file type.

4. **Choose Comma Separated Values (Windows) and click Next.**

   The Wizard prompts you for the folder to export from.

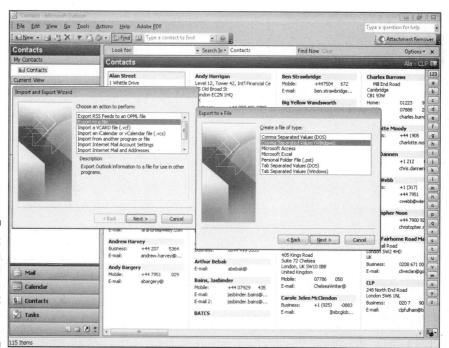

Figure 5-4:
Outlook's Wizard helps you export contacts as a CSV file.

5. Choose Contacts and click Next.

The Wizard prompts you for the file name.

Windows attaches the extension `.csv` to the filename, and uses it to identify the file type, but does not show the extension in most displays of the filename.

6. Type a name for the file and click Browse to choose a location for the file to be stored in. When you've entered the name and location, click Next.

The Wizard displays a confirmation message, just to be sure. It also Displays the Map Custom Fields button, you the opportunity to edit the fields that will be exported, to remove fields from what gets exported and to reorder the fields in the exported file.

7. If you want to edit the list and order of fields to be exported, click the Map Custom Fields button. If not, skip to Step 10.

The Map Custom Fields dialog appears, as shown in Figure 5-5.

8. Edit the list of exported fields and drag and drop fields to reorder them.

Use the Previous and Next buttons to view specific entries. To start from an empty list, click Clear Map. To return to the original map, click Default Map.

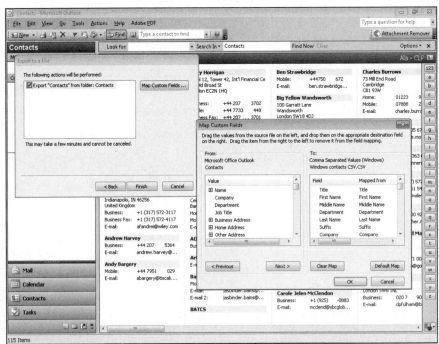

Figure 5-5:
You can tweak the exported file a field at a time.

Fields of dreams

Here are the fields in the Google address book: Name; Title; Company; Email-Home; Email-Work; Email-Other; Phone-Home; Phone-Work; Phone-Mobile; Phone-Home Fax; Phone-Work Fax; Phone-Pager; Phone-Other; Address-Home; Address-Work; Address-Other; plus several entries for Website, Birthday, additional fields that can be added, and Notes.

In a CSV export process, or when editing a CSV file, you can simplify what's exported to make it as close as possible to the fields and field names that Google's address book stores. This makes it more likely that Google will import the file correctly, with fewer problems and with less need for editing the resulting individual contacts.

9. **When you're finished, click OK.**

   You return to the Export to a File dialog box.

10. **To export the file, click Finish.**

   The export proceeds.

11. **Open the exported file in a spreadsheet program, inspect it, and re-export if needed.**

12. **Edit the file in a spreadsheet program if you wish. You can delete rows and columns you don't need and/or edit the field names to more closely match Google's. Use the fields listed in the "Fields of dreams" sidebar, as a guide. When you're done, save the file as a CSV file.**

Entering data into a CSV file

You can edit a CSV file or create one from scratch, using it to hold information you type in, for example, from an address book or business cards.

The easiest way to edit or create a CSV file is in a spreadsheet program, such as Microsoft Excel. You work with the file as usual, then save it as a CSV file. You can then import it into Google.

Follow these steps to create and enter data into a CSV file:

1. **Open your spreadsheet program and open a new file.**

2. **Enter the field names across the top, in row 1.**

   Use field names similar or identical to the Google field names shown in the sidebar, "Fields of dreams." Leave out less-used fields such as Phone-Pager.

If you need a model, export contacts from Outlook or Google and use the field names as a starting point. Google can recognize these formats and some others.

3. Type the data for a few contacts in the rows below.

You can copy and paste the data from sources on your PC or type it in from paper sources such as an address book or business cards.

4. Save the file as a CSV file.

To start, choose File➪Save As. In the Save As dialog box, use the pull-down menu to choose CSV (comma delimited) as the file type. Navigate to the destination you want to save the file to and click Save.

5. Test the importing capability for the CSV file.

Follow the steps in the "Importing data from a CSV file" section.

Make sure that your new contacts come in the way you expect them to. Adjust the field names in the first row if needed and retry.

6. Continue importing and entering data.

Your spreadsheet fills in and looks something like the spreadsheet in Figure 5-6.

7. Save the file, as described in Step 4 above, and import it into Google, as described in the next section.

Importing data from a CSV file

You can use CSV files from various sources to update Gmail.

Figure 5-6:
Create your
own input
data.

	A	B	C	D	E	F	G	H	I	J	K	L	M	N	O
1	Title	First Name	Middle Nar	Last Name	Suffix	Company	Departmen	Job Title	Business	Business	Business	Business	Business	Business	Business (Ho
2		Miles													
3		Alicia							Balboa Avenue					92111	United States
4	Dr	Daniel	P			Earthwatch	Institute	Head of Cl	Earthwatc					OX2 7DE	United Kingdo
5		Anjali				HSBC		Manager, I	Level 36, 8 Canada Square					E14 5HQ	United Kingdo
6	Dr	Tim				Scripps Institution of Oceanograf		9500						92093	United States
7		Edward				CB Richard	Ellis	Surveyor - Valuation Advisory							
8		Brian				Cisco Systems		Consulting Systems Engineer							
9		Ryan							Morris St.					46203	United States
10		Amy				Wiley Publishing	Acquisition		Crosspoint Blvd.					46256	United States
11		Harshad				Computer	Step	Managing	Southfield					CV47 0FB	UK
12	Dr	Colin				North End	Medical Centre	211 North End Road						W14 9NP	United Kingdo
13						David Lloyd	Leisure		Unit 24,					SW6 1BW	United Kingdo
14		John				VTC		Product Manager							
15		Nicole				Wiley Publishing, Inc.	Project Ed		Crosspoint Blvd.					46256	United States
16		Teddy				Video expert									
17						Blackwells									
18						Foyles									16:
19		Floyd													
20		Carole	Jelen			Waterside	Production	VP/Literary Agent							
21		Brenda				BBC London	Tonight								
22		Carol	Madison												
23		Carole							405 Kings					SW10 0BE	United Kingdo
24		Jessica													
25		Floyd													
26		Richard							5 Moncks Bay Lane					8081	New Zealand

Gmail can import a maximum of 3000 contacts at a time. If your CSV file has more than 3,000 contacts, you need to split it into parts. You can import a CSV file into a word processing or spreadsheet program, edit it, and then save one or more CSV files to get under the 3000-contact limit.

After you have the CSV file the way you want it, import it into Google:

1. **Open the Google Voice Web site and click Contacts in the left-hand menu.**

   The Contacts page appears.

2. **Click the Import link in the upper-right corner of the page.**

   The Import page appears, as shown in Figure 5-7.

3. **Click the Browse button to find the CSV file to import.**

   The Choose File to Import dialog appears.

4. **Find the file and click Open.**

   The file path appears in before the Browse button.

5. **To also add the contacts to a specific group, click the checkbox, and chose the group name from the pull-down menu, or specify that contacts will be placed in a new group.**

   The contacts are placed in the All Contacts list in any event, from which you can place them into specific groups relevant to Google Voice. They are only placed directly into a specific group if you click the checkbox here.

   You may want to create a new Group for the contacts you are importing to go into. See the section on Groups below for information about how to create a new Group.

6. **Click Import to import the contacts.**

   The contacts will be brought into Google. Some contacts may not be brought in; if so, one or more error messages will describe the problem(s).

Combining contacts in Google Voice

There's a potential challenge in using Google Voice: most computer-based contacts lists are e-mail centric, because that used to be the only way you could use a computer to communicate with other people.

But with Google offering Gmail, Google Talk, and Google Voice — as well as an online calendar for which address information is most useful — there's a need for more complete contact information. In Google Voice, you're likely to combine phone-oriented contacts (potentially imported from GrandCentral, if you were a GrandCentral user) with contacts that are e-mail centric.

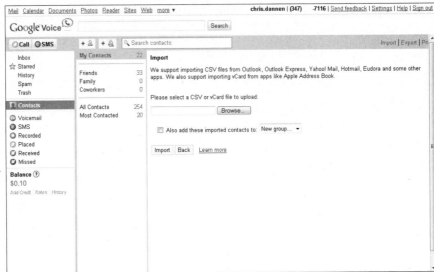

Figure 5-7:
Time to
bring in your
not-so-long-
lost data.

After you get your contacts right in Google Voice, they automatically become available in all Google applications. You can also export them for use in other tools such as Microsoft Outlook and Apple's Address Book.

Follow these steps to combine contacts in Google Voice:

1. **Open the Google Voice Web site and click Contacts in the left-hand menu.**

   The Contacts page appears.

2. **Click All Contacts.**

   You can combine two or more contacts from any of your groups of contacts but to make sure you don't miss any, choose All Contacts.

3. **Click the first contact you want to merge.**

   The checkbox next to the contact name is selected. Review the contact details.

4. **Click the second contact you want to merge.**

   This removes the selection highlight and the check from the first contact, but displays the second contact's details. Review the contact details. Ensure that you really do want to merge these two specific contacts.

   You can merge more than two contacts at once, but it's a bit of a stupid pet trick because the chance that you'll lose information in the merge increases. If you have more than two contacts to merge, do it in several merge operations, checking at each step of the way.

5. **Hold down the Ctrl key and click on the first contact again.**

   The two contacts will be highlighted and the Merge these two contacts link appears, as shown in Figure 5-8.

   Hold down Ctrl to maintain the existing selection and add the new contact you click to it. Hold down Shift to maintain the existing selection and add the new contact *and any contacts in between.* For adjacent contacts, either way will work, but using Ctrl is more flexible. We recommend using Ctrl at all times to maintain, well, control.

6. **Click the Merge these two contacts link.**

   Google Voice displays a proposed merge of the two contacts, as shown in Figure 5-9.

7. **Edit the information carefully.**

   Note that most fields are preserved. However, for the contact name, the name of the first contact in alphabetical order is used; the second name is discarded.

8. **Click Save to save the contact.**

   The revised contact is saved and the two contacts you merged to create it are deleted.

9. **Click the new contact and check to make sure the information is correct. Click the Edit button if you need to change anything.**

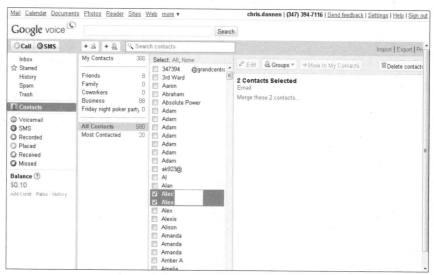

Figure 5-8:
Time to transmogrify two contacts to one.

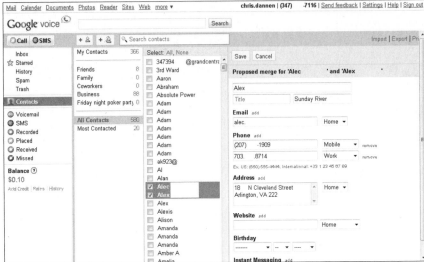

Working with Groups

Groups in Google Voice are collections of one or more contacts that can take on the same settings for call handling. Groups created in Google Voice can also be used in other Google products.

You find several default groups — four that you manage yourself, and two that Google maintains for you:

✔ The groups you manage yourself are My Contacts and Friends, Family, and Co-workers.

✔ The groups that Google maintains for you are All Contacts, which is an all-inclusive group, and Most Contacted, the 20 contacts you are in touch with most frequently.

A contact can be assigned to one of the default groups from among the four you manage yourself or to a new, custom group you can create.

A contact can be assigned to more than one group; for example, someone can be in both the Friends and Family groups. Also, you can have My Contacts, Friends, Family, Co-workers and/or members of custom groups in a special-purpose custom group, such as a group that you name "Poker Night." However, managing overlapping groups can be confusing, and it can be difficult to be sure which group settings are in effect for contacts that belong to multiple groups.

Contact management for centurions

Google Voice offers as useful a way to hand-edit contacts as we've seen. However, if you're a centurion — if you have 100 contacts or more — it may take too long to do everything in Google Voice.

Instead, you may want to export contacts to one or more CSV files and then combine them in a program that can handle CSV files, such as a spreadsheet or word processor. Then reimport the new file(s) into Google Voice. Where you can go through them, check that everything's OK, and hand-edit anything that's a problem!

If you're a Centaurian, though, rather than a centurion, your address fields are going to be a bit complex, and we don't know your phone numbering system — so you're on your own.

Like individual contacts, a group can have:

✔ Specific settings for which of your phones ring when a member of the group calls.

✔ A specific greeting played when a member of the group leaves a voicemail.

✔ Call presentation — the potential for call screening and the ability to listen in when a caller is leaving a voicemail — turned on or off for members of the group.

When you change the settings for an individual contact, it overrides the settings for the group(s) that the contact belongs to.

The following sections share instructions for adding an individual contact to a group and for creating a new group.

Creating and deleting groups

A new, custom group that you create can contain contacts that are separate from the other groups you manage directly — My Contacts, Friends, Family and Coworkers — or intermixed among them.

Follow these steps to create a new group:

1. **Open the Google Voice Web site and click Contacts in the left-hand menu.**

   The Contacts page appears.

2. **Click the New Group button (marked with a + symbol and two heads).**

   A dialog box appears, asking what you want to name this group.

3. Enter a name for the group and click OK.

The new group name appears in the list of groups you manage directly, as shown in Figure 5-10.

4. To remove a custom group, highlight a group name in the list of groups.

If the selected name represents a custom group, the Delete Group button will be highlighted for selection.

5. Click the Delete group button to delete the highlighted group.

You are asked to confirm whether you want to delete the group.

6. Click OK.

The group is deleted. The group's contacts are still available through the All Contacts group and whatever other groups each contact may belong to.

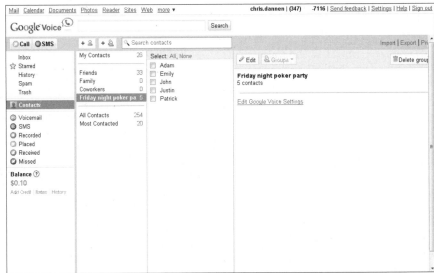

Figure 5-10:
Your new group takes its place among pre-defined ones.

Adding and removing contacts from groups

Follow these steps to add or remove contacts from a group:

1. Open the Google Voice Web site and click Contacts in the left-hand menu.

The Contacts page appears.

2. **Click the group, such as All Contacts, that has contacts in it that you want to assign to another group.**

   The group name is highlighted and the contacts in the group are listed with empty checkboxes next to their names for selection, as shown in Figure 5-11.

3. **Click the All link to select all the contacts in the displayed group; click the None link to deselect all of them; and click individual checkboxes to select or deselect individual contacts.**

4. **Click the Groups button to display options for managing the Group memberships of the selected contacts.**

   The relevant options appear.

   Not all of the choices shown in the Groups pull-down menu are necessarily relevant to all the selected contacts, but each of the choices shown is relevant to at least one of the selected contacts. For instance, you are given the option to remove the selected contacts from the My Contacts group even if as few as one of them is actually a member of that group.

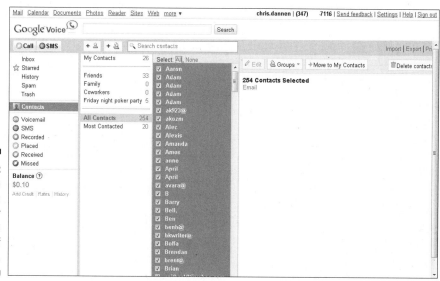

Figure 5-11: You can work with All, some, or None of the members of a group.

5. **Click the Groups button to display options for managing the Group memberships of the selected contacts.**

   The Groups pull-down menu appears, with choices relevant to the selected contacts displayed, such as moving the contacts to another group.

6. **Highlight the desired action with the mouse and click to select it.**

   The action will be carried out.

Changing settings at the group level

Google Voice allows you to change settings at the group level, but only for three of the pre-defined groups: Friends, Family, and Coworkers or new groups that you create and populate yourself.

Google Voice does not allow you to change Google Voice settings at the Group level for the groups My Contacts, All Contacts, or Most Contacted.

When you specify settings at the group level, one option you have is to pick up the settings used at the overall level, as set in the General and Phones tabs, as described in the previous chapter. Doing it this way gives you a lot of power at the overall level to change settings for not only your non-contacts — calls from numbers not listed as belonging to one of your contacts — but for those contacts in your Friends, Family, Coworkers or custom groups as well.

So review those settings, if you need to, before or as you change the settings at the group level.

Follow these steps to change settings for a group:

1. **Open the Google Voice Web site and click Settings in the left-hand menu.**

   The Settings page appears.

2. **Click the Groups tab.**

   A list of the groups for which you can change settings — Friends, Family, Coworkers and any custom groups you've created — appears, as shown in Figure 5-12. The list displays phone forwarding, greeting, and call presentation settings for each group.

   You can also get to this screen by choosing Contacts and then highlighting the name of a relevant group by clicking it in the list of groups that appears. Then click the link, Edit Google Voice Settings. The screen shown in Figure 5-12 appears.

   The settings displayed here do apply at the group level, but may have been overridden for specific contacts within the group.

3. **Click the Edit button under the name of the group whose settings you with to edit.**

   The settings for the group appear, as shown in Figure 5-13.

Figure 5-12:
Quickly view
current
settings
on the
Groups tab.

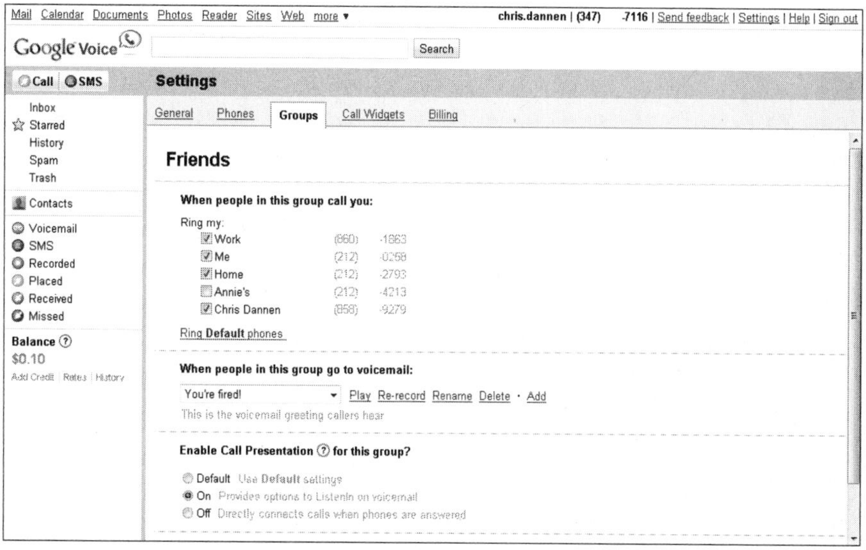

Figure 5-13:
Change the
settings for
a group.

4. **Change which phones are set to ring by clicking and clearing check-boxes. To use the settings defined in the General tab, choose Ring Default Phones.**

The change applies to new contacts you create within the group and existing contacts that are set to use the group setting. It will not apply to contacts in the group for whom you've created customized settings.

5. **Change the voicemail greeting from the pull-down menu. Use the links to play, re-record, rename, delete, or add a greeting.**

6. **Set call presentation options for the group.**

    Turn call presentation on or off for the group. To use the settings defined in the General tab, and continue to use them if they're updated, choose Default.

7. **Click Save to save the group settings.**

    The group settings are changed.

Managing Settings at the Group Level

Managing your settings for Google Voice is where its power comes from, but also where there's the most potential for confusion.

You can easily have hundreds of contacts in Google, growing to include all the people you exchange e-mail with. Only some of these people are likely to call you, and many of those will call only occasionally. Yet conveniently managing this "long tail" of occasional callers is one of the main benefits of Google Voice.

Harvesting phone numbers

One of the key advantages of Google Voice is the way it lets you move seamlessly between "live" phone calls, voicemail messages, text (SMS) messages, and e-mail. But this only works if you have people's phone numbers.

Google Voice encourages a move from phone calls to e-mail. For example, Google Voice's transcription feature, in which voicemail messages are transcribed and sent to you as e-mail, is an outright invitation to send an e-mail in some instances where you would have made a return phone call in the past.

But it works the other way, too. As more people use Google Voice, you may get phone calls and text messages where people would have e-mailed you in the past. As e-mail In boxes pile ever higher, a phone call can be a good

way to cut through the noise. Google Voice encourages this.

Having people's phone numbers — both so you can call them, and so you (and Google Voice) can recognize who's on the other end when they call you — becomes ever more important. Moving to Google Voice is a good opportunity to get your contacts' complete and up-to-date information. If you are getting a new Google Voice number, when you contact people to let them know your new number, ask for their numbers as well. If you move your cell phone to Google Voice, send an e-mail to your e-mail contacts who you might also wish to call, or who might call you, asking for their phone number.

Google Voice has a nice summary presentation of settings for all groups from the Groups tab but nothing similar for individuals. So consider getting your groups set up correctly and changing Google Voice settings by group as much as possible. Then you can manage your *high value* such as close family members, close friends, and key co-workers individually when needed.

Gaining control of your phones is great. But losing track of settings such that you're not getting calls you should be getting can be extremely frustrating. So give some thought to how you set things up.

It may seem extreme, but consider creating medium-sized groups, and even a couple of very small groups. You may even want to have one or a few groups with only one contact. The idea is to make the groups small enough that you manage all your settings at the group level. Then you can use the Groups summary presentation to quickly review all your important settings and make changes at the group level where needed. Doing this prevents you from having to go through potentially dozens of individual contacts one after another just to confirm what their settings are.

Chapter 6

Changing Settings in Google Voice

· ·

In This Chapter

▶ Settings strategies

▶ Taming your phones

▶ Making ListenIn work for you

▶ Customizing voicemail greetings

▶ Changing settings for text messages

· ·

*O*ne of the great advantages of the telephone is its simplicity. But people also want power. Google Voice is the best *power tool* so far for phones. It puts you above the action, managing your phones like players on your own personal team of devices. You can even add a *ringer* — a nearby phone that you want to use for just a little while — to help you win!

This chapter focuses on services available while using Google Voice on any phone and what you can do with the Google Voice Web site, whether you're using it on a PC or using the mobile version on a smartphone. However, you won't find any information on what you can do from your smartphone with various Google Voice dialer programs; you can find information on dialers in the chapters in Part III.

Adjusting Settings and Strategies

Basic telephone service: dialing, ringing, talking; is called *POTS*, for "plain old telephone service." The great advantage of POTS phones is that they "just work." And an advantage of a mobile phone is that you can turn it off — but one of the worse things is that you can forget you turned it off.

Google Voice gives you a whole new set of ways to *break* each of your phones — that is, to block calls from getting through. One of the benefits of being geared up with a home phone, an office phone, and one or more cell phones is that people have many ways to reach you. With Google Voice, you can control all of them centrally.

But there's a basic tension here: The best way to avoid problems with Google Voice is to *set and forget*, to come up with a group of settings and to stick with it. On the other hand, much of the benefit from Google Voice is to change the settings frequently (for example, changing settings and messages when you travel).

You can get the best of both worlds by learning how to control the settings for Google Voice — and by having ready access to the settings you might not have memorized yet.

Don't be afraid to limit how much twiddling you do, to set simple and clear rules even if your phone does ring occasionally when you didn't necessarily want it to. Even then, with Google Voice you have more options than you would without it.

The settings for Google Voice contacts and phones are explained in detail in Chapter 3. In this chapter, we just briefly mention what a function does; the focus is on changing settings.

Google Voice has several levels of settings: a top level, in either the General tab of settings or the Phones tab; a middle level, where you manage Groups; and a lower level, individual Contacts. Keeping on top of what your settings are can get confusing. There are three settings that can be managed at all three levels:

- ✔ **Phone forwarding:** This setting is the most basic element of Google Voice: which phones ring when different people call you. You set a default for which phones ring at the top level, in the Phones tab. At the Group level, you can create different settings, or use the settings in Phones as a default. At the Contact level, you can create different settings again, or use the Group setting — which might refer back to the top-level, Phones setting.

- ✔ **ListenIn settings:** ListenIn, referred to as Call Presentations in the Settings area, is a very powerful feature of Google Voice, but it puts your callers through extra steps to call you. Controlling ListenIn settings is just like controlling phone forwarding: You set a default for ListenIn at the top level; you can then use that default or specific settings at the Group level, and use Group settings or Contact-specific settings at the Contact level.

- ✔ **Voicemail message settings:** Your voicemail messages that can be used in any part of Google Voice can be managed — added to, renamed, and deleted — from the General tab, within a Group setting or at the Contacts level. After you have your messages list right, you can choose a message in the General tab as a default; use or override it at the Group level; and use the Group setting (which may be the overall default) or a new, specific setting for a given contact.

These three types of settings are covered in their own sections below, but thinking about them holistically is also important, so that you can make your settings as complex as you need — but not so complex as to cause you confusion.

Changing Which Phones Ring

Having the ability to decide which phones ring when someone calls your Google Voice number is the most important function in Google Voice. Google Voice honcho Craig Walker described it as allowing you to "never miss a call you do want, and never take a call you don't want." This vision creates a power struggle: people want to be able to call and, potentially, interrupt you; you want to control when and how that happens.

Google Voice gives you a lot of power in managing this crucial capability. And after you get this right, it's like a dream; your phones are finally tamed. The second is, with voicemail notifications via e-mail — and, if you so choose, via text — the penalty for missing a call is lower, as you get notification and a transcription shortly after. You can revert to the caller quickly and accurately, completing the communication.

We recommend that you be generous in allowing calls through initially. You are, in essence, trying to train your contacts to call you at a number that's based in "the cloud" — on the Internet — rather than tied to a particular phone. If you're usually available, they (and you) learn to trust this approach. If not, people either get frustrated, or just keep calling you on your direct phone numbers — in which case Google Voice just becomes another phone number and voice message mailbox that you have to manage along with the others.

Quickly changing a pair of Generals

At the General level, two settings don't interact directly with other settings at the Group or Contact level, and you may want to change these settings frequently, and in concert with one another. These are

✔ **How you're alerted to new voicemails.** Your choices are by email and/or by SMS text message to a cell phone.

✔ **Do Not Disturb.** This setting sends all calls to voicemail. Unfortunately, you can't set up Do Not Disturb to have exceptions for emergency calls.

Most of the time, you probably won't want SMS text message alerts for voicemails to be turned on; if you're billed for text messages by your wireless carrier, the charges add up. But you may want to turn on SMS text message alerts for voicemail when Do Not Disturb is on — that way you can quickly respond to any calls that seem urgent, without allowing them to actually ring your phone.

We also recommend that you manage phones at the overall level as set in the Phones tab of the Settings area wherever possible; and that, when that's not enough, you use Groups rather than individual Contacts. (See the "Group strategy" sidebar for an interesting twist on this approach.) Otherwise, you may have to review each and every one of your Contacts on a regular basis just to remind yourself how phone forwarding is set up for each of them!

Finding out about phone forwarding

The phone forwarding settings for a Contact can be set at three levels, with more capabilities at the lowest level, specific Contacts:

- At the Contact level, you can set each of your phones to ring or not ring; send that Contact to Voicemail, treat as Spam or block the caller entirely; or default to the setting for that user's Group.

- At the Group level, you can only set phones to ring or not ring, or default to the top-level setting in the Phones tab of the Settings area. You can't send all the Contacts in a Group to Voicemail, treat them as Spam or, block all the callers in the Group entirely.

- In the Phones tab of the Settings area, you can only control which phones your Google Voice number rings through to, assuming that the default setting is used at the Group level and the Group setting is used at the individual Contact level. You can't send calls through to Voicemail, treat them as Spam, or block them entirely at this level.

However, in the General tab, you can turn on the Do Not Disturb option, which does have the effect of sending all calls to voicemail (overriding Group and Contact-level settings).

Group strategy

In Chapter 3, we recommended a strategy for managing which phones ring, and we'll repeat it here. Google Voice makes it very easy to see, at the Group level, which phones are set to ring, which greeting is played, and whether call presentation (i.e. ListenIn) is on or off.

We suggest that you control as much as possible at the Group level; and that you even go to extremes and create one-person Groups for the very few people who call you most. That way you rarely, if ever, need to override Group settings at the individual Contact level, because your key Contacts are Groups of their own. And you can always get a quick display of the current settings in effect by looking at the Groups screen, because you know you rarely if ever override them at the individual level.

A phone can be set to On or Off at the Contact level. But if the phone is set to Ring <group> phones at the Contact level, the actual setting depends on the Group and/or General setting, as shown in Table 6-1.

Table 6-1		Setting Phone Forwarding for a Contact to Ring <group>phones		
		Group setting for phone forwarding		
		Default	*On*	*Off*
Phones setting for phone forwarding	Off	Contact set to ring <group> phones: **Off** **(vm)**	Contact set to ring <group> phones: **On** **(vm)**	Contact set to ring <group> phones: **Off** **(vm)**
	On	Contact set to ring <group> phones: **On** **(vm)**	Contact set to ring <group> phones: **On** **(vm)**	Contact set to ring <group> phones: **Off** **(vm)**

Changing phone forwarding settings

The following sections explain how to use the Google Voice Web site or Google Voice mobile site to change phone forwarding settings for all of Google Voice, a group of callers or a single caller quickly and effectively.

Creating a "sin bin" or several

You can create one Group for users who are blackballed or even — if you have a lot of people you want to treat harshly — separate Groups for people who are always sent through to voicemail, always treated as spam, or always blocked.

If you use Groups in this way to control ringing phones, you can also use the same Groups to ease setting up your ListenIn settings and your voicemail messages, which again are likely to

be more controlling for people you are making sure never reach you directly.

Using Groups for people who share certain Google Voice settings is a bit different than the original intent of Groups — "Friends" and so on. But people always find ways to make systems do what they want them to do. Google Voice is involved in a very important part of your life, and you should bend it to your will any way you can.

Setting the default forwarding setting for all Groups

The settings you assign in the Phones tab can be used by Groups or overridden by Groups. Settings at the Group level can be used by individual Contacts or overridden by settings at the Contact level. So the settings in the Phones tab only take effect if they're not overridden by Group or Contact settings.

Follow these steps to set the default forwarding setting for all Groups:

1. **Click the Settings link in the upper part of your screen.**

2. **Click the Phones tab.**

   You see a list of your phones, as shown in Figure 6-1.

3. **Click in each checkbox to set the phone as On for forwarding or Off as a default setting.**

Turning forwarding for each phone On or Off here *only* affects the phone if its Group setting is Ring Default phones and the individual Contact is set to Ring <group> phones. It doesn't function as a control panel from which you can turn phones on or off regardless of other settings.

Changing the settings for a Group:

Settings at the Group level can override settings at the top level, under Phones. If you use the default setting, Ring Default phones for most or all Groups, then the top-level setting has more effect. That also means you have less to remember about which Groups are set to do what when you want to change settings, for instance before a vacation or business trip. Follow these steps:

1. **In the Settings area, click the Groups tab.**

2. **Under the name of the Group you want to change settings for, click Edit.**

3. **Then turn forwarding for each phone On or Off; or click the Ring Default phones link to adopt the setting in the Phones tab.**

Turning the phone ringing on or off for a Contact

Settings at the Contacts level can override settings at the top level, under Phones or at the Group level. If you use the default setting, Ring <group> phones, for most or all Contacts, then the Group settings have more effect. This prevents you from having to inspect, and potentially change, the settings for many contacts when you make a change in your routine, such as taking a day off.

1. **Click Contacts in the left-hand menu.**

2. **To reach any Contact directly, choose All Contacts in the middle pane and then click an individual Contact.**

3. **Click the Edit Google Voice Settings link.**

Figure 6-1:
Google
Voice puts
your phones
on offer.

For the specific Contact, as shown in Figure 6-2, begin by checking the pull-down menu at the top, Use settings from: <group>. For Contacts that are in multiple Groups, you can choose the allegiance of the various kinds of settings. It does not automatically change that Contact's settings to the applicable Group's settings; it controls where Google Voice looks for the Contact's settings if you choose to default to the Group's phone forwarding, voicemail message or ListenIn ("Call Presentation") options.

Figure 6-2:
The Contact
level has the
most power
to ring your
phones.

You can turn forwarding On or Off for various phones or send that Contact straight to Voicemail, treat them as Spam, or block them entirely. The final option is to choose Ring <group> phones, in which case ringing uses the Group setting, as described earlier.

Turning forwarding for each phone On or Off here *only* affects the phone if its Group setting is Ring Default phones and the individual Contact is set to Ring <group> phones. It doesn't function as a control panel from which you can turn phones on or off regardless of other settings.

To determine the phone ringing setting for an individual Contact:

- ✔ Look at that Contact first, as described earlier. If it's set to On or Off, Send to Voicemail, Treat as Spam or, Block Caller, you have your answer.

- ✔ If the Contact is set to Use <group> settings, you have to look at the setting for the chosen Group, as described earlier. If the Group is set to On or Off for each specific phone, you have your answer. If the Group is set to Ring Default phones, you have to look at the setting in the Phones tab, as described earlier.

Using ListenIn

Phones are social instruments, and ListenIn strategy is a tricky part of the social aspect of using Google Voice. It allows you to continue the old practice, from answering machine days, that allows people to screen calls before picking them up.

Think of it from the caller's point of view. Instead of just calling you and having the phone ring, the caller might be asked to identify themselves. Then they might get sent to voicemail. Then you might or might not bother to pick up the call while they're leaving a message. What a message that sends!

The wording is tricky, too. Google Voice promotes ListenIn as an important feature of Google Voice, but in the Settings area it refers to the same feature as Call Presentation, a soporific term that sounds like something entirely different.

So keep your callers' needs in mind when setting up ListenIn (using the Call Presentation settings) and using it. Some Google Voice users even report abandoning ListenIn entirely out of concern for how their callers might feel about it. But most Google Voice users will use ListenIn at least some of the time, so it's worth learning how to use the feature well.

Changing ListenIn settings

The ListenIn setting for a Contact can be set, using the options labeled Call Presentation, at three levels:

- ✔ At the Contact level, you can turn ListenIn On or Off, or default to the setting for the Group.
- ✔ At the Group level, you can turn ListenIn On or Off, or default to the General setting.
- ✔ At the General level, you can set the default that may or may not get used by various Groups and, via the Group setting, by various Contacts.

ListenIn can be set to On or Off at the Contact level. But if ListenIn is set to Default at the Contact level, the actual setting depends on the Group and/or General setting, as shown in Table 6-2.

Table 6-2   Results of setting ListenIn for a Contact to Default

		Group setting for ListenIn		
		Default	*On*	*Off*
General setting for ListenIn	**Off**	Contact set to Default: **Off**	Contact set to Default: **On**	Contact set to Default: **Off**
	On	Contact set to Default: **On**	Contact set to Default: **On**	Contact set to Default: **Off**

Here's how to use the Google Voice Web site or Google Voice Mobile site to change ListenIn settings for all of Google Voice, a Group of callers or a single caller quickly and effectively:

Setting the default ListenIn setting for all Groups:

Here are the steps to change the default setting across all Groups.

1. **Click the Settings link in the upper part of your screen.**

2. **Click the General tab.**

Ring Friends' phones?

The wording of some of the prompts and options of Google Voice is potentially confusing. The option to Ring <group> phones — for instance, to Ring Friends' phones — is one such example.

If you choose Ring Friends' phones, Google Voice does not, in fact, ring the phones of your friends when that Contact calls you. It *uses the settings in the Friends Group* to determine which of your phones ring.

When you think about it, this is easy enough to remember when you're fully paying attention. But perhaps some of the medicines that can make you drowsy, and that say "do not drive or operate heavy machinery while using this medicine" on the packaging, should add: "or change your Google Voice settings."

3. **Halfway down, look for Call presentation. Turn it On to allow ListenIn to be used for Groups with the Default setting; turn it Off to turn ListenIn off for Groups with the Default setting.**

(A Group setting of default can still be overridden at the Contact level.)

Turning ListenIn on or off for a Group

Here are the steps to change the ListenIn setting for a Group.

1. **Click the Settings link in the upper part of your screen.**

2. **Click the Groups tab.**

3. **Click the Edit button under the Group you want to change. Choices appear, as shown in Figure 6-3.**

4. **Under the heading, Enable Call Presentation for this group?; choose Default (the effect of which is determined by the General setting in Step 1), On or Off.**

Turning ListenIn on or off for a Contact:

Here are the steps to change the setting for a Contact.

1. **Click Contacts in the left-hand menu.**

2. **To reach any Contact directly, choose All Contacts in the middle pane, then click an individual Contact.**

3. **Click the Edit Google Voice Settings link.**

One screen to ring them all?

Because you can send calls to voicemail, treat them as spam, or block them entirely at the Contact level — not at the Group nor at the top, Phones level — you have to look at individual Contacts before you can be sure what the settings are. There are only two ways to avoid this.

One is to put everyone who's sent to voicemail, treated as spam, or blocked entirely in one overarching "bad" Group, or three separate Groups, as described earlier in the sidebar, Creating a "sin bin."

The other is to never use these options at the Contact level and use the Do Not Disturb setting in the General tab of the Settings area to send *everyone* to voicemail when you don't want to be disturbed. Because you can get e-mail alerts and, if you choose, text message alerts, this is a practical option you may want to consider.

For the specific Contact, begin by checking the pull-down menu at the top, Use settings from: <group>. For Contacts that are in multiple Groups, this allows you to choose the "allegiance" of the various kinds of settings. It does not automatically change that Contact's settings to the applicable Group's settings; it controls where Google Voice "looks" for the Contact's settings if you choose to default to the Group's phone forwarding, voicemail message or ListenIn ("Call Presentation") options.

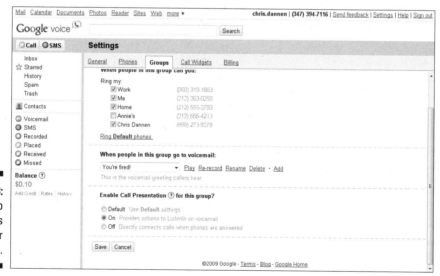

Figure 6-3: The Group level is crucial for ListenIn.

Under the heading, Enable Call Presentation for this Contact?, select the setting. Click the Edit link to change it to Default. To determine the ListenIn setting for an individual Contact:

- ✔ Look at that Contact first, as described earlier. If it's set to On or Off, you have your answer.

- ✔ If the Contact is set to Use <group> settings, you have to look at the Group setting, as described in Step 2. If the Group is set to On or Off, you have your answer. If the Group is set to Default, you have to look at the General setting, as described in Step 1 earlier.

Pushing buttons for ListenIn

You're quite likely to use ListenIn at least some of the time. Here's how to push buttons when ListenIn kicks in.

Your phone rings, and Google Voice announces that you have a call. It also announces the name of your caller — either reading it out of your Contacts, or playing back a name it recorded from the caller. It then starts reading out the options you have for handling the call.

Now you may be in a stressful situation — driving, or in a meeting (but using Google Voice to allow at least *some* potentially important calls to come through). So you want to decide whether to take the call as quickly as possible. Here are the options that you want to memorize:

Option 1: Accept the call. You can press 4 during the call to start recording it.

Option 2: Let the call roll into voicemail.

Option 3: Let the call roll into voicemail and ListenIn on the voicemail; press * to pick up the call after ListenIn has begun.

Option 4: Accept the call and start recording it from the beginning. (The caller will hear a message to alert them.)

To sum up, Options 1 and 4 both accept the call, with 4 also turning recording on. Options 2 and 3 both send the call to voicemail, with 3 also turning on ListenIn.

The easiest way to use ListenIn is to set all your Contacts to Use <group> setting, and all your Groups to Default. Then you can turn ListenIn on or off for all your callers at once by changing the On/Off setting at the General level.

If you do it any other way, you get more fine-tuning of control, but risk having to do a lot of looking around at settings to know what's going on. This is an example of the convenience versus control balance you need to consider for many Google Voice settings.

Changing Voicemail Greetings

When phone answering machines first appeared a quarter-century ago, they were not only popular, but they became a cultural phenomenon. You may remember *Friends* episodes that turned on answering machine greetings and messages.

With people having to juggle multiple phones — a home phone, work, and cell phone, in many cases — just trying to retrieve and return messages from different answering services became an exhausting task, and people tended to keep their outgoing messages simple. But as you get more and more of your voicemail messages through a single source (your Google Voice online mailbox) you may want to consider having some fun with voice messages again.

Google Voice is very clever this way. It lets you record a number of messages (as we describe in Chapter 3) and assign them by using the same three-level structure as ringing phones and ListenIn settings — an overall default setting, Group-level, and Contact-level control.

Voicemail greeting messages are inherently personal, and you may have a very good reason for not wanting your friends and family to hear the same message as your work colleagues. You may also want to give timely information about trips and so on in a different way to different people.

You can create a new voicemail message at any time, from any point in Google Voice where the list of voicemail messages is available — in the General tab of the Settings area, in a Group, or in a Contact. A voicemail message you create in any of these places can be used there, or in any of the others.

It's possible to end up with fragments of Google Voice error recordings on the answering machines of any and all phones you don't answer when a call rings them. To prevent this in at least some cases, make your voicemail greeting at least 15 seconds long.

You can also use voicemail greetings as a kind of message board: for your Friday night poker party, you can put the specific refreshments assignment in a voicemail greeting, and then have people leave a message to commit or bail.

So unlike the more serious settings described above, for which we advise caution, for voicemail messages we say: go flipping nuts. This kind of playing around helps you enjoy life and learn how to use Google Voice better. And having someone hear the wrong message is not likely to be a very big deal.

Some people have asked for control down to the level of having different settings, not just for Groups or specific Contacts, but depending on *which* of the Contact's phones the person calls you from. This isn't promised, but luckily there's a workaround: Just create several Contacts for the same person, with each one having a different phone number. Then you can really take Google Voice to the max.

Finding out what you can do with voicemail messages

First, remember that there are three ways people can get a voicemail message from you:

- ✔ You send them straight to voicemail by using your phone forwarding capabilities at the individual Contact level, or by setting Do Not Disturb in the General tab of the Settings area.

- ✔ You can see and/or hear that they're calling, but let them go through to voicemail after several rings, with or without ListenIn on.

- ✔ You're not paying attention to the relevant (phones) at the time, so the call goes through to voicemail after several rings.

You can control what greeting people get at three levels, similarly to the way you can control ringing your phones or ListenIn:

- ✔ At the Contact level, you can choose from any of your voicemail messages and assign it to that Contact. So you can have a specific message for your sweetie, but don't use the same message for your boss! ("Hi darling" could put your job on the line, so be careful!) You can also choose to use the meeting for the Group that Contact is in; the; or the completely generic System Standard greeting.

- ✔ At the Group level, you can choose from any of your voicemail messages and assign it to that Group. This includes the Default Greeting, set at the top level, in the General tab of the Settings area. However, the Group-level setting only affects the Contacts in that Group that are set to use the Group's voicemail greeting.

- ✔ At the top level, in the General tab of the Settings area, you can choose from any of your voicemail messages. The settings you choose affect only Groups assigned to use Default Greeting. At the level of individual Contacts, it then affects Contacts set to use Default Greeting or the greeting of the Group the Contact is in.

UI UI, oh no, sayin' me gotta go

A very common mistake at parties is to play the song "Louie, Louie" over and over. And over. And over....

A very common mistake in user interface design is to mix "set and forget" settings that you might only need to ever see once with settings that need to get accessed in a hurry. When you sit down in your car, you set the mirrors before you go, but you shift gears constantly, which is why the controls aren't next to each other.

Unfortunately, Google Voice's relatively clean, attractive, and easy-to-use interface makes all options seem as if they're created equal. Let's look at how often you're likely to change various settings in the General tab of the Settings area:

✔ Language: Set and forget.

✔ Time zone: Only change when you travel — and maybe not only then, as it only controls time-of-day-specific Google Voice settings that many people won't use.

✔ Voicemail Greeting: Set and forget for some people, constantly changed (at several levels of control) for others.

✔ Recorded Name: Set and forget.

✔ Notifications (how voicemail alerts are handled): Most people say yes to e-mail notifications once and change the target e-mail address very rarely, whereas the text message notification setting may be changed fairly often.

✔ Call Screening: Set and forget.

And so on. This mix of fast and slow functions can be really frustrating when you're in a hurry and trying to make a quick change. In our humble opinion, Google Voice needs a control panel for settings that are likely to be changed frequently. You can sort of use the Groups tab for this if you use Group-level settings where possible, an option recommended throughout this chapter.

Voicemail greetings work differently from how your phones ring and how you set ListenIn in one important way: Individual Contacts can be set to use the voicemail greeting set at the top level, in the General tab of the Systems area. So you can use the top-level setting as a control panel for the greeting that you want to use throughout the system.

Changing voicemail greeting settings

Here's how to use the Google Voice Web site to change phone forwarding settings for all of Google Voice, a Group of callers, or a single caller quickly and effectively:

1. **Click the Settings link in the upper part of your screen.**

2. **Click the General tab, shown in Figure 6-4.**

3. **Use the pull-down menu next to the prompt, Voicemail greeting, to choose a greeting as the system-wide default.**

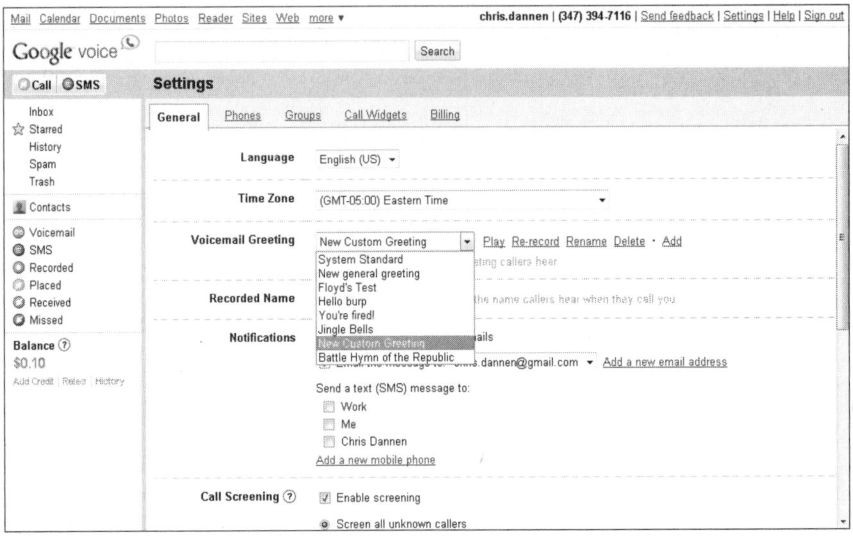

Figure 6-4:
Plot
strategy at
the General
level.

TIP

Note that this is the system-wide default, but that the choice you make here can be overridden, or used, by specific Groups and specific Contacts, separately or in conjunction.

4. **To change the settings for a Group: In the Settings area, click the Groups tab. Under the name of the Group you want to change settings for, click Edit. Then choose the greeting you want from the pull-down menu; choose Default Greeting to always use the greeting chosen by the process described in Step 1.**

5. **To turn the settings for a Contact: Click Contacts in the left-hand menu. To reach any Contact directly, choose All Contacts in the middle pane, then click an individual Contact. Click the Edit Google Voice Settings link.**

6. **Choose the greeting you want from the pull-down menu: Choose Default Greeting to always use the greeting chosen by the process described in Step 1. Choose <Group> Greeting to always use the greeting chosen by the process described in Step 2.**

To determine the voicemail message setting for an individual Contact:

 ✔ Look at that Contact first, as described in Step 3 above. If it's set to anything except <Group> Greeting or Default Greeting, you now know the answer.

 ✔ If the Contact is set to <Group> Greeting, you have to look at the setting for the chosen Group, as described in Step 2 above. If the Contact is set to Default Greeting, or if the Contact is set to <Group> Greeting and the Group is set to Default Greeting, you have to look at the setting in the Phones tab, as described in Step 1 above, to find out which greeting is in use.

Working with voicemail messages on the line

One of the great plusses of Google Voice is having all of your voice messages unified — once you've gotten everyone switched over to using your Google Voice number instead of your cell phone, home phone, work phone, and so on. So checking messages should be easy.

Unfortunately, although Google Voice only offers a few options, remembering them is not that easy. With a little practice, you can get it. Follow these steps:

1. **Call your Google Voice number. If necessary to access your account, press * and enter your PIN.**

   If you're calling from one of your registered phones that connects directly to your Google Voice account — usually, this is your cell phone — Google Voice offers you options directly; if not, you need to press * and enter your PIN to access your account and hear options.

2. **Press 1 to access voicemail.**

   Google Voice tells you how many messages you have and then reads off the first one.

3. **Then press the following options:**

   - 2 to return the call.

   - 7 to archive the message.

   - 8 to mark it as "spam" (which marks the caller's number as spam as well).

   - 9 to keep the message as new.

   You can archive any messages you don't want to return from your voice-mail list, because you will still have the message notification, link, and transcript. If you delete the message, you still have the message notification and (possibly illegible) transcript, but the link to the message will no longer work.

4. **Repeat for each of your messages.**

People like Google Voice because it gives them tools to handle voice messages in a variety of different ways. If this describes you, actually returning the call from your voicemail box might seem almost quaint. But it's a great way to get things handled. If you're not going to deal with the message from your voice mailbox, though, archive it rather than deleting it; you'll still want the link to work from your e-mail notification.

Was GrandCentral better? Discuss!

Google Voice has a lot of capabilities that its predecessor, GrandCentral, lacked. One of the few things that didn't make the leap from GrandCentral to Google Voice was RingShare.

RingShare allowed GrandCentral users to create custom greeting music for callers. Instead of a ring, callers would hear whatever MP3 file the GrandCentral user wanted them to hear.

Extra work for the GrandCentral user? For sure. Potentially confusing? Very much so. A lot of fun? Definitely.

GrandCentral sign-ups were always tightly restricted, first by typical start-up growing pains, then by a sensible Google-imposed cutoff after it acquired GrandCentral in 2007 (and quietly started building Google Voice on the GrandCentral foundation). And, unlike other desired features, Google has not made any encouraging noises about reviving it.

Why? Speculation is rampant (among the few thousand of us who even care). There may be copyright problems with people grabbing random (and potentially copyrighted) MP3s and using them for RingShare. Such concerns have hardly stopped Google in other ventures. Perhaps the true answer will never be known.

Changing Text Message Settings

One of the huge improvements in Google Voice over GrandCentral is support for text messaging. GrandCentral simply ignored text messages; who knows how many texts were sent to GrandCentral numbers and lost in the ether, never to be received? Google Voice, on the other hand, does a great job with texts.

At least one GrandCentral user has complained in online forums about their Inbox filling up with text messages now that she's upgraded to Google Voice. She must have been happier just losing the messages before!

However, now there is an alternative to receiving texts on your cell phone. All texts sent to your Google Voice number show up in your Google Voice Inbox. If you don't forward the text message to your cell phone(s), they don't count against your text message allowance(s) or cause charge(s) on your cell phone bill(s).

There are several ways you can handle text messages without ever forwarding them to your cell phone:

- ✔ Handle them in Google Voice Inbox on a PC.
- ✔ Handle them in Google Voice Inbox on Google Voice Mobile on a smartphone.
- ✔ Reply to the e-mail notification you get for the text message by calling or e-mailing the person, not texting them at all.

You can use all of these methods when they're convenient for you.

Remember to keep a small allowance for text messages on each of your cell phones so you don't pay an inordinate charge for the occasional text that does go straight to your cell phone.

With all this flexibility, you may find yourself wanting to change your cell phone settings frequently as your needs for receiving text messages directly on your cell phone change. Here's how to do it:

1. **Click the Settings link in the upper part of your screen. Click the Phones tab.**

   A list of your phones appears.

2. **Click Edit under one of the phones listed (probably one designated as Mobile).**

   The phone description appears, as shown in Figure 6-5.

3. **Click in the checkbox labeled Receive SMS on this phone to turn SMS reception on or off.**

4. **Click Save.**

   You return to the list of your phones.

5. **Repeat for all your cell phones.**

One of the toughest issues for Google Voice and for you as a Google Voice user is to keep sending calls and texts through your Google Voice number, so people don't see the phone numbers of your actual, physical phones.

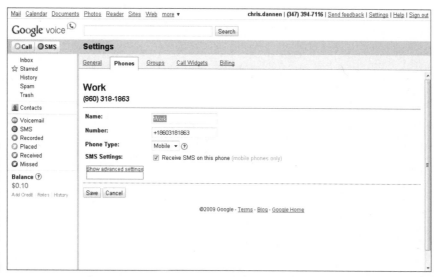

Figure 6-5: Make your phone SMSy, or clean text messages right off it.

Replying to a text is fine, as long as you do it the right way. As a Google Voice user, there are five ways you can send a text through Google Voice, and the only one you should avoid is the easiest and most familiar:

- ✔ **Do:** Reply to a text from your Google Voice Inbox.

- ✔ **Do:** Send a text from Google Voice on your PC.

- ✔ **Do:** Send a text from Google Voice Mobile on your smartphone.

- ✔ **Do:** Send a text from a dialer program running on your phone (see Part III).

- ✔ **Don't:** Send a new text directly from your cell phone "the old-fashioned way." This is the easiest and most familiar technique, but unfortunately it's the only one in which the recipient will see your cell phone number and possibly start using that instead of your Google Voice number.

Not sending texts from your cell phone is going to be tough if the phone doesn't run Google Voice Mobile and doesn't have a dialer program available — but if you want to get the most out of Google Voice, you have to avoid doing this. Given how smartphone sales are rising, one way to avoid this is obvious . . . though hardly a way to save money.

When you reply to a text from a PC, with its nice, comfortable keyboard, it's easy to go over the limit for text messages of 160 characters. Keep texts short, even if you're sending them from a PC!

Some cell phone providers have refurbished phones available and provide warranties for them as well. Both of the authors make a point of buying refurbished equipment, including cell phones, whenever possible. It's not only cheap; it's *green* (better for the environment). Check that a dialer program is available for the phone you choose before committing, and that you have a window of time for making sure you're satisfied, not least with using the phone with Google Voice, after you receive the phone.

You're not frozen out from even the most talked about equipment with refurbished gear. Apple is one tech manufacturer that has long made a point of offering refurbished equipment, and the iPhone is no exception. Other providers also offer refurbished phones.

Consider a pay-as-you go plan with Google Voice, because many of your minutes and texts will be through Google Voice or shifted to landlines rather than through your cell phone. This option can work well with a new phone or a refurbished phone, from a carrier or on the open market and unlocked, though some smartphone providers won't allow this.

Chapter 7

Saving Time and Money

· ·

In This Chapter
▶ Saving money with phone flexibility

▶ Calling other countries

▶ Figuring out rates for other countries

▶ Managing your phones

· ·

Google Voice is great for saving time and money and reducing anxiety, especially if you keep your settings simple and know how to change them quickly, as we describe in the previous chapter.

Google Voice phone calls are different than most. Control of the call resides with the Internet and all the servers and other computers connected to it. But the actual call is handled over traditional phone networks. You gain better call quality and reliability, but you may get some usability hassles. The control layer can't always make the traditional phone networks do what you might want them to do.

This is why Google Voice can't, ironically, do as much with calls you make — which would seem to be more under the control of Google Voice — than with calls you receive. It's easier to manipulate the incoming voice stream than the outgoing one.

This chapter tells you how to use Google Voice to save time and money. Everything involved is easy to do, but does requires changing some of your phone habits. The benefit is that you save ever more time and money as you get better at using Google Voice.

Saving Money with Phone Flexibility

In just the last 20 years, we've seen the maturing of one revolution in phone use and the beginning of another. The first revolution was the move from using landline phones to using mobile phones. Then came the burgeoning move from both types of phones to voice over Internet protocol (VOIP) calls, made over a computer through services, such as Skype. And now a service is available that combines traditional telephone lines and Internet-based control, Google Voice.

We aren't sure how to help you avoid getting Google Voice and Google Talk confused because the difference still sometimes eludes us, too.

The control and convenience of the cell phone is trumping the advantages of old-fashioned POTS (plain old telephone service) phones, which remain better on call quality and reliability. And the cost savings of VOIP calls — along with convenience, for those of us who have come to like talking on the phone using full headphones — sometimes trump the advantages of cell phones, even with their convenience.

Table 7-1 summarizes the advantages of each type of phone, reminding you when best to use each.

In this chapter, we show you how to use Google Voice to get the mobility and control advantages of the cell phone, while taking advantage of the quality and low cost of a landline. You can even use Google Voice to move calls to and from your computer with Gizmo 5, which is described in Chapter 11.

Table 7-1	Typical advantages by type of phone		
	Landline	*Mobile phone*	*VOIP on PC*
Call quality	√		
Low cost	√ (when used with GV)		√
Mobility		√	
Control		√	√
Low-cost gear			√

Shifting a call to another phone

Shifting a call that you've received to another phone that's registered with Google Voice is seemingly easy; just press * at any time during the call. Doing this makes all the phones registered to your Google Voice account ring at once, provided they're selected to ring; just pick up the other phone you want to use with Google Voice and continue your call.

By using the * key, you can easily switch a cell phone call to your home landline, for example, when you're sitting comfortably at home; you can switch it back if you need to free up your home phone or continue the call while you go on the move.

This technique also works for shifting a call to an assistant or colleague, if their phone is registered to your Google Voice account.

A phone can only be registered to one Google Voice account at a time, so having your assistant's or friend's phone registered to your Google Voice account may become impossible if they register for their own Google Voice account.

But this is where some bad news can bite: with the words, "rings all the phones attached to your Google Voice account at once." You don't necessarily want your assistant's and best friend's phone to ring when you're switching a call from your cell phone to your home phone. And you don't want to bother the people at home with spurious rings of the landline while you're switching calls at work.

Saving money live with Google Voice

Cell phones are great for flexibility, control, and convenience. But they cost you; recent analyses of the cost of a smartphone and service plan over a two-year period show the total adding up to thousands of dollars. And that's without even counting the sticker shock on your bill when you make a few international calls without the benefit of a special rate or go over any limits your plan has on talk time, SMS text messages, or data transfer.

There's another dirty little secret of cell phones: they aren't as good at supporting conversations — the core purpose of a phone — as a landline phone. Signal quality varies; heavy compression of sound, inherent in the technology, can damage the quality of speech for you and the other caller.

Get the best possible results from cell phones and landlines by using Google Voice to save money when you're getting phone calls. Follow these tips:

✔ When you get a call on Google Voice, your mobile and a landline may ring at the same time. By picking up the landline phone, you avoid using cell plan minutes, get better call quality, and use a more comfortable handset.

✔ Start a call on your cell phone if you want to take advantage of built-in contacts or to use a Google Voice dialer to make the call easier. When you use the dialer, you can assign your nearby landline phone to ring instead of your cell, so you can actually conduct the call on the landline.

✔ If you receive a call on your cell phone and find it's going longer than you thought, press * during the call and pick up from a nearby landline phone.

✔ If your cell phone doesn't work or has poor call quality, whether at home or at the office, Google Voice solves the problem; calls to your Google Voice number ring your cell phone and landlines as well.

As you may well know by now from experience, Google Voice doesn't work with extension numbers in offices.

Dialing into Google Voice directly

The "hard way" to use Google Voice is to pick up a landline handset or a cell phone without a dialer, dial your Google Voice number, press 2 to make a call, and then dial the outgoing number.

The extra steps involved are considered to be so difficult that no one will ever do them, meaning that Google Voice calls will almost always be initiated from a computer or a Google Voice dialer program running on a cell phone.

However, in certain situations dialing into Google Voice to make a call is worthwhile:

- ✔ **When you're making a call to another country.** You may want to make an appointment to make sure the other person will be there. Making an appointment first saves you the hassle of doing the two-step dialing process too many times. It also avoids making the other person call you back, potentially at great expense to him, and helps you avoid time difference concerns that narrow the desirable calling window for each of you.

- ✔ **When you're using someone else's phone.** One of the great hassles in life is not having a phone number nearby from which you can make a call without leaving a charge (for a long-distance U.S. call or for an international call) on someone else's phone. Even if the cost isn't all that high, the phone's owner may be too polite to take money from you for the call, and you're probably too polite to impose on them by taking them up on the offer, so the call just doesn't get made. Go through the two-step dialing hassle to avoid leaving even a small charge on someone else's bill.

You can greatly speed up the process of using Google Voice for long-distance calls with two tricks. The first trick is to set up a speed dial number on your landline phone(s) and cell phone for your Google Voice number. Doing this makes dialing out much quicker.

The second trick is to use your cell phone as a phone book, so you read out the number you need from your cell phone screen. You still have to dial, but you're leveraging the hard work you do to keep your contacts current on your cell phone.

Evangelizing Google Voice

Apple is the only non-religious organization we know of that has hired people with the job title of "evangelist" — someone to not only sell products, but actually get people to believe in a technology offering. If the evangelist does his job right, developers, customers, and other stakeholders don't just buy Apple's products, they think of new ways to use them and the technologies underlying them, provide feedback to the company on bugs and needed new features, or even start their own new company to build on the base offered by the technology.

Google Voice is the kind of offering that has the potential to make evangelists of its users because it's well-designed, robust, and easy to use.

Some key Google Voice features including the ability to switch a call to a different phone, the ability to record calls, and the ability to set up a conference call only work for calls you receive on Google Voice, not for calls you make using Google Voice. (And they certainly don't work for calls you make directly from a phone, bypassing Google Voice, even if the phone is registered with Google Voice.)

So that means you want people to call *you*, not for you to call them, so you have more flexibility. But why should they, if the call might cost them money? This is not as big a problem for cell phone calls, which usually are on plans that allow free nationwide calling. But it is for home phones (where the call might cost, depending on the plan it's on) and for business phones (where the caller may not know whether there's a cost or not but not want to risk hassle about it).

If you get your friends, family, and colleagues in the same country to use Google Voice, they can call you from any of their phones for free — and you can change phones, record the call, or create a conference call. Even better, if they use Google Voice, either of you can record the call and share the recording after, or either of you can host the conference call, so it matters less who called whom. (The callee is still the only one who can switch phones on the trot.)

All this may well make you an evangelist, getting everyone around you to adopt Google Voice because it increases the functionality available to you, directly or with the help of your friends.

For callers from other countries, the issue is even bigger. International calls are very cheap for you to make through Google Voice, but they may be very expensive indeed for the party on the other end, for instance, the call is being made from a mobile phone (as they tend to say overseas) with no international calling plan. So they will be reluctant to call you unless it's absolutely necessary. Instead, they may call you and ask you to call them straight back through Google Voice, once they know how cheap it is for you.

Now it's time for some trickier evangelism. Get in touch with Google and let them know you want them to offer Google Voice in the countries you're in touch with most often. You'll be pushing on an open door. Google no doubt wants to expand their service area as well.

Using GOOG-411 from the voice menu

GOOG-411 is a Google directory assistance service for finding businesses. With the exception of the ugly-sounding and ugly-looking name, it's great. It uses voice recognition and Google's vast databases to help you get information while you're on the move or in a hurry.

GOOG-411 is free, unlike most directory assistance services. It doesn't charge you for the search, and it doesn't charge you after it connects you with a business either. But, because it's automated, the results may not be as useful to you as calling a live person via a paid-for directory assistance service. And it doesn't include residential information.

GOOG-411 has gotten rave reviews. And Google keeps extending it; at this writing, the service has been extended to optionally include information about nearby intersections, help you orient yourself.

The technology developed for GOOG-411 powers Google Voice's voicemail transcriptions as well. It is also promising as a possible front end for any Google search, not just a search for local businesses. (But even a big company like Google has to start somewhere.)

A Google vice president said, "The reason we really did it is because we need to build a great speech-to-text model. . . that we can use for all kinds of different things, including video search." For the research paper, visit: `http://research.google.com/archive/goog411.pdf`.

You can use GOOG-411 from the Google Voice touchtone menu or by calling 1-800-GOOG-411. (That's 1-800-466-4411.) Or just dial into Google Voice and access GOOG411 from the voice menu.

We recommend that you use GOOG-411 through Google Voice. Why? Here goes:

✔ **GOOG-411 text messages can be archived in Google Voice.** Getting information by text message is a key feature of GOOG-411, but texts can only be received if you're calling from a cell phone, unless you are calling via Google Voice, in which case the phone you're calling from doesn't matter. The text messages go to any and all cell phones that you have registered with Google Voice and to your Google Voice Inbox as well. From there, it's easy to store them, forward them to people, or use them to drive looking up more information.

✔ **GOOG-411 map links work better in Google Voice.** Links to Google Maps (naturally) are a key feature of GOOG-411. But map links are useless on landline phones and only moderately useful on mobile phones, with their small screens. However, map links are fantastic on PCs; with Google Voice, you can get the map link on both.

So get in the habit of using GOOG-411 through Google Voice so that you can take advantage of your shortcuts to your Google number while getting all these cool features.

To access GOOG-411 from the Google Voice touchtone menu, follow these steps:

1. **Call your Google Voice number. If necessary to access your account, press * and enter your PIN.**

   If you're calling from one of your registered phones that connects directly to your Google Voice account — usually, this is your cell phone — Google Voice will offer you options directly; if not, you need to press * and enter your PIN to access your account and hear options.

2. **Press 3 to access GOOG-411.**

   GOOG-411 asks you for your city and state.

3. **Say your city and state, or enter a five-digit zip code.**

   It's not just what you tell GOOG-411, but how you tell it; speak slowly and clearly.

   It's good to enter the zip code if you know it and you're not sure just how otherwise to describe your location. (For example, many areas are on the boundary between two towns, or you could know the large city you're in but not which neighborhood.)

   Don't think you have to enter a zip code as a workaround if you have an accent, though; speech recognition systems working in limited domains, as in this case, are pretty good at cutting through accents.

   GOOG-411 asks you for the business name or category. It sometimes performs better on categories (surf shop) than business names (Zog's Houz of Tubez).

4. **Say the name or type of the business. To spell the name or category, press 1, and then enter the name with the phone keypad.**

   (For example, "pizza" would be 74992 on your phone keypad.)

   Google Voice responds with a list of businesses, clearly numbering them: "Number 1, ...; number 2, ...".

5. **Respond by saying:**

   • "Number 1" or "Number 2", or press the listing number, to get details of a specific listing.

   • Add the phrase "text message" to get the business information as a text message.

   • Add the phrase "map link" to have a map link sent to your phone.

   • Add the phrase "details" to get cross streets.

The "number" part is important; speech recognition systems have a tough time with single-syllable words, including digits, whereas the "number" part makes it easier.

GOOG-411 connects you to the business and, if you requested, send you business information and, again if you requested, a map link.

For a quick pointer to shortcuts for GOOG-411, visit the Mobile Help Web page for GOOG-411 at:

```
www.google.com/support/mobile/bin/answer.
py?hl=en&answer=76436
```

The page is shown in Figure 7-1.

Using a cell phone with a headset is legal in most states, and Google Voice doesn't demand that you use your phone keypad if you call directly, so it's probably legal to use GOOG-411 while driving in a given state. However, the concentration needed to "format" your request, to speak it clearly, and to understand and act on the information you get back, could be quite distracting. (For example, you could be momentarily tempted to make a bootleg turn if you just passed the pizza parlor you want!) Consider pulling over before calling GOOG-411 while in your car.

Microsoft has a similar service, which you can reach at 1-800-BING-411 (1-800-246-4411). It includes directions. Try both to see which works better for you.

Figure 7-1: Help for GOOG-411 is at hand.

Don't use GOOG-411, BING-411, or other such services for emergencies. Dial 911 or another locally relevant emergency number.

If 911 doesn't work on cell phones in your area, consider finding out your police hotline number and storing it on your cell.

Saving – or losing – on your cell phone text count

Google Voice can save you money on text messages, but if can also cost you money if you're not careful.

Most people have monthly service plans for their cell phones, and many of these plans have fairly generous SMS text message allowances. But going over the limit, if you have one, is still expensive. And if you can reduce your text message count, you can potentially switch to a cheaper plan, or go on a pre-paid or post-paid plan in which you only pay for the texts, talk time, and data transfer you actually use.

Also, many people, especially younger people, have gotten in the habit of sending and receiving dozens (if not hundreds) of texts a day. Switching some of this to the PC, which is easier to type on, is easier on your eyes, wrists, and thumbs.

Here's how Google Voice can *cost* you money on texts:

✔ **Text message notifications:** Google Voice can alert you to voicemail messages by sending a text message to one or more cell phones. These are additional text messages over and above what you'd normally get.

✔ **Message multiplication:** Google Voice sends a text message sent to your Google Voice number to as many cell phones as you set it up to. In the past, that message would have gone to just one phone. You might not have seen the message for a long time if it went to a less-used phone, but at least you wouldn't be paying for it multiple times.

✔ **Message expansion:** Getting your text messages both through the Google Voice Web site and on one or more cell phones makes it easier for you to reply quickly, which may just elicit more messages and multiple copies.

Here's how Google Voice can *save* you money on texts:

✔ **Minimize text message notifications:** Unfortunately, you can't only get notified on messages from specific callers, but you can turn text message notifications off completely. You can rely on notifications by e-mail instead (especially if you have a cell phone with e-mail support).

  ✔ **Turn off SMS support for some of your phones:** On the Phones tab of the Settings area, select a mobile phone. You can turn off SMS from any of your cell phones, as shown in Figure 7-2.

  ✔ **Turn off SMS support for all of your phones:** You can turn off SMS support for Google Voice for all of your phones and just rely on the copies that show up by e-mail notification and in your Google Voice Inbox. This method is a particularly viable if you're a responsible person who, like the authors, regularly checks for new e-mails on her smartphone.

See the next section for how to weave your SMS text strategy into your other money-saving plans.

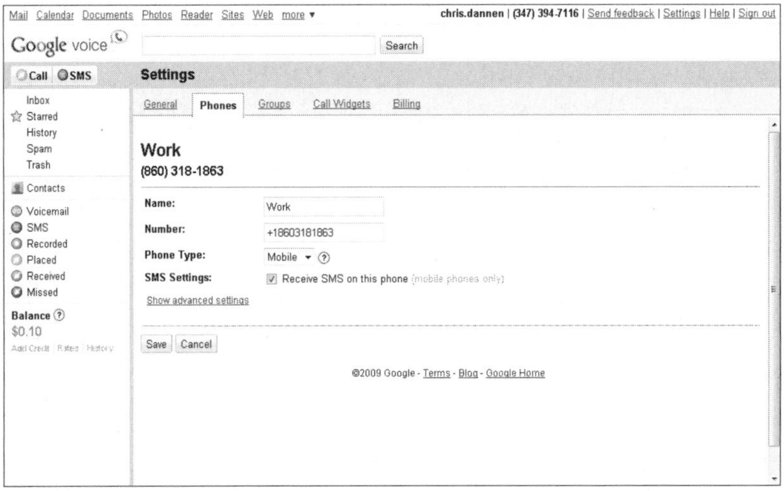

Figure 7-2:
SOS: Cut
down on
SMS.

Can you go prepaid?

Being a technophile has always been expensive, but at least buying a PC puts the cost right up front, with the blow often softened by financing or the use of a credit card.

But cell phone pricing is sneakier. Most of us pay a (subsidized) cost of a cell phone — a nice, easy-sounding number like $99 or $199 — and easy-sounding monthly numbers like unlimited voice calls for $99, unlimited data for $30, and so on.

Only the small print reminds us that this is a commitment for, perhaps, two years, making the total cost more like $2,500, or more. And at the end of that two-year period, with phones changing so fast, you're no doubt going to want to get a new phone and commit to a monthly plan all over again.

You can save money with more limited service plans, but if you go over the plan's limits, the costs mount right back up. And overseas calls are often considerable extras from any kind of plan. (A call to Europe might cost $1.50 a minute if not made within an international calling plan of some sort.)

Google Voice offers some relief right up front. Overseas calls are only a few cents a minute to most countries, almost eliminating one of the main potential "gotchas" in either a landline or cell phone bill. Text messages can be greatly reduced or even, with discipline, almost eliminated, as described in the previous section. And the ability to move calls from cell phones that may charge for minutes to landlines that don't is a big plus.

But the big win is to get off the new cell phone plus monthly plan treadmill. Instead, consider getting an unlocked, mid-range, or refurbished cell phone and get a prepaid plan for it, then manage your minutes, texts, and data usage carefully. A goal might be to get a phone for up to $200 and keep monthly costs down to a maximum of $50, which has recently become a benchmark figure for contract-free services. Total two-year cost: $1400, about half the cost of a top of the line new phone and a high-end monthly plan.

In the following list, we look at the elements needed to move from the all-you-can-eat plans to the hopefully less expensive a la carte plans:

- ✔ **Phones:** Unless you're at a PC most of the time, Google Voice wants — almost needs — a smartphone that can receive e-mail. Budget $200 or so for a lower-end or refurbished smartphone.

- ✔ **Minutes:** Google Voice can help you cut cell phone minutes by spending more of your phone time on landlines and by using PC-based VOIP services, especially Gizmo (see Chapter 11). Google Voice can also help you respond to voicemail messages by e-mail, avoiding minutes entirely.

- ✔ **Texts:** Used appropriately, as described in the previous section, Google Voice can help you cut your text count to almost nothing. Texts can be handled via a dialer application on your smartphone, using your data plan rather than counted as text messages, or on a PC for free. This leaves only a few texts and a small number of minutes to pay for.

- ✔ **Data:** This is the weak spot of an a la carte approach, as data costs are hard to predict and control. However, you can make good use of an unlimited data plan that might cost about $30 a month by using a smartphone. With this you can handle many calls as e-mail on the phone or a PC.

If you like to talk, love having the newest phone, and hate sweating the small stuff, a new phone and a pay monthly service plan is probably the better bet. But if you like to use some of your technical expertise to find the best used or refurbished phone model, and like the prospect of using a new tool like Google Voice to save money as well as to do more, the a la carte approach may be very good for you.

If you have an employer-provided cell phone, much of your phone time is going to be paid for anyway. You can probably handle your personal needs on an a la carte basis.

Making Calls To and From Other Countries

Google Voice's performance with overseas calls reminds one of a brief verse about a little girl with a little curl.

We don't know if Google Voice has a little curl right in the middle of its virtual forehead, but the rest fits. Google Voice is very good indeed if you are in the U.S. and need to make calls to other countries, because it brings VOIP calling rates — a few cents a minute, in most cases — right onto all your phones, including your mobile phones in particular.

But when you're traveling, Google Voice is horrid. Calls to your Google Voice number don't ring your phone at all. Texts get to your Google Voice account online, but never reach your cell phone. There's no amount of money you can pay or setting you can tweak to change this; it just doesn't work.

Getting a SIM card or a whole phone for use in the country you're visiting doesn't make any difference; Google Voice won't forward calls to an American number when the phone is overseas, and it won't forward calls to a foreign number at all. (Though this may change for Canadian numbers, which have the same +1 country code and the same formatting of area codes and local numbers as America, and for calls to Alaska and Hawaii, which are 100 percent American, in the near future.)

Wi-Fi and VOIP calling

Most cell phones don't yet support Wi-Fi (wide area network) support for voice over IP (VOIP) calling, and for those few that do, hotspot usage often carries costs of its own. VOIP calling over a PC, through services such as Skype, Gizmo 5, and Google Talk, is a real option though. This area is maturing rapidly, so it's hard to give specific advice, but you can handle a good share of your phone needs at very low cost over VOIP today, and it's only getting better. See Chapter 12 for specifics on Gizmo 5, a VOIP service that uses a virtual phone number and can therefore be thoroughly integrated with Google Voice. See Chapter 14 for specifics on Google Talk and how to use it in tandem with Google Voice.

So we have the agony and the ecstasy here. In the next section, we tell you how to add very small amounts of money to your Google Voice account to make very long calls to overseas numbers. We also explain how to manage when you're overseas and your Google Voice number stops ringing through on your cell phone.

Adding credit where credit is due

Adding credit to your account is easy, using Google Checkout, a battle-tested and reliable online payments service used by thousands of merchants.

Google always adds credit in "chunks" of $10, which is a whopping 500 minutes to the cheapest countries, at 2¢ a minute, and about 20 minutes to the very few most expensive counties, which peak at 56¢ a minute — less than landline rates and far less than what some cell phone service providers charge. And you don't need to specify what countries you'll be calling in advance.

Google's selling credit in $10 increments gives you plenty of time for the more common and less expensive calls, but cuts you off fairly quickly if you're unknowingly clocking up minutes to a (relatively) expensive destination.

Follow these steps to add credit to your account:

1. **Click the Settings link in the upper part of your screen. Then click the Billing tab.**

   You see your current credit balance and a billing history, as shown in Figure 7-3.

Figure 7-3:
Add credit before credit is due.

You may want to look at your billing history to decide whether to add just one $10 "chunk" of credit or more.

2. **Click the Add Credit link.**

   A Google Checkout screen appears, as shown in Figure 7-4. If you have a Google Account and are already signed into it, as you typically will be while using Google Voice, you will be asked to re-enter your password; if you do not have a Google Account yet, you'll be asked for complete name, address, credit card and other details.

3. **If you are using an existing Google Account, type your password and click Sign in and continue. If you are creating a new Google Account, type the requested personal details, review the Terms of Service, and click Agree and Continue.**

   The final screen appears, as shown in Figure 7-5.

4. **Set or clear checkboxes relating to e-mail offers and privacy. Type any coupon code you have and click Apply.**

   Most people, already receiving too much e-mail, will deselect the first and third checkboxes, which relate to special offers and promotional e-mail. The middle checkbox is the critical one. If you select it, your e-mail address will be kept confidential from the seller. It doesn't matter for this transaction, as the seller is Google, but in other cases you may want to check this checkbox to shield your e-mail address from that specific seller. (Google handles the e-mail traffic between you and the seller in a way that keeps your e-mail address confidential.)

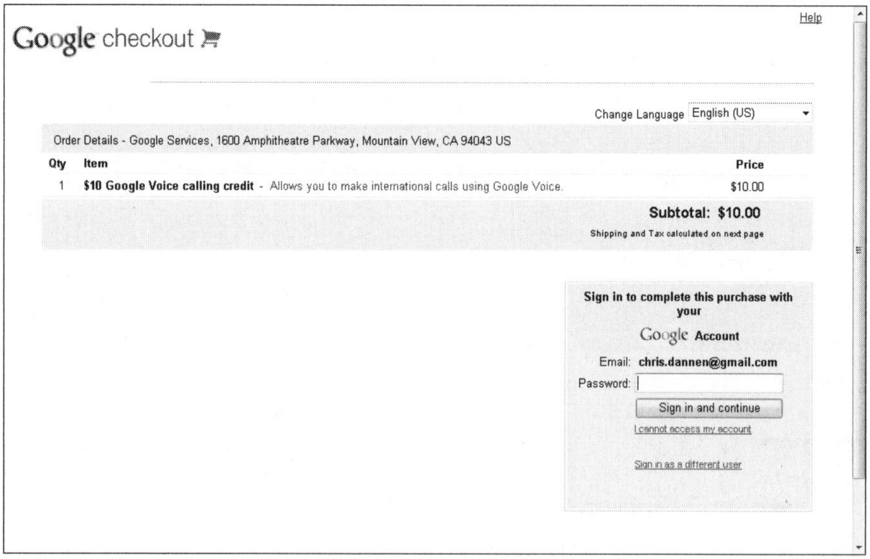

Help

Google checkout 🛒

Change Language English (US) ▼

Order Details - Google Services, 1600 Amphitheatre Parkway, Mountain View, CA 94043 US

Qty	Item	Price
1	**$10 Google Voice calling credit** - Allows you to make international calls using Google Voice.	$10.00

Subtotal: $10.00

Shipping and Tax calculated on next page

Sign in to complete this purchase with your

Google Account

Email: chris.dannen@gmail.com

Password: [   ]

[Sign in and continue]

I cannot access my account

Sign in as a different user

Figure 7-4:
Google
makes it
easy to buy.

5. **Click the Place your order now button.**

   Google adds the credit to your account and sends you an e-mail message confirming the purchase.

6. **Repeat the process, beginning at Step 1, if you want to add another $10.**

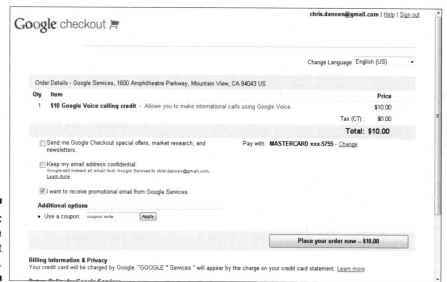

Figure 7-5: Google makes it easy to pay.

Checking the rates

You can check the calling rates by country from almost any screen in Google Voice. Your current account balance for long-distance calls appears in the left-hand panel. Simply click the Rates link under your balance to check current rates by country.

There is often a dramatic difference in calling rates between landlines and mobile phones, even in the relatively low-cost world of Google Voice. For example, calls to a U.K. landline are 2¢ a minute; calls to a U.K. mobile phone, as the Brits call it, are 19¢ a minute.

The difference between a landline phone number and a mobile number is usually obvious to residents of the country, but not to outsiders. (In the U.K., mobile phone numbers begin with 075, 077, 078, or 079 at this writing.) So check the rates before calling and, if you need to, ask the recipient whether he is on a mobile; he'll understand if you then keep the call brief.

Table 7-2 shows countries organized by calling rate, with mobile rates, where different, shown in parentheses. This makes it easier for you to find the country you need to call and to avoid "gotchas" for the most expensive countries for both landline and mobile calls.

Table 7-2 Landline calling rates in ¢/minute U.S. & North America

Cost/ minute	Country (mobile cost/minute, if different)
0¢	**US ex-Alaska, Hawaii, Puerto Rico, US Virgin Islands, American Samoa**
1¢	**Canada ex-Yukon Territory**
2¢	**Hawaii; Puerto Rico; Mexico-Guadalajara & Monterrey;** Austria (19¢); China; Denmark (19¢); France (15¢); Germany (18¢); Greece (22¢); Guam; Hong Kong; Hungary (19¢); Ireland (19¢); Italy (25¢); Netherlands; New Zealand (26¢); Norway (19¢); Poland (24¢); Portugal (24¢); Puerto Rico; Singapore; Spain (19¢); Sweden (18¢); Switzerland (29¢); Taiwan (09¢); United Kingdom (19¢)
3¢	**US Virgin Islands**; Argentina (16¢); Australia (17¢); Belgium (24¢); Chile (19¢); Czech Republic (19¢); Estonia (29¢); Iceland (25¢); Israel (15¢); Japan (14¢); Korea; South (06¢); Luxembourg (21¢); Malaysia (04¢); Monaco (29¢); Russia-Moscow & St. Petersburg (08¢); Slovakia (22¢); Thailand; Venezuela (16¢)
4¢	**Alaska**; Bahamas; Brazil (19¢); Bulgaria (33¢); Guadeloupe (33¢); Northern Mariana Islands; Slovenia (37¢)
5¢	Andorra (25¢); Bahrain (20¢); Brunei; Colombia (09¢); Cyprus; Finland (15¢); Jordan (12¢); Macao; Martinique (37¢); Panama (12¢); San Marino; Saudi Arabia-Riyadh (19¢); Turkey (18¢)
6¢	Croatia (23¢); Georgia (15¢); Gibraltar (29¢); Latvia (29¢); Liechtenstein (49¢); Lithuania (19¢); Romania (19¢); Russia ex-Moscow & St Petersburg (08¢); South Africa (18¢); Vatican City
7¢	Costa Rica; India; Laos; Saudi Arabia-Jeddah (19¢); Trinidad & Tobago (12¢); Uruguay (21¢); Zambia (17¢)
8¢	**Canada-Yukon Territory; Mexico ex-Guadalajara & Monterrey;** Malta (25¢); Mexico; Zimbabwe (29¢)
9¢	**American Samoa**; Armenia (24¢); Bermuda; Bolivia (15¢); Dominican Republic (14¢); French Guiana (35¢); Ghana (18¢); Honduras (16¢); Indonesia (14¢); Iraq (16¢); Pakistan; Paraguay (15¢); Turkey; North Cyprus; Uzbekistan; Vietnam
10¢	Jamaica (25¢); Kazakhstan (15¢); Seychelles; Ukraine (16¢)

Cost/ minute	Country (mobile cost/minute, if different)
11¢	Iran (11¢); Kyrgyzstan; Lebanon (22¢); Namibia (25¢); Philippines (17¢); Saudi Arabia ex-Riyadh & Jeddah; Serbia & Montenegro (29¢); Swaziland (20¢)
12¢	Aruba (19¢); Bangladesh; Botswana (19¢); Ecuador (24¢); Kuwait; Sri Lanka; Tajikistan
13¢	Barbados (20¢); Macedonia (33¢)
14¢	Dominica (22¢); Guatemala; Moldova (21¢); Netherlands Antilles (23¢); Uganda
15¢	Albania (25¢); Antigua & Barbuda; Azerbaijan (19¢); Bosnia & Herzegovina (29¢); Burundi; Kenya (20¢); Malawi; Mongolia; Peru (24¢); Tanzania (15¢); Turkmenistan; Virgin Islands; British (19¢)
16¢	Algeria (25¢); Grenada (25¢); Mauritius; Nicaragua (26¢); Niger; Rwanda; Sudan (29¢); Yemen (16¢)
17¢	Angola (23¢); Egypt; Nigeria; St. Kitts & Nevis (25¢)
18¢	Anguilla (20¢); Cameroon; Gabon; Morocco (29¢); Reunion (31¢)
19¢	Burkina Faso; Cayman Islands (19¢); Congo; Republic of the; Guinea; Haiti (25¢); Nepal; Oman; Senegal; Tunisia (29¢)
20¢	Bhutan; El Salvador; Faroe Islands; Ivory Coast; St. Lucia
22¢	Belize; Benin; Cambodia; Suriname
23¢	United Arab Emirates
24¢	French Polynesia; Mozambique; Palestine; Syria
25¢	Belarus; Cameroon; Equatorial Guinea; Israel; Palestine (25¢); Liberia; Libya (27¢); Mali; Micronesia; Montserrat; Turks & Caicos Islands (25¢)
26¢	Lesotho (26¢); New Caledonia; St. Pierre & Miquelon
27¢	Fiji; Qatar; St. Vincent & The Grenadines
29¢	Afghanistan; Cape Verde; Chad; Congo; Democratic Republic; Eritrea; Ethiopia; Madagascar; Maldives
30¢-60¢ (no cell phone rates)	30¢: Guyana; Togo; 31¢ Marshall Islands; 32¢: Sierra Leone; 33¢: Gambia; 35¢: Myanmar; 37¢: Palau; 39¢: Central African Republic; Djibouti; 40¢: Tonga; 44¢: Comoros & Mayotte; Guinea-Bissau; 49¢: Samoa; 50¢: Ascension Island; Greenland; 53¢: Somalia; 55¢: Tuvalu; 56¢: Vanuatu; 60¢: Cuba-Guantanamo Bay; North Korea

Traveling to other countries

Managing phone calls when you travel has always been a small — or even a large — nightmare of inconvenience, expense, hassle, and missed opportunities. Google Voice helps in some ways, but makes things harder in others.

If, as in *The Godfather*, your boss "insists on hearing bad news at once," here it is: if someone calls your Google Voice number while you're in another country, your cell phone won't ring. If someone sends you a text, it won't appear on your cell phone.

There's no setting you can change or payment you can make to make these basic things, the very core of what a telephone or cell phone does, happen. Except for one trick.

If you have a landline, direct all your Google Voice calls to your landline. Then have your phone company forward your landline to your cell phone. Doing this may cost some money, but it does work. Check what the costs are with the phone company.

Some advantages are worth listing:

✔ You won't pay roaming charges for calls or texts you receive, because you won't actually receive any calls or texts.

✔ People who call you according to your home time zone won't wake you up at 3 a.m. in Istanbul or interrupt important business with trivia. (Those "wazzup?" calls from high school friends may not impress your foreign contacts, acquaintances, or family members.)

✔ Google Voice's e-mail notifications, voicemail transcriptions, and cheap international calls can be quite helpful in keeping you in control.

The following section cover how to make Google Voice work for you, even when you're abroad.

Using Google Voice in other countries

When traveling in other countries, you want to use Google Voice to save time and money and maintain control of when your phone rings and your costs. For this, you want to have either a smartphone with e-mail access or frequent access to a PC.

If you have e-mail access through your smartphone, through your dumb-phone, or any other data transfer capabilities, check with your cell phone service provider before traveling. Phones often check for new data, and some people have been hit with bills for hundreds of dollars after a trip overseas. Establish how your phone works with regards to data, purchase a "travel abroad" add-on data plan to save money or learn how to turn off data access completely, and check your cell phone charges regularly during your trip.

After you've got your data costs under control, you can use Google Voice on your smartphone to manage many of your phone calls and texts via notifications and respond by e-mail. You can also use a PC instead. Given time zone differences, responding by e-mail is probably a better way to manage many interactions than actually receiving and making phone calls.

But how can you make real, live phone calls when you need to? Foreign countries tend to have more Internet cafés than the U.S., and VOIP calling with Skype is more popular. So when in Rome, do as the Romans do, and use an Internet café for international phone and video calls. It's also common for hotels to have wireless Internet access — sometimes at high cost, so check when you book. Many also have business centers with PCs, Internet access, and printing capability.

Try to avoid using your hotel room phone for outgoing calls. Experienced travelers are aware of how easy it is for a brief phone call to stretch to 10 or 20 stressful minutes, putting a hole in your wallet (or an embarrassing line on your expenses form) of $50 or more.

So Google Voice can help you handle most of your phone needs without actually using your phone. But what about those times when you really do need it?

Using your cell phone for calls overseas

You still may need to make or receive phone calls overseas. For making calls, consider calling your Google Voice number first.

Before you travel, contact your cell phone service provider to find out about prepaying or using an add-on to your plan to reduce charges for roaming calls from other countries to your Google Voice number in the U.S.

After you call (and pay for the call to) your Google Voice number, the onward part of the call from Google Voice to U.S. numbers will be free. It may also be cheaper to call numbers in your destination country by calling your Google Voice number in the U.S., and then making a call from it to your destination country at Google Voice's low international rates.

So that takes care of making calls from your cell phone. First, get cheap rates for roaming calls back to the U.S. Then call via your Google Voice number to mask your cell phone's number with your Google Voice number. This also gives you the onward part of your call free (to U.S. numbers) or at low rates (internationally).

What about receiving calls?

You can have people call your hotel room, with the hotel switchboard acting as your secretary. You can also have people call any businesses or friends you're visiting. Of course, in these days of ubiquitous cell phone access, borrowing a phone might get embarrassing.

In the worst case, you have two alternatives:

✔ Give out your "real" cell phone number and ask people to use it only while you're traveling. This is cheaper and easier for your U.S.-based contacts.

✔ Rent a mobile phone in the country you're traveling to; renting a phone is easier, less expensive, and more commonly done in most other countries than in the U.S. Renting a phone is especially good for your contacts in the country you're visiting, as they then don't have to make an international call to reach you.

In either case, you can't forward the calls from Google Voice; it won't ring your U.S.-based cell phone while you're overseas, and it won't forward calls to a foreign number.

You can use Google Voice to *soft forward* calls. Just leave a message — for selected people only, if you prefer — stating that you're traveling, the time difference, and the number you're using while traveling. (Your "real" cell phone number or your rent-a-phone number.) Doing this not only gives people a way to reach you, it might help them call you at sensible times and only when really needed.

A checklist for the Google Voice-equipped traveler

Managing phone calls while you're traveling is never easy. Here's a checklist for reducing hassle and expense by using your usual cell phone and, if you wish, an additional rented local phone. Use some or all of these techniques as needed:

✔ **Before you travel, contact your cell phone provider.** Ask for add-ons to reduce costs of data transfer while roaming, so you can manage voice call and text notifications via mobile e-mail and buy an add-on to reduce the cost of calls back to your Google Voice number while roaming, so you can cheaply make calls after dialing into Google Voice.

✔ **Use your own cell phone.** Before you travel, set up Google Voice voice-mail messages, customized as appropriate. A suggested script: "While traveling, I'll have limited phone access, so please send e-mail or leave a voicemail message. If urgent, call me on…" and give the time difference and your cell phone number.

✔ **Use a rented phone.** After you reach your destination, rent a mobile phone or rent a SIM card if you have a phone that uses the local cell phone technology standard. Set up Google Voice voicemail messages, customized as appropriate, giving the temporary mobile phone number as your "urgent" number.

✔ **Avoid using the phone.** Use your cell phone's e-mail capability, Internet cafés, wireless access in your hotel and any business center your hotel has to manage your voice message and text notifications, respond by e-mail or using Google Voice's texting capability, and make calls using a VOIP service such as Skype, Google Talk, or Gizmo 5.

These techniques allow you to operate with the least cost and inconvenience for yourself and the least change in habits for your callers.

Chapter 8

Managing Phones with Google Voice

• •

• •

Google Voice changes the way you use your phones. You can begin Google Voice calls by dialing into Google Voice from your phone, by using a Google Voice dialer app, or by using the Google Voice mobile Web page from any cell phone with even a basic Web browser.

This chapter explains how to use Google Voice from your phone or from the Google Voice Web site to make calls and send text messages. We describe a couple of very cool things you can do with your Google Voice phone number and call recordings on the Web. We then tell you about the exciting things you can do with calls that come to you through Google Voice.

This chapter is the last one to cover the basic information on how to set up and use Google Voice — which has taken up eight chapters and more than half the book!

If you're brand new to Google Voice, consider going through this chapter a couple of times; once to get a feel for what Google Voice can do, then again to actually try the things that you want to use right away. Learning takes time, but you're likely to find that the investment of time you make is well-rewarded with Google Voice.

Calling with Google Voice Is Different

The biggest issue that Google Voice presents users seems to be the added steps in dialing out. Understanding exactly what's involved and how to work around it may help you get more out of Google Voice.

The first step in getting the most out of Google Voice is to get people to call your Google Voice number. This is like herding cats; people are likely to revert to old habits. However, if you do your part, you may be able to make this stick.

After you get people calling you on your Google Voice number, the key to using Google Voice successfully is *always* making calls from Google Voice. That way, people see your Google Voice number as the number you called from and, when they return calls, they come back to you through Google Voice. You have to do this consistently to get the advantages that Google Voice offers you.

However, consistently calling from Google Voice is hard work. The most unusual aspect of Google Voice is that to place a call from a phone, you call your Google Voice number first, then Google Voice calls first you, and connects you to the other party. This change in how phone calls work is disconcerting at first.

Even after you get used to the change in how things work, the extra effort is daunting for many. It's enough to put many people off using Google Voice consistently for their outgoing calls. But if you start returning calls directly to one or more of your phones without using Google Voice and you'll lose the advantages, too.

Using Google Voice consistently is easier when calling from a smartphone using a dialer, as we describe in Part III. The extra work is eliminated — you enter a number, and then the dialer calls Google Voice for you. After that step is saved, a dialer that closely mimics the way the smartphone works when not using Google Voice — giving easy access to contacts and so on — gives you an almost unchanged experience compared to calling directly from your cell phone. There's still the change in interaction, with Google Voice calling you and then the other party, but that by itself is not a stopper.

Dialing out using Google Voice

It's relatively easy to dial out using Google Voice if you have a smart phone, or even from a dumbphone that can run a browser, by using the Google Voice mobile Web site. But what if you have a dumb phone, or if you want to use a landline for the call to save cell phone minutes or get better call quality, take advantage of your landline handset's features, and/or have a more comfortable call?

The indirect way to do this is to use your cell phone and the Google Voice Mobile Web page or a cell phone dialer application (see Part III) to drive calls to your landline phone. On your cell phone, enter the number you're dialing — you can often pick it out of your contacts — then use the scrolling list in the dialer to specify your landline as the ringback number. Google Voice rings your landline first and, after you pick up, it calls the number you're trying to reach. So your cell phone works as a remote control for landline phones!

Figure 8-1 shows a Blackberry user choosing a dialer application to route a call through a landline phone.

Figure 8-1:
Start your outbound call on your cell phone and continue it on a landline.

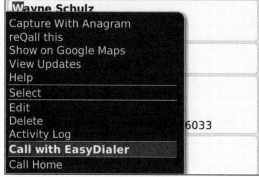

Another, complementary method is to set up your Google Voice number as a speed dial number on your phone. Many phones have a speed dial feature. Unfortunately, for many landline phones and office phone systems, the speed dial feature is just hard enough to use that some of us never use it. (The fact that speed dial works slightly differently on different systems is much of the problem.)

Take the time to set up a speed dial to Google Voice on all your phones. Then use your cell phone as a mobile directory. Doing this allows you to most easily make free (in the U.S.) or cheap (international) calls wherever you are.

When you use Google Voice, you can use any landline to make your call. As long as you're in the same area code, or the phone you're using has free national long distance, you won't leave behind an unpleasant reminder of your visit in the form of a line on someone else's bill. You can even borrow a mobile for an international call; you will be burning minutes, but not running up a potentially huge bill on someone else's phone.

Landline phones can be frustrating!

People have missed an important point about the popularity of cell phones. It's great that they're mobile, yes, but they're also just plain better phones than landline phones in many ways. Even the simplest cell phones make it much easier to call people back, keep contact phone numbers, and more.

I (Smith) have as a home phone a Supersonic XZ-FC245. (Slightly renamed to protect the guilty.) The main body of the unit has a built-in fax machine and copier and a decent handset attached. This handset preserves the curve that traditional phones have always had, which puts the earpiece close to your ear and the mouthpiece close to your mouth, giving you comfort, clarity, and privacy (on the incoming part of the call).

But the mobile handsets that come with the phone, and that I actually use most of the time,

are mobile-phone-like: straight, with no comforting curve. The handsets are at least longer than a typical cell phone, which helps.

When I tried to figure out how to set up speed dial on this phone, it wasn't pretty. The manual is long gone, and I couldn't find it online. (How do I know if it's a 2.4Ghz phone or a 5.8GHz phone, or maybe an expandable system?) [Modern household phones are predominantly 2.4Ghz.]

Finally, pushing buttons, I was able to put my Google Voice number in the thing's on-board phonebook. Not as good as just pressing one button, but not bad. Hopefully you'll have better luck with your phones!

Using forwarding for Google Voice

Forward your home phone, business phone, and mobile phone to your Google Voice number to save some of the effort of getting people to call you on Google Voice. Then set up Google Voice so that it doesn't ring any external phones. (You can't have Google Voice ring a phone that's forwarded to Google Voice.)

The bad news is that, if you do this without making any other changes, none of your phones will ever ring. If you are phone-phobic, this is not a bad thing.

You can still make calls from all your phones; you can even use them to call Google Voice and then dial out from there, keeping up the Google Voice illusion that you need to preserve for people who might call you back. But you can't receive calls directly through your Google Voice number.

We doubt that many of you are willing to do this full-time. But it might be useful when you're very busy or unavailable (for example, during a trip).

If you take an extra step, you can make this work better. Forward all your existing phone numbers to Google Voice; then get a new cell phone SIM card. Put the old SIM card someplace safe. Then put the new SIM card in your cell phone and assign Google Voice to ring the new number when you want to receive calls. That way, people who call your previous cell phone number are patched into Google Voice, and Google Voice can make your cell phone ring by using the new number.

Figure 8-2 is a conceptual diagram of how incoming calls flow to your new SIM card and phone number.

When using this workaround *always* use the Google Voice Web site, a Google Voice dialer, or dial into your Google Voice number by phone to make calls from the new cell phone. That way, you preserve the Google Voice illusion for people who note your number and call you back. Otherwise you have to forward the new number to Google Voice, too, and get yet another new SIM card!

But with this approach, if you're conscientious, you can save some of the effort of getting people to call you on Google Voice. You lose the ability to move incoming phone calls to your usual work and home landlines, but you get all of Google Voice's other capabilities and control, all the time.

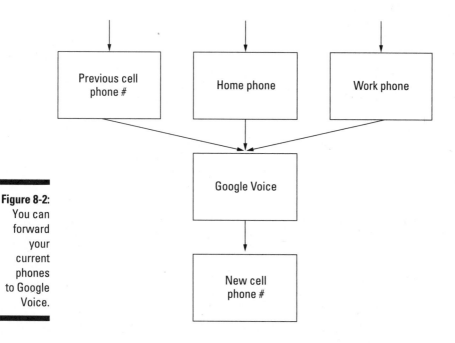

Figure 8-2:
You can forward your current phones to Google Voice.

With this approach, you can't have Google Voice ring any of the phones that are forwarded to it; Google Voice doesn't allow that kind of circular logic. This may cost you cell phone minutes on your new SIM, because you can't reassign incoming cell phone calls to your landline as you might otherwise do.

Always keep any phone SIM card someplace safe and easy to remember. They're obviously easy to lose, and surprisingly easy to damage, outside the protective casing of a phone.

Porting a phone number to Google Voice

Google Voice already offers *outbound* phone number portability: that is, portability of your Google Voice number to another provider, such as a cell phone provider. This feature is Google's insurance for people with tepid interest: they know that they can try having Google Voice in their life for a while, and if they don't like it, they don't have to abandon their new number when they go elsewhere.

And although outbound portability is nice, what people really want is inbound phone number portability. That means the ability to move your cell phone number to Google Voice.

What would inbound phone number portability do for you? It would mean that people could keep calling your cell phone to reach you. People are getting increasingly stubborn about not giving up their cell phone numbers; young people today often seem bent on keeping theirs for life. Younger people often have cell phone numbers with the area code based not on the city where they all live and work, but on where they come from.

So having your cell phone number become your Google Voice number is attractive. With this feature, you keep your business cards the same and your friends, colleagues, family, old boyfriends, and girlfriends can keep using the same old number because you get the calls through Google Voice.

Some people say that the central benefit to porting your number into Google Voice is that you won't have to change your business cards. However, true Google Voice fans will end up changing their business cards anyway, as people who get used to Google Voice don't like to list any other numbers. They want *all* calls to them to come in through Google Voice.

However, if you port your current number to GV, your old phone is left without a number; the carrier will have to assign it a new one. If you port your phone number to Google Voice, then keep your new, actual cell phone number totally secret. Try to ensure that no one but yourself ever has it, because if they do, they'll call your cell phone directly, bypassing all the convenience and control that Google Voice gives you.

Other people's problems

Some people, usually more technically minded, love the features of Google Voice and the control it gives them so much that they don't mind the extra work.

For many others, the extra steps and the differences in the model of how phones work with Google Voice present too much mental effort to be practical in day-to-day scenarios.

So if you're a classic early adopter type, or just love Google Voice, you may find Google Voice to be powerful, capable, and fun to use even in its initial state. Those who are not may want to wait until more integration with existing phones is offered or until everyone they know is using Google Voice and they feel more comfortable joining in.

And this rule applies to outgoing calls, too — to maintain the illusion, you have to dial Google Voice first, then your outbound number. A dialer program on your cell phone can shorten the steps but not eliminate the difference.

A Google Voice phone number is in an important sense not a real phone number. It's not tied to a real phone but just calls up specific associations and service in the network of servers that store Google's information. What's really needed is full phone number portability *and integration*. Not only would your cell phone number become your Google Voice number; it would also remain your "true" native cell phone number. Calls from your cell phone would be direct calls out and would still display your Google Voice number as your cell phone number, because they would be one and the same.

Because Google makes a cell phone operating system, Android, that's already running on over 1 million phones, this kind of capability may be made available soon.

Unfortunately, this capability still wouldn't solve the entire problem. If you wanted to use a landline for outgoing calls, you would still have to dial your Google Voice number first.

What you really need is the ability to spoof any phone you choose to appear as if it were just another phone using the same Google Voice number. This is currently illegal in many jurisdictions, because it can be used to perpetrate fraud. There may be a workaround that eventually allows many phones to simply work as extensions on your Google Voice number. But until then you'll still have to do extra work to take full advantage of both Google Voice and all the phones around you.

Using the Google Voice Web Site for Calls

Many people have gotten in the habit of using a computer for phone calls and even video calls due to Skype, Google Talk, and similar services. The easiest way to use Google Voice for making calls or sending texts is to make the call or send the text from your computer, assuming you're near one that is connected to the Internet. This way, the call or text comes directly from your Google Voice number, without extra steps.

Calls to domestic numbers from Google Voice are free; calls to international numbers are at very low rates (see Chapter 7). Texts sent from Google Voice can only be delivered to U.S. cell phones and are free as well for the sender. Neither calls nor SMSs sent from Google Voice count against your cell phone airtime minutes or text message limits, a further savings. (But they may count against the recipient's.)

You can't send an SMS text message to an international number from Google Voice. You may be tempted to send an SMS directly from your cell phone, but doing so may be expensive and will reveal your cell phone number, distracting the person from consistently using your Google Voice number. Consider sending a (free) e-mail message instead.

Going back to the future with Google Voice

In the movie *Back to the Future*, Marty McFly goes back in time to the years before he was born and ends up a spectator to his parents' budding romance. While nothing that upsetting is likely to happen to you while using Google Voice, it may make you pine for the days of landline telephones.

Many people, especially young adults in what's called Gen Y, don't have a landline, but use their cell phone instead. If you're one of these cell-only minimalists, you may find that, with Google Voice available, you suddenly want a landline in your life. Or, if you already have a landline, you may want another one.

Google Voice's ability to ring several phones at once or, by pressing the * key during an incoming call, to switch it to any of "your" phones gives you the option of switching between phones, taking away all the inconvenience that once defined hard-wired phones.

Why would you want a (or another) landline? Here are a few reasons:

- ✔ Landline phones don't use your cell phone plan's minutes.
- ✔ Landline phones have gotten extremely cheap since cell phones became widely used.
- ✔ Landlines don't use up your cell phone's battery.
- ✔ Landlines have a more reliable connection (this will be a clincher for some cell phone users).
- ✔ Landlines are more comfortable.
- ✔ Landlines have other features lacking in Google Voice, such as conference calling on outbound calls.
- ✔ Landline phones have better speakerphones.

These features make for more relaxed, more enjoyable, and less tiring phone calls. And these features may encourage you to be on the phone longer, for better or worse.

You may find that you are not only more comfortable but that you save money by having a landline, or an additional landline, versus doing without it. Certainly if you make business calls on your cell phone, and have a better quality of conversation by switching some of those to a landline, you may make more money, even if you don't save money directly.

As mentioned above, you can use Google Voice Mobile or another cell phone dialer application to drive calls to your landline phone. Just specify your landline as the ringback number, and Google Voice can connect the call through to your landline instead of to your cell phone.

Calling or texting from the Google Voice Web site

The people at Google use the term Click2Call for making a call from the Google Voice Web site. You can Click2Call or send a text from the Web site:

- ✔ From your Contacts
- ✔ From a Google Voice message
- ✔ From the body of a Google Voice message transcript
- ✔ For calls only: from the Call box on the Google Voice Web site. (That's an accidental pun, as a "call box" is a box, usually metal, with a phone in it that only dials a predetermined number.)
- ✔ For SMS text messages only: from the SMS button on the Google Voice Web site. (No pun intended or committed.)

If you're familiar with the quality of automatic transcripts of voice messages in general, or even of Google Voice's voicemail transcripts in particular, dialing a phone number from within a Google Voice voicemail transcript may sound like a joke.

However, in the computer version of "let's put our best people on it," Google Voice has apparently devoted extra computational resources and its very best algorithms to decoding phone numbers. Phone numbers are therefore more likely to be correct than the rest of the text.

So it's quite likely that you can successfully use the decoded phone numbers in voicemail transcriptions to return calls. If you're concerned, listen to the voicemail message and check the transcription against what you hear. In some cases you may not be sure what's being said either!

Calling your Contacts

Making a call to one of your Contacts from the Google Voice Web site is easy:

1. **Open the Google Voice Web site.**

2. **Click Contacts in the left-hand pane.**

   A list of your contacts appears.

3. **Click the needed group and then click the name of the contact you want to call.**

   The contact name and phone number(s) appears.

4. **Click the call link next to the phone number you want to use.**

   The Make a Call dialog appears and displays the number you've selected, as shown in Figure 8-3.

5. **Use the pull-down menu to choose which of your phones to ring.**

6. **If you want to always ring the same phone on calls to this person, select the Remember my choice checkbox to set it.**

   You will still have access to the pull-down list when making a call from your Contacts, but the default will be determined by the selection that was in force when you clicked Remember my choice.

   When you get a message from this person, the choice you make here is be preselected as well.

7. **Click Connect.**

   The dialog box disappears, and the call is connected.

Replying to calls and texts

Replying to a call or text to your Google Voice number is even easier than making a call, whether it comes from a Contact or not. Follow these steps:

1. **From the Google Voice Web site, click in the left-hand pane to access your overall Inbox, your Voicemail, or your SMS In box, as shown in Figure 8-4.**

   A list of your incoming messages appears, showing all your messages in your Inbox (shown in Figure 8-4) or only your voice messages or SMS text messages if you chose one or the other.

2. **Scroll to the call or text message you want to reply to.**

3. **Click the Reply button to be given a choice between calling or replying with an SMS text message.**

For SMS text messages only, and to reply directly by text without making a choice, click the Reply link below the message, not the Reply button to the upper right. You can see the Reply link and button on the same SMS text message in Figure 8-4.

Unlike in some other countries, the American (and Canadian) phone numbering system does not give you or Google Voice any way to distinguish between a landline (which, as a rule, cannot receive text messages) and a cell phone (which can) based on the number alone. Be aware that if you send an SMS text message to a phone you're not sure of, and the phone turns out to be a landline, the message will not be received. (This problem occurred a great deal with the old Grand Central service that predated Google Voice, because it simply ignored incoming text messages.)

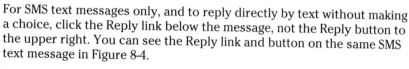

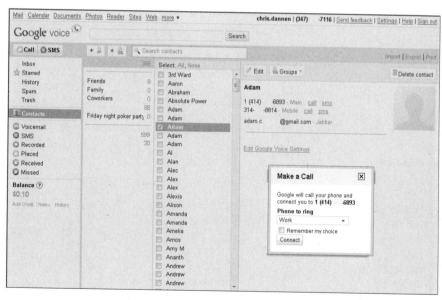

Figure 8-3: Calling is easy from Google Voice.

Figure 8-4:
Replying
from the
Google
Voice Web
site is
easy, too.

4. Choose Call or SMS.

If you choose Call, the same dialog as shown in Figure 8-1 appears; if you choose Text, a dialog for texting appears, as shown in Figure 8-5.

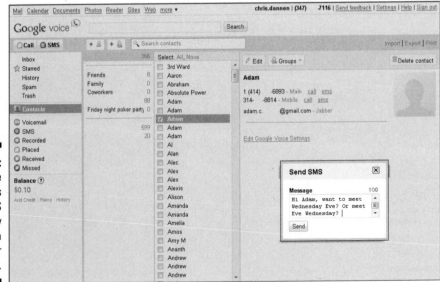

Figure 8-5:
Google
Voice's
SMS
capability
includes a
character
counter.

5. **If calling, choose which of your phones to ring and, optionally, click in the checkbox to remember your choice; then click Connect.**

   The phone you chose will ring; pick it up and then Google Voice will dial the party you're calling.

6. **If texting, enter your message and then click Send.**

   Equipped with a computer keyboard and the ability to easily cut and paste, it may be tempting to go well over the 160-character limit for a single text message. Resist temptation!

There's no easily available shortcut that you can use to transfer phone numbers you enter into the Call or SMS boxes, or phone numbers that appear in messages, into contacts. However, we recommend that you take the extra time to create contacts because doing so makes dealing with calls from these numbers in the future much easier. (If you are using call screening, it will be easier for the caller as well, because they won't potentially have to state their name when calling.)

Using the Call button

Using the Call button is very similar to calling a contact or replying to a call:

1. **Open the Google Voice Web site.**

2. **Click the Call button.**

   You are presented with the Call balloon, as shown in Figure 8-6.

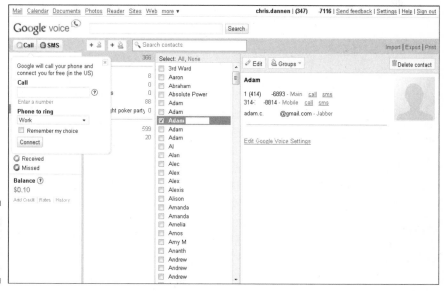

Figure 8-6:
Use the Call balloon for a quick call.

3. **Enter the phone number you want to use.**

   You can cut and paste the number if you have it on your computer.

4. **Use the pull-down menu to choose which of your phones to ring.**

5. **If you want to always ring the same phone on calls to this person, click the checkbox, Remember my choice, to set it as the default.**

6. **Click Connect.**

   The dialog disappears, and the call is connected.

Using the SMS button

Using the SMS button is very similar to texting a contact or replying to a call or text via SMS:

1. **Open the Google Voice Web site.**

2. **Click the SMS button.**

   You are presented with the SMS balloon, as shown in Figure 8-7.

3. **Enter the phone number you want to use.**

   Be sure it's an SMS number; if you can't be sure, you can still send an SMS, but be prepared to follow up in other ways as well.

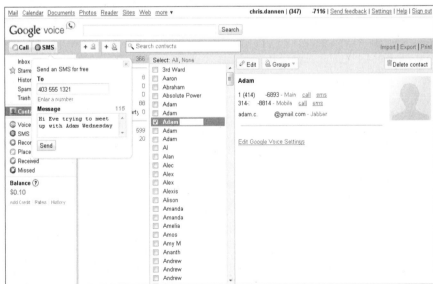

Figure 8-7:
Use the
SMS bal-
loon for a
quick text.

4. **Enter the message.**

   Sending SMS text messages from Google Voice is free, but that doesn't mean people want to pay for or take the time to read extra-long text messages. Take the 160-character limit seriously.

5. **Click Send.**

   The dialog disappears, and the text is sent.

Whether you enter the phone number from the Google Voice Web site or by using a dialer from a smartphone, you can only enter domestic U.S. numbers in the classic ten-digit format: a three-digit area code and a seven-digit number. Doing this prevents you from using some shorter numbers, such as when you're requested to SMS a confirmation code for online banking and other transactions, or for using Twitter. In these cases, you need to use your cell phone directly throughout the transaction, and not Google Voice.

What the HTML is going on here?

As you use Google Voice more and more, you may get a bit tired of repeating the mouse clicks needed to reach Settings, Contacts, and other areas in the Google Voice site.

If you know a bit of HTML, you can make yourself a convenient control panel for Google Voice that goes to key parts of Google Voice with many fewer clicks. Just create a Web page whose text is the names of the parts of Google Voice you want to reach. Then link the appropriate URL from that area to the text.

In fact, you don't even need to know HTML. You can do the same thing in most word processors, including any non-antediluvian version of Microsoft Word. Just type the text you want to appear in your control panel. Then use the menus to assign a URL to each piece of text. (In Word, the command is Insert⇨Hyperlink; the shortcut in Windows is Ctrl+K).

Any part of the Google Voice Web site that has its own unique URL can be linked to from an HTML page that you create. Individual Contacts and Groups do not have their own unique URLs, so you can't link to specific people or specific groups.

Whether you create the file directly in HTML or by using a word processor, save it to your hard drive. (In Word, be sure to use the option Save as Web page if you want to open the file in a browser.) Then open the resulting file in a browser.

If you want to use the file on your smartphone, you can either transfer it to your smartphone or publish it to the Web if you have a hosting account, or use a free host such as Blogger. (No one else can use it unless they know how your username and password to sign into your Google account.) Once on the Web, you can surf to the page and then use it to access Google Voice functions with a single click. (After the clicks needed to sign into your Google account, of course.)

Some of you older nerds out there may recognize a similarity between this and the old .BAT batch files that some of us used to create in DOS. Some of you younger nerds will not know what any of the previous sentence means. Be (mostly) thankful.

Getting (Secret) Calls from the Web

You can use Google Voice to easily create a Call Widget, which is HTML code that appears on a Web page as a button labeled "Call Me." The HTML code that can be placed in any Web page you control, such as your blog. When the Web page user clicks the button, Google Voice connects to the caller's phone and then calls one or more of your phones.

A Call Widget hides your number, so the person who calls never sees it. And the call can be set up to go straight to voicemail or to ring one or more of your phones, all of the time or at different times of day.

A Call Me button is much cheaper than setting up a free 800 number but is just as effective and more flexible — backed by all the capabilities of Google Voice, including flexible ringing of phones, customizable voicemail greetings, voicemail transcriptions, text message alerts, and more. And just like any other phone call, you can see the number of whoever is calling you on your phone's caller ID. It also gets logged in your Google Voice account.

The good news is that the HTML code for the Call Me button does not show your number in plain sight. However, it can be decoded or otherwise hacked from the HTML. This useful feature has the ability to hide phone numbers but it is not bulletproof.

Although hiding your Google Voice number can be a good thing, you don't *have* to hide it. You can also give the number in plain sight on the Web page. This gives Web page visitors the option of calling directly, which will be more familiar to them, and also gives them the option of sending a text. (You should make this clear in the text on the Web page; for example, use text like this: "Click the Call Me button to call us for free, or call or text directly to. . . ".)

Following is the HTML code for an example Call Widget, for your amusement:

```
<object type="application/x-shockwave-flash"
        data="https://clients4.google.com/voice/embed/
        webCallButton" width="230" height="85"><param
        name="movie" value="https://clients4.google.
        com/voice/embed/webCallButton" /><param
        name="wmode" value="transparent" /><param
        name="FlashVars" value="id=5e52fdd1c86ca89477c9
        1f43c31a7ab3e35609db&style=0" /></object>
```

Follow these simple steps to set up a Call Widget:

1. **Go to the Google Voice Web site.**
2. **Click the Settings link.**

3. Click the Call Widgets link.

The Call Widgets area appears, as shown in Figure 8-8.

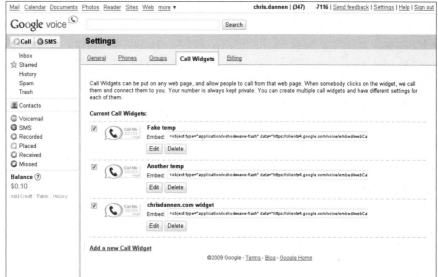

Figure 8-8:
See
your Call
Widgets.

4. Click the Add a new Call Widget link.

The fields for adding a Call Widget appear, as shown in Figure 8-9.

Figure 8-9:
Create
your Call
Widgets.

5. **Specify the settings for your Call Widget: Name, which phones to ring (or send straight to voicemail), which greeting to use, and whether to use Call Presentation.**

   Remember that you can assign a ringing schedule to a phone, so you can assign the Call Widget to a phone that only rings at certain times of day. It's the World Wide Web, and prospects — or suspects — could call you at any time of the day or night!

   Consider having a special greeting just for Call Widget users that's specific to them, such as: "Thank you for calling us from the Call Me button on our Web site. Please leave a message describing. . ."

6. **Click Save Changes to create the Call Widget or Cancel to stop the process.**

   Your Call Widget appears in your list of Call Widgets.

7. **Select the code next to the prompt, Embed. Place this code in any Web page you care to.**

8. **Test the Call Widget to make sure that it works and that it rings the correct phones and triggers the right voicemail message. Consider how the phone will be staffed. Take responsibility for the user's entire experience when they use the Call Widget.**

Consider inviting your Web visitors to give you feedback about their experience using the Call Widget. Otherwise, any problems with the experience could go undetected until a long time has passed and quite a few customers have gone away angry or confused.

To edit a Call Widget, follow the same steps, but begin by clicking Edit under an existing widget rather than clicking the Add a new Call Widget link.

Be sure to use the other features of Google Voice in conjunction with Call Widgets, such as voicemail transcriptions. These features can help you deliver a superior, "right first time" response to your callers.

You might want to consider setting up a special Google Voice account with its own phone number to connect Call Widgets to your business phone number. Be aware, though, that you may run into two limitations of Google Voice: you can only assign any one phone number to a single Google Voice account, and you can't assign a Google Voice number to a phone extension. The use of a business phone number with Google Voice demands some thought and planning, as explained in Chapter 15.

Consider getting a specific phone line just for your Call Widget to ring to. Then you can control the ring times for this phone specifically in tune with the needs of your Web visitors and yourself!

Forwarding Voicemail Messages and Recordings

You can easily e-mail any Google Voice voicemail message or recording, or put it on the Web.

Google Voice stores both types of recordings and sends you a link. You can easily download the audio file and edit it, and you can do all sorts of things with the link, including forwarding it to people via e-mail.

You can also put the link to the stored file, or a new link to the downloaded (and possibly edited) file, on an intranet page, or even a public-facing Web page for all the world to hear. There are some times when this is a good idea and some times when it's a lousy one.

A time when it's a good idea is when you have a meeting with several people, but additional people can't attend. You can send them a link to a recording of the meeting. You can even edit the recording to catch the high points.

A time when it might be a bad idea is when you record a customer service call, and the customer gets angry in a way that strikes you as funny, and the idea hits that you can put this on the Web and have a good laugh about it with your Web site visitors.

You can make people hurt, upset, and really, really angry if you surprise them by publicly sharing a recording of them on a phone call. They might even threaten to sue. Think through any potential embarrassments before doing this. In some cases, you may want to ask for permission.

Chapter 9

Using the Inbox and Handling Calls

Google Voice does so much for you, but you need to take the time to master all of the features to get the most from the service. During the early, steep part of the learning curve, you may wonder who's working for whom — Google Voice for you, or you for Google Voice!

We've all had the experience of trying to remember the location of a command or how to use a feature. Google Voice includes commands for its Web interface, for the Google Voice dialers on mobile phones, and even commands that only work from a phone. With options scattered about, taking advantage of all of them can be confusing.

This chapter brings together the options for the parent of all Google Voice interfaces, the Google Voice Inbox. We go through each option thoroughly and to a moderate level of detail, so that you can master the tool.

This chapter also describes keyboard commands and emergency phone registration, a quick and dirty process that can only be initiated from a phone, by calling your Google Voice voice mailbox. (It can be cancelled online or by phone.)

We conclude with Google Voice keyboard commands, the power user's tool for getting around within Google Voice and other Google services more quickly.

Using the Google Voice Inbox

The Google Voice Inbox is much like Gmail. The Google Voice Inbox is long-term storage for all your voice messages. This record only becomes more valuable with time and increased use, as it accumulates more information you can retrieve when you need it.

The Google Voice Inbox is easy to use and clean. In fact, we prefer it to Gmail's interface, which is highly capable but crowded and busy. The Google Voice interface might be Google's second best so far, after the stripped-down Google Search home page. (The Google Search home page is particularly notable because it initially appeared around the turn of the century, at a time when search rivals were creating complex home pages on busy portals at a rapid rate.)

Like others among the best interfaces, the Google Voice interface incorporates tremendous amounts of functionality presented as simple options for the user. We look at it in two parts: the individual message notifications for calls and text messages and then the controls and options surrounding the notifications.

This book and the Google Help documentation refer to the Inbox as all views on Google Voice notifications, even views through folders other than the Inbox, as shown in Figure 9-1. We follow that practice here as well; the Inbox is both any view that shows Google Voice notifications (basically, any view that isn't Settings) and the specific Inbox folder, which only shows notifications you haven't archived, marked as spam, or deleted. When we refer specifically to the Inbox folder, we call it the Inbox folder.

Message notifications

The Google Voice Inbox includes text message exchanges, call notifications, voicemail message transcriptions and links to call recordings.

Figure 9-1:
A Google
Voice Inbox
message
alert has
hidden
depths.

A Google Voice Inbox message includes several elements that are worth paying attention to:

✔ **Originating phone number and contact name and Add link:** Google Voice uses caller ID to get the incoming phone number and uses your Contacts list to associate a name with it. If the phone number is not associated with a contact, Google presents an Add link option to let you add it to a new contact or an existing one.

Use e-mail instead of a return call or SMS text message to deal with calls whenever it makes sense. There's no direct link to do this, but it only takes two clicks to do it for existing contacts: Click the contact's name to see contact details; click the contact's e-mail address to send an e-mail. See the "The Missing Link" sidebar for details.

✔ **Date and time of the call; number of days ago:** A very useful feature that would be even more useful if it included the day of the week. (A three-letter abbreviation would do nicely, pretty please, Google?) We tend to remember when, for example, a work colleague calls on a Saturday, and that would be a lot easier to scan for than a date. The number of days ago does help, though.

✔ **Star marker:** You can star a message by clicking the barely visible star outline that appears way over to the right within the message notification. (On a widescreen laptop, where you might display your Inbox full-screen, you may miss the outline entirely.)

Everyone uses (or ignores) stars in their own way. Starred voicemails are one of four classes of messages: Starred, regular Inbox messages, messages in the History folder, and deleted messages. Starred messages show up in the Inbox; they are the only messages in the Starred area, and they show up in History as well.

✔ **SMS — more messages link:** Google Voice displays the most recent message exchange and makes others available through a link; clicking the link expands the exchange. The current and past messages are rolled up into a single entry. This is often convenient, but it can drive those of us who want to see all messages one at a time nuts. (It's not done as aggressively as in Gmail, thank goodness.) Also, after you expand an exchange of messages, there's no control in the Inbox to contract it again. (Refreshing the browser window will do it, though.)

✔ **Voicemail message transcript:** Google's sometimes-amusing, but generally-useful transcript is shown below the message audio bar. Google puts extra computational resources into getting phone numbers and other digits correct. Google provides buttons for you to vote on whether the transcript is useful, although the light green Yes button is much more inviting than the grayed out No button.

The missing link

Google Voice is useful because it makes phone calls more like e-mail. But the best way to make voice interactions more like e-mail is to move them all the way into e-mail.

Google Voice notifications give you a Call link and an SMS link for replying to callers, but there's another link that should be there: an E-mail link. E-mail is often the best way to respond to voice.

Why? E-mailing moves messages from real-time interruptions to messages you can deal with asynchronously, at a more convenient time for you. E-mails can more easily be saved, tracked, searched, copied, and forwarded.

The E-mail link may be missing, but e-mail is never far away. Just click the name of the caller, and her contact information appears.

Click on her e-mail address and you're off and running. You can copy other people to update them, or even forward the message to someone who can handle it better.

It's probably best to acknowledge the transfer from phone to e-mail in your message; you can begin the e-mail message, "In response to your phone call. . .", then respond. If you're still the appropriate contact, don't be afraid to ask, politely, that they e-mail rather than call. Appropriate language for this purpose may be some version of the following: "Please reply by e-mail rather than by phone, as I'll find it easier to deal with your request quickly and effectively." The purpose is not to "diss" the caller but to help them; if they continue to contact you by phone, continue to respond in whichever way is most effective for both parties.

- ✔ **Call link:** Click to call the person from your Google Voice number. Google lets you select which of your phones to ring. This handy feature not only lets you use Google's low international calling rates, it also lets you send a phone call to a landline phone and avoid using up cell plan minutes.

- ✔ **SMS link:** Click to reply with a free SMS text message, which can appear to come from your Google Voice number.

- ✔ **Mark as read link:** Unread messages give you a Mark as read link to click when you've read (and perhaps dealt with) a message. Consider archiving it at this time, as described in the next section.

- ✔ **More drop-down menu — Mark as Unread:** If you choose to mark the call as unread, the caller's phone number appears in bold and the blue surround around the content is subtly darkened.

- ✔ **More drop-down menu — Add note:** Adding a note is great for clarifying what's going on in an exchange or tagging the notification for later searches. For example, if Google's voice message transcription has misspelled a name, you can put the correct spelling here.

- ✔ **More drop-down menu — Block caller:** Great for getting rid of people who are bothering you, but don't be too hasty. Not only can this be a harsh step; it's easy to forget you've blocked someone. So your intent to temporarily block someone can accidentally become permanent.

You can do a lot with notes by treating the words in them as tags for later scanning and searching. We recommend that you apply some simple rules. For example, tag every recording with a mnemonic such as "recording"; tag every conference call. That way you can quickly find all your recordings and conference calls. This is also a good place to make a note if you followed up by e-mail.

Because Google Voice is so new, exactly how people will use the service is unclear. Gmail is a pretty good analogy, though, and what happens in Gmail is that people keep years' worth of e-mail messages, totaling in some cases several gigabytes, as a huge searchable archive of their online activities.

Experienced Gmail users are pretty confident that they can find a given e-mail about a business deal, a home purchase, and so on. People don't seem to edit their inboxes down much, but some of the successful ones do tag e-mails, as we're suggesting you do for Google Voice.

Performing multiple-item actions

You can perform certain actions on multiple notifications at a time. Each notification has a checkbox; click to select, or use the Select pull-down, combined with the page right and page left buttons to select many messages at once. Select as many messages as you want. Then choose an action, as shown in Figure 9-2.

✔ **Select pull-down:** This pull-down allows you to select or deselect messages by choosing all (select all), none (deselect all), read (select all read, deselect unread) or unread (select all unread, deselect read).

Use this in combination with the page-left and page-right buttons on the right edge of the Inbox, at the same level, to quickly act on messages in a crowded inbox or other folder.

✔ **Archive:** Archive takes an item out of the Inbox, but keeps it available in the History list. This is just like the All Mail/Inbox buckets in Gmail.

✔ **Report Spam:** Google Voice may inspire whole new types of phone spam, inspired by (and perhaps carried out by) e-mail spammers. Here's our chance to fight back; every time you report spam you help fellow users as well as yourself.

Figure 9-2:
You can act
on several
notifications
at once.

You can add your Google Voice number to the "do not call" list for spammers at www.donotcall.gov. Then, if you do get spam calls, report them; the holder of the number may get a big fine.

✔ **Delete:** You can delete messages, but in most cases it's preferable to archive them. You never know when you might want to reply to just about any message that isn't spam. Google Voice deletes the message without asking you to confirm.

✔ **Starred folder only — Move to Inbox:** In the Starred folder, a Move to Inbox folder allows you to quickly move a message to the Inbox.

Why might you need to move a starred message to the Inbox? Because you can delete a starred message; it's removed from the Inbox and History, but remains in the Starred folder.

✔ **More actions — Mark as read:** This feature gives you a quick way to mark several messages as read but not much quicker than clicking the Mark as read link on each.

✔ **More actions — Mark as unread:** The Mark as unread link is somewhat hidden in messages, so it might be quicker to perform this operation by using the checkbox method than one at a time for individual messages.

✔ **More actions — Add star:** You can quickly star multiple messages.

✔ **Show: All:** This is the default setting, showing every message in your Inbox.

✔ **Show: Unread:** Showing only unread messages is good for focus, but it's easy to leave the display in this mode and then wonder why the read messages in your Inbox aren't showing up.

Use Show: Unread with caution, and try to remember to return to Show: All as soon as you're done. Otherwise, messages that are in your Inbox but read might seem to disappear.

✔ **Page-right, page-right-end, page-left and page-left end.** You can quickly scroll through pages of your Inbox here.

These controls at the top of the page are easily used in combination with the Select pull-down and checking or unchecking individual messages to rapidly choose groups of messages for actions.

Searching messages

The Search box is a small part of the Google Voice Inbox, but it's given pride of place at the top and rightly so.

Using your browser for the right answer

You can use your browser to create an e-mailed response to a caller by using your default e-mail client, if that's not Gmail.

Create a bookmark in your favorite browser with the following, instead of a Web page address:

mailto:subject=Re: your voicemail

This code opens a message from your default e-mail client, with the subject line filled in as "Re: your voicemail." Just drag and drop the person's e-mail address into the To: line, add the e-mail addresses of any people you want to copy, and you're off and running.

Searching your calls is one of the new functions of Google Voice that you could never do before. Try it a few times; it has a pretty strong "wow!" factor. After you try it, use these tips to understand searching better and make your searches more effective:

- **Search by text.** You can search by text in a text message or voicemail transcription or Note. However, if Google has misspelled the text, the accuracy of your search will obviously suffer.

Correct misspelling of key terms in a voicemail transcription for search by entering the correct spelling of the term as a Note to that message. Also enter key terms for recorded calls as Notes so they can be searched for as well.

- **No From or To Search:** Google Mail has special search categories such as the person who sent you mail, or who you mailed to. Google Voice doesn't have these special categories.

You can search by the name of the person who called you. You can get the calls from that person, but also the calls to that person, as well as calls in which that name is mentioned in the voicemail transcript, in an SMS text message, or in the Note you add to a call. Still useful, but this can be frustrating if you're a florist with two different friends named Bud and three named Rose!

- **Search by number:** You can search by part or all of a person's phone number. However, the search text has to be formatted exactly as the number is displayed in the notification in the Inbox.

- **Search by name:** You can search by a person's name as a text string.

- **Search by date:** You can't search by date.

Don't get us wrong; being able to search your phone traffic is amazing. However, it's still quite limited, not yet nearly as effective as using search with, say, Gmail.

The best hope for searching effectively in Google Voice is "hard" information: the person's name, (parts of) their phone number, and text you enter in Notes with the notification.

Using folders

Google Voice offers 11 folders for your phone traffic through Google Voice. Five are storage for managing your Inbox messages; six are different views on your calls.

The five folders for managing your Inbox messages are:

- ✔ **Inbox:** Holds all incoming messages except the ones you archive or delete. The name Inbox is displayed in bold when there are one or more unread messages, and the number of unread messages is displayed next to Inbox. This is the only one of the top five folders for which unread messages are highlighted.

Only the Placed and Received folders show the length of a call.

- ✔ **Starred:** Adds the Move to Inbox top-level button to those described in the previous section. All messages you star are kept in the Starred folder, even if you archive or delete them. If you unstar a deleted message, it disappears from the Starred folder and exists only in the Trash.

- ✔ **History:** Also has the Move to Inbox top-level button. History holds all messages that aren't deleted. When you archive a message it removes it from the Inbox but leaves the existing copy in the History folder. You can archive a message while looking at it in the History folder, which removes it from the Inbox.

- ✔ **Spam:** Has different top-level buttons, Delete Forever (see next bullet) and Not Spam. This folder holds messages that are suspected by Google Voice of being spam, including incoming messages that go straight to the Spam folder and messages that come to the Inbox but that you mark as spam. Using the Not Spam button moves selected messages to the Inbox and History folders.

- ✔ **Trash:** Holds deleted messages only. Extra buttons for managing selected messages are Delete Forever and Undelete (which works the same as Not Spam in the previous bullet). When you click Delete Forever, you receive a dialog asking "Are you sure?" If you click Yes, the selected messages are removed from your system, even if starred.

The six folders that provide different views on your messages are views on all the messages in your History folder; they don't reflect what is or isn't in your Inbox. They also don't include messages in the Trash or Spam folders. Each of these six folders is highlighted if it contains unread messages.

Unlike the set of five folders I previously detailed — Inbox, Starred, History, Spam and Trash — that means you can have unread messages in several different folders. You can have more unread messages in these folders than show up in your Inbox if you move unread messages out of your Inbox into, say, History.

The six folders names are largely self-explanatory:

- ✔ **Voicemail:** These are calls you received through Google Voice, did not answer, and received a voicemail for. Includes all your transcripts.
- ✔ **SMS:** Includes all your SMS text message notifications.
- ✔ **Recorded:** Includes all calls you recorded even a brief part of. This folder contains a subset of the calls in Received.
- ✔ **Placed:** Includes all calls you made out through Google Voice. This folder and Received also show the length of the call.
- ✔ **Received:** All calls you received through Google Voice and answered. This folder and Placed also show the length of the call.
- ✔ **Missed:** All calls you received through Google Voice and neither answered nor received a voicemail message.

Optimizing your Inbox

You can use your whole Inbox (in the overall sense, including all the folders) to manage, archive, and retrieve all your voice traffic that goes through Google Voice. Here are a few tips you can use to get the most out of it:

- ✔ **Add callers to your Contacts.** When calls come in from numbers not in your Contacts list, use the Add link on the notification to add the number to an existing contact if you have one, or create the needed new contact if you don't. Doing this regularly makes both Google Voice and Gmail steadily more useful.
- ✔ **Move all your phone traffic to Google Voice.** Put it all through Google Voice. The more your calls go through Google Voice, the more it can help you. See Chapter 6 for details.

Stop answering your other phone numbers and leave voicemail greetings on them telling people to call your Google Voice number.

- ✔ **Move Google Voice traffic to e-mail.** Many calls to you can be replied to — or delegated to someone else — through e-mail. E-mail is easier to track, search, copy people on, and manage than voicemail, even with Google Voice to help you. This also saves time, interruptions, and money.

✔ **Don't move e-mail traffic to Google Voice.** Some Google Voice users give out their Google Voice number more freely than they previously gave out their phone number because, hey, Google Voice generates e-mail notifications, too. Don't do this, because it just adds a layer to what may well become an e-mail conversation anyway and generates more phone calls for you to decide what to do with. Keep using your e-mail address as your first line of defense against intrusion.

✔ **Manage the Inbox folder.** Use the Inbox folder specifically as a control panel for active voice traffic, with the star to designate the really urgent ones. Deal with messages quickly and archive them.

✔ **Tag messages.** Use the Notes field to tag notifications, including notifications of calls you placed. Doing this makes your overall Inbox far more valuable. If you're a consultant or someone who otherwise bills for your time, this capability can help with invoicing. (Remember, everything you don't explicitly delete is in the History folder.)

Handling Calls with Google Voice

Google Voice has so many features that you may have trouble remembering which one is best for the situation you're in. Here are some calling scenarios you might encounter, and how to best use GV in each.

Options for all incoming calls

You have certain options in Google Voice only for incoming calls. The two key such options are recording calls and starting conference calls.

Recording calls

Recording an incoming call in Google Voice is easy. Just press 4 at any point during the call. The caller receives a warning message that the call will be recorded.

After the call, you receive a notification with a link to the recording, as shown in Figure 9-3.

Google Voice does not send you a file with a recording of the call as, say, an MP3. It sends you a *link* to such a file. However, it allows you to download the recording to an MP3 file. You can copy this file to an MP3 player, such as an iPod — or, these days, an awful lot of mobile phones — edit it in sound editing software and so on.

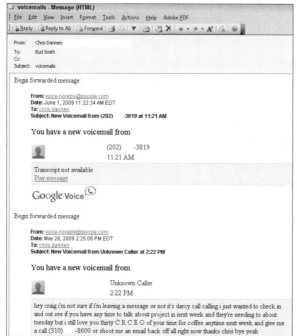

Figure 9-3:
Make a
record of
any
incoming
call.

Mac computers come with programs for editing audio. You can easily find freeware, shareware, and paid programs for Windows. One good source for such programs is `download.com`.

Google Voice also allows you to embed the link in a Web page so the conversation can be shared widely without the necessity of hosting or otherwise moving the file around.

The etiquette and legalities of publicizing Google Voice recordings have not been threshed out thoroughly yet. We recommend that you get permission from the participants before sharing a call recording online. Give the participants an opportunity to review the version that you intend to publicize, including any edits you make. If possible, provide a transcript as well.

Conference calls

Google Voice makes conference calls easy — again, for incoming calls only. If you don't have a smartphone, such as the iPhone, that can merge calls, have people call you so that you can initiate the conference. Google Voice announces the caller on call waiting:

"Call from: Jane."

(The words "Call from" are spoken by Google Voice. The caller's name is read out by Google Voice if the phone number used is in your Contacts; it is spoken in the person's own name if call screening is on and the phone number used is not in your Contacts.)

"To add this caller to your current call, press 5."

Just press 5; it's as easy as that. You can have up to three incoming calls on the line, for a total of four people on the call.

You can also use Google Voice's recording capability by pressing 4 at any point during an incoming call.

We suggest that you make a habit of recording conference calls. This step is good for alleviating confusion about who said what, providing support for any agreements reached, and sharing the call with people who missed the meeting.

If you want to add more than three participants to a call, use a smartphone to handle the call. Add the maximum with Google Voice, then have the rest call your true cell phone number and conference them in this way. Try this before you depend on it for an important call.

Google Voice conference calls offer tremendous money and time savings compared to most other ways of having conference calls. Many providers make a great deal of money charging organizations in particular for overpriced conference calling capabilities that are limited, hard to use, require advance notification, get oversubscribed and therefore are unavailable when you need them most, and so on.

Google Voice saves you most of this trouble. Existing services will not go out of business entirely. Google Voice is limited to just 4 lines at once and lacks some of the scheduling and media sharing capabilities of other services. But for small and casual conference calls, and with its built-in recording capability, Google Voice can't be beat.

Have the conference call on a comfortable phone with good reception or a good connection and good voice quality. Avoid conference calls on the move if at all possible; you'll just frustrate yourself and others.

Emergency phone registration

The normal process of registering a phone for use with Google Voice, as described in Chapter 3, is sensible but cumbersome. You specify a phone number; Google Voice makes sure that the phone isn't registered to anyone else for use with Google Voice and then calls you on that phone. You enter a code that Google Voice displays onscreen, and the phone is then available for you to manage within your Google Voice account.

But what if you're visiting an office somewhere or a friend's house, or staying in a hotel? What if your cell phone is out of range of a signal or out of charge, but your friend's or colleague's isn't? You may want all your Google Voice calls to go to one number — either so you get them, or so they can be answered for you.

Google Voice offers a quick and easy way to do this, and there's no need to even register the phone you're using. This feature, called temporary call forwarding, forwards all your Google Voice calls to the temporary number.

The steps for setting or clearing temporary call forwarding from the Google Voice touchtone menu are very similar, so they're given one after another here.

Setting temporary call forwarding

You can't set up temporary call forwarding from the Web interface; you have to call your Google Voice number and use Google's touchtone menus.

You can't use a phone registered to your Google Voice account for temporary call forwarding.

Follow these steps to set temporary call forwarding:

1. **Choose which phone to call from.**

   If you call from the number that you want the calls to be forwarded to, you won't have to enter the number you're calling from. But if you do this, the phone may incur long distance charges for the (brief) call. To avoid this, calling from your cell phone is likely to be quickest and to avoid long distance charges.

2. **Call your Google Voice number. If necessary to access your account, press * and enter your PIN.**

   If you're calling from one of your registered phones that connects directly to your Google Voice account (usually, this is your cell phone), Google Voice will offer you options; if not, you'll need to press * and enter your PIN to access your account and hear options.

   • Press 4 to access the main settings menu.

   • Press 4 again to access temporary settings.

   • Press 2 to set a temporary forwarding number.

      You can use the number you're calling from or enter a different number.

3. **Specify whether to use the number you're calling from, or enter the other number you wish to use.**

When you receive a call to your Google Voice number, your temporary phone number rings *in addition to* your other phones — depending on their settings. You have to turn off ringing for these other phones in Google Voice if you don't want them to ring while your temporary phone number is in effect.

Clearing temporary call forwarding

You can clear temporary call forwarding from a phone, by using Google's touchtone menus, or from the Google Voice Web site.

Follow these steps to clear temporary call forwarding using Google's touchtone menus:

1. **Call your Google Voice number. If necessary to access your account, press * and enter your PIN.**

2. **Press 4 to access the main settings menu. Choose from the following:**

   • Press 4 again to access temporary settings.

   • Press 2 to edit or remove your temporary forwarding number.

   • Press 3 to turn off your temporary forwarding number.

Follow these steps to clear temporary call forwarding using the Google Voice Web site:

1. **Go to the Google Voice Web site at** `voice.google.com`**. Sign in if needed.**

   The Google Voice Web site appears.

2. **Click the Settings link in the upper part of your screen to go to the Settings area.**

3. **Click the Phones tab.**

   A list of your phones appears, showing your temporary number at the top, as shown in Figure 9-4.

4. **Click Delete to remove the temporary number.**

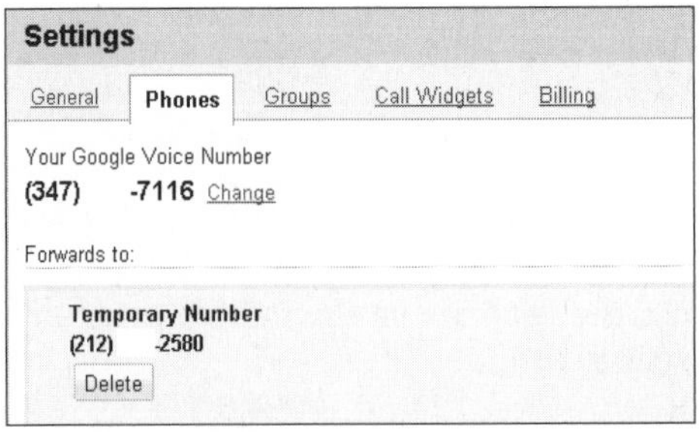

Figure 9-4:
Your temporary number shows up right at the top.

Settings				
General	**Phones**	Groups	Call Widgets	Billing

Your Google Voice Number
(347)   -7116 Change

Forwards to:

Temporary Number
(212)   -2580
Delete

Using keyboard commands

Google offers keyboard commands in many of its programs. Google Voice is particularly well-suited to them because of the repetitive nature of much work with phone calls.

Table 9-1 sums up keyboard commands for Google Voice. If you handle a lot of calls, it may well be worth the effort to learn them.

Table 9-1	Keyboard Commands for Google Voice	
Type Of Shortcut	*Keystrokes*	*Results*
Calling and texting	c	Open Quick Call
Calling and texting	m	Open Quick SMS
Calling and texting	<esc>	Close Quick Call/SMS
Message selection	*, a	Select all
Message selection	*, n	Select none
Message control	!	Mark message(s) as spam
Message control	#	Move message(s) to trash
Better dead than unread	<Shift>+i	Mark as read
Better dead than unread	<Shift>+u	Mark as unread
Better dead than unread	*, r	Select read
Better dead than unread	*, u	Select unread
Relative navigation	/	Jump to search box
Relative navigation	-> or n	Go to next page
Absolute navigation	g, i	Go to Inbox
Absolute navigation	g, s	Go to Starred
Absolute navigation	g, h	Go to History
Absolute navigation	g, p	Go to Placed calls
Absolute navigation	g, r	Go to Received calls
Absolute navigation	g, m	Go to Missed calls
Absolute navigation	g, c	Go to Contacts

Google Voice for the deaf

Phones are a hugely important tool for most people and are a big source of frustration for people who are hard of hearing or deaf. While most states have regulations supporting phone accessibility for the deaf, still more could be done.

E-mail and text messaging, on the other hand, have been hugely helpful to deaf people, and Google Voice is another step in this direction. It allows interactions that begin in voice to be continued in text, which is perfect for anyone who needs or prefers text.

E-mailed notifications of voice messages are great as an alert, and transcriptions of voice messages, while far from perfect, can still be helpful.

Google Voice is additionally useful for those who are hard of hearing, rather than more fully deaf, as Google Voice makes it easy to play back a voicemail message repeatedly, through headphones and/or at high volume, to help the recipient parse the contents.

Part III
Maximizing Your Handset

The 5th Wave   By Rich Tennant

Cell Phones

"This model comes with a particularly useful function – a simulated static button for breaking out of long winded conversations."

In this part . . .

Google Voice is ideal for people who juggle a cell phone or two and one or more landlines. There's a special Google Voice Mobile Web site that anyone can access and specific Google Voice dialers for your smartphone. We show you how to make the most of the rich range of offerings out there.

Chapter 10

Using the Google Voice Mobile Web Site

Google Voice is made to work across all your phones; however, you can also use it as a power boost for your cell phone.

Many people use their cell phones to handle calls and, by doing so, get the convenience of a single interface and suffer through the hassle of mixing between friends and family, personal business, and work through a single device, often at all times of day. Much of the power of Google Voice is in helping you untangle the spaghetti and get only the calls you want and only when you want them.

But this means that the make-or-break factor for changing over to a Google Voice number is having all calls and texts from your cell phone appear to be from your Google Voice number, making your communications easier to manage consistently.

To make all that easier, there are two solutions for cell phones: the Google Voice mobile Web site is one, and dialer apps for BlackBerry and Android phones is the other. A *dialer* is a smartphone application that lets you use your phone just like you'd use the Web interface of Google Voice.

The iPhone once had several dialers of its own, as we describe in Chapter 11, and a fourth was expected directly from Google. However, in a move that got a lot of attention in mid-2009, Apple rejected the Google Voice application from Google itself and, perhaps more shocking, yanked the existing Google Voice apps from the App Store.

So users of the GV mobile site will include iPhone users, some of whom will be quite unhappy at having the dialer apps pulled, along with users of other phones that don't have dialer support.

In addition to supporting dialing and texting, the Google Voice mobile Web site and dialers have another purpose as well: to allow you to manage Google Voice from your phone instead of from a computer.

Of course, the original purpose of GrandCentral (and now, Google Voice) was to control all your phones by using your computer. But with the advent of the BlackBerry, the most important computer for many people became the one in their pocket, not on their desktop.

A cell phone-centric approach spread to, and even intensified with the arrival of the iPhone. But because not everyone has a smartphone, Google gives you the option of controlling Google Voice from your desktop, your smartphone, or both.

Benefitting from Google Voice

The Google Voice mobile Web site, which we refer to here as the GV mobile site, is surprisingly capable, but it's still a compromise. It's not as good for making calls as using a dialer and it's not as good for managing Google Voice as using the full Google Voice Web site. For a report describing the tradeoffs, see `www.boygeniusreport.com/2009/04/12/gvdialer-puts-google-voice-on-your-mobile-handset/.)`

The GV Mobile site serves two purposes:

✔ **As a dialer:** The GV mobile site is your best choice for a dialer on most phones out there today, as shown in Figure 10-1. On Android and BlackBerry, you should use Google's customized dialer for your phone or, if you prefer, a third-party dialer. On iPhone, you can use one of two third-party dialers, but only if you got your copy before they were pulled from the App Store in mid-2009. These dialers are much better integrated in terms of their user interface appearance and their integration into the phone's native functionality and in some cases can work just as well as dialing a normal call.

If you're paying high charges for data transmission on your non-smartphone, using the Google Voice Mobile Web site may be expensive. If so, consider dialing out to your Google Voice number and making calls from there instead.

✔ **For managing Google Voice:** You can accomplish many tasks in managing Google Voice through the GV mobile site. On smartphones with dialers, you can manage Google Voice through the dialer instead; for smartphones without them you may use the more capable Google Voice Web site some of the time and the faster GV mobile site at other times.

If you use an Android phone or a BlackBerry, or if you have an iPhone and got a dialer app before they were pulled, go to the specific chapter for your phone. (Unless you have a dumbphone, too, or are a manager, a software developer, or just want to know what people with lesser phones will have to suffer through.) See Chapter 11 for information on how to use a Google Voice dialer on iPhone, Chapter 12 for BlackBerry information, and Chapter 13 for Android details.

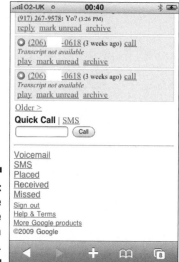

Figure 10-1:
Using the GV mobile site as a dialer.

To use the GV mobile site as a dialer, it has to know which number to dial to reach you. The site doesn't "know" what the number is of the cell phone it's being used on. Use the My Mobile Number setting of Google Voice Mobile, under the Settings tab, to specify which phone you're running the GV mobile site on.

What makes a smartphone?

Smartphones are all the rage, but the very definition of one is somewhat up in the air.

Most people understand a smartphone to be a phone that has a platform: a well-defined operating system that outsiders can program to; hardware that enables at least some PC-type capabilities; and strong functionality as a phone. Also, for most people to consider it, it has to look like a winner in terms of sales and application support.

Capabilities that people buy smartphones for include on-the-go e-mail and Web surfing. The hardware and software that support these capabilities include a full keyboard — on a touch screen, with real buttons, or both — and a screen large and high-resolution enough to allow at least limited Web surfing.

By these measures the clear winners among smartphones are the phones we cover in the following chapters: the iPhone, BlackBerry phones, and all the Android-based phones we've seen so far. (With the latter two types advantaged by still having dialers available.)

Palm Pre is capable enough to qualify as a smartphone, but it's quite new, so it's still up in the air as to whether it will become a winner. Windows Mobile phones are smartphones but seem to be fading in sales after some strong early starts.

If the leaders in smartphones remain iPhone, BlackBerry, and Android, what are their specialties? The iPhone is best for Web surfing; BlackBerry phones are beloved for e-mail. Perhaps top-notch Google Voice integration will become the distinguishing feature for Android phones.

Finding Out What the GV Mobile Site Can Do

The GV mobile site is nothing except a stripped down version of the Google Voice site that is optimized for smaller screens. Although the GV mobile site does less than the full site, it's more compact and focused only on key tasks. Therefore, it's much easier to use from the small screen and the poor-to-awful keyboard and positioning controls of a mobile phone.

Here's what the GV mobile site can do:

✔ **Dial!** Dial all your outbound calls by calling your Google Voice number first, through the GV mobile site or the full Google Voice site. That way, the people you call will see your calls originating from your Google Voice number. Return calls will come back through Google Voice, so you can answer them just like any other call.

✔ **Send SMS text messages.** Send and receive SMS text messages, again with recipients seeing your texts as originating from your Google Voice number.

✔ **See and use your Inbox.** The GV mobile site, shown in Figure 10-2, shows your Inbox right up front, with recognizable (but less functional) versions of your call notifications in it. Voicemail transcripts are the same ones you see in the full Google Voice Web site.

✔ **Turn Do Not Disturb on and off.** You can control this crucial global setting from GV Mobile.

✔ **Use your Contacts.** See a list of your Google Voice Contacts (only the full list, unfortunately, not smaller lists like Friends or Family), search the list, and then call or SMS them. Again, the call or SMS text message appears to come from your Google Voice number.

✔ **Change global and top-level settings.** You can change many general settings and global phone, call presentation and call screening settings. See Figure 10-3.

✔ **Add credit for calls.** Crucially, you can add to your credits for international calls from GV Mobile. Otherwise, you could easily run out of credit to use for international calls and be out of luck until you could get to a computer and add more credit.

Figure 10-2:
Getting your
Inbox on
your mobile.

You can only play back calls in your Google Voice Inbox on your phone if it can play MP3 files. You may well not know if your phone can play back MP3 files until you try playing back a call from your Google Voice Inbox, so if you're not sure, try it right away so you know.

Too many contacts?

One of the difficulties of having multiple-device access to shared resources such as the Web is that things that make sense on one system don't work the same way on another.

Having a long list of contacts in Google Voice works well on a computer where you can quickly move through them or use various folders with shorter lists. From the GV Mobile site, you'd be better off with a hotlist of frequently called numbers. But that doesn't exist, unfortunately; you have to search to cut down the size of the list, which can be painstaking. The smaller the phone, in general, the harder it is.

If you have HTML skills, or even a word processor that can save a Web page, you can create an HTML document with hyperlinks to your top contacts. You can then publish it, for example, on a blogging site or another site you control, then use it for quick access to your top contacts. Not quite as convenient as using the hotkeys on your cell phone keypad, but better than nothing.

If your phone can't play back MP3 files, you can't use the Play link in incoming messages to play them back. You can still see that calls have come in and read the transcripts of voicemails that Google provides. You can also still use the other functions of the GV mobile site.

Figure 10-3:
Changing the Do Not Disturb setting.

Understanding What the GV Mobile Site Can't Do

Google Voice has so many capabilities that it can be tough to remember and manage them all, especially under the pressure of a ringing phone. Trying to remember what the GV mobile site can and can't do is enough to bring tears to one's eyes. (Or maybe we've just been spending too much time with Google Voice and are becoming a bit fragile.)

Never fear, *For Dummies* is here! We've created a handy table listing the major features of Google Voice major features from the Google Voice Web site that are available on GV Mobile. The table can help you decide when to use GV Mobile, when to use the full Google Voice site, when to use a phone directly, and when to stop and take a rest.

Table 10-1	Functions: GV Mobile site versus GV full site only	
Category	**The GV mobile site & GV full site**	**GV full site only**
Quick Functions		Call; SMS; Do Not Disturb; Search
Notifications	Play message; Reply by phone*; Reply by SMS*; Mark as unread; Archive	Email caller; Add to contacts; Add note; Block caller; Download MP3; Report spam; Delete; Star
Notification folders	Inbox	Starred; History; Spam; Trash
Notification types	Voicemail; SMS; Placed; Received; Missed Recorded	
Credit	Check balance; Add credit	Check rates; See history
Voicemail greetings	Change default greeting	Play; Re-record; Rename; Delete; Add
E-mail notifications	Change address	On/off; Add destination

(continued)

Table 10-1 *(continued)*

Category	The GV mobile site & GV full site	GV full site only
SMS notifications (by destination)	Turn on/off	Add destination
Screening	On/off; Screen unknown/blocked callers	
Call presentation	On/off; Show caller's #/my GV #	
Contacts	Search	Edit contact information Edit GV settings per contact: phones to ring, voicemail greeting; call presentation
Group access	All contacts	My contacts; Most contacted; Friends; Family; Coworkers; Custom groups
Group settings		Edit GV settings per group: phones to ring, voicemail greeting, call presentation Merge contacts; Add contact; Add group; Import; Export; Print
Call widgets		Create; Edit; Delete
Miscellaneous		Change language; Change time zone; Record name; Change voicemail PIN; Enable voice-mail transcripts

Working with Limitations of the GV Mobile Site

The GV mobile site does a lot less than the full site. This isn't to knock it; it's a specialized tool built for minimalism. If you want to master Google Voice, though, you need to have a handle of what is *only* available on the full site. Things that you can't do on GV Mobile:

- ✔ **Flexible replies:** The full site supports flexible replies to either a call or an SMS by calling back, sending an SMS reply, or replying by e-mail. The GV mobile site only supports calling back a caller or sending SMS replies to SMS messages.

- ✔ **Contacts management:** The GV mobile site doesn't allow you to easily add a caller as a contact. Nor does it allow you to edit contact information.

- ✔ **Call control by group or by contact:** In the GV mobile site, you can only change global settings for which phones to ring, which voicemail greetings to play, and call presentation; you can't fine-tune settings at the group or contact level. Since group and individual settings often override global settings, this can cause difficulties.

- ✔ **Group access:** You can only scroll through or search your All Contacts group; other groups, including your own custom groups, are inaccessible.

- ✔ **Call widgets:** You can't do anything with call widgets on GV Mobile.

- ✔ **Miscellaneous settings:** On the GV mobile site you can't change language or the timezone you're operating in.

The GV mobile site also lacks some features compared to the custom dialers for Android, BlackBerry, and iPhone, including:

- ✔ **Dialer interface:** You enter phone numbers for calls and SMS into a small strip using your phone's keypad; there's no onscreen dialing interface to make it easier to see what you're doing, and no interaction with any touchscreen support your phone might have.

- ✔ **Look and feel:** The GV mobile site is a generic mobile Web site, lacking the same look and feel as applications native to a given phone.

- ✔ **Speed:** An application runs faster because it's all native to the phone. A Web site has inherent delays in sending information back and forth to and from the Internet.

- ✔ **Integration:** The GV mobile site knows nothing about contacts, call logs, quick dialing keys and so on that you might have on your phone; you're working in two different worlds on the GV mobile site versus the phone's built-in capabilities.

Using GV Mobile

Using the GV mobile site is fairly easy at first, and becomes even easier with practice. There's a big caveat to this, though. On most phones except the very best smartphones, doing *anything* on the Web is difficult. Here are some of the barriers you face:

- ✔ **Small screens:** The iPhone has a full 6 square inches of screen space; Android, Windows Mobile, and some BlackBerry screens are almost as big. Other phones tend to have much smaller screens, making it very hard to use even a specially designed mobile site on very small screens.

- ✔ **Difficult text entry:** BlackBerry smartphones with full keyboards are famous for relatively easy text entry; other smartphones tend to have full keyboards of some type, either onscreen or with keys. Where text entry falls well below the BlackBerry standard, texting or e-mailing from the phone gets harder. Where there's number-pad entry instead of a full keyboard, entering text is slow and error-prone for most.

   Difficult cursor control: Moving smoothly around any Web page is very important, and only a few phones have controls that really make it easy. (BlackBerrys such as the Bold and the iPhone with its touch screen are two of the best.)

- ✔ **Slow response time:** Web access time is much slower on a mobile phone than on a computer with wireless access.

The better the Web support on your phone, the easier the GV mobile site will be to use. Only on a few phones with really good Web support is it practical to consider using the full Google Voice Web site from the phone, and most of those phones have custom dialer apps as described in the next few chapters. You only need to consider using the full site when you need to do something the dialer can't do.

Given that each step in using the GV mobile site is difficult, you want to make the most of each step you take. Part of doing that successfully is knowing what you can and can't do in GV Mobile, as described in the previous section. Another part of it is going straight to the function you need.

Here's a menu tree for the GV mobile site to help you get straight to what you want:

- ✔ **Every page:** On every page of the GV mobile site you can find a strip across the top with links: Inbox, Contacts, Search and Settings. At the bottom of every page, you find Quick Call / SMS and links to Notifications folders: Voicemail, SMS, Placed, Received, and Missed. You can also find links Sign out, Help & Terms, and More Google Products.

- ✔ **Inbox:** Call and SMS notifications with SMS text contents and voicemail transcriptions.

- ✔ **Contacts:** Your contacts are shown; first is a contact-specific search box, and then a list with 40 contacts per page. See Figure 10-4.

✔ **Search:** The Search tab at the top level searches your Inbox, not your Contacts.

✔ **Settings:** Five links are under the Settings tab, as shown in Figure 10-5:

- **Settings-General:** Change Voicemail Notifications, Call Screening, Default Voicemail Greeting, Call Presentation and Caller ID display.

- **Settings-Phones:** Change default Forwarding Settings for your Google Voice number to the phones you've registered with Google Voice.

- **Settings-Add Credit:** Current Balance shows, and there's an Add Credit button.

- **Settings-Do Not Disturb:** Enable/disable Do Not Disturb.

- **Settings-My Mobile Number:** Specify which phone you're using as your mobile phone. This is important; it's the phone that rings when you place a call using the mobile Web site, so it needs to be the number of the handset you're running Google Voice on.

✔ **Quick Call I SMS:** At the bottom of every page.

✔ **Notifications folder link:** Voicemail; SMS; Placed; Received; Missed. At the bottom of every page.

✔ **Links:** Sign out, Help & Terms, More Google Products. At the bottom of every page.

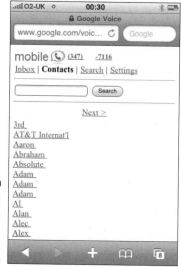

Figure 10-4:
Getting in
Contacts is
easy.

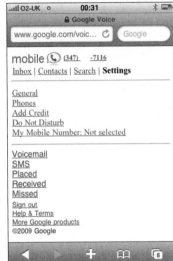

Figure 10-5:
Settings for
GV Mobile.

Use this information to help you find the function you need quickly.

The stripped-down functionality of the GV mobile site also might make you think twice about a few other aspects of how you use Google Voice overall, especially if you find yourself managing Google Voice from the GV mobile site a lot.

One key element is Contacts. A pared-down All Contacts list — shorter than, say, 40 contacts — will be much easier to navigate in GV Mobile, even though you might like having it larger when you use the full Google Voice Web site. A tough call! (No pun intended.)

The other element is your customization strategy. As we describe in Chapter 6, you can set up your Groups and individual Contacts so they have their own settings for which phones to ring, which voicemail greeting to use and whether to use call presentation. You can also, though, set them to use the Group setting. Because the Group setting is the only level you can change from GV Mobile, you may want to set up your Groups and Contacts to always reflect the Group setting. Then you can quickly change the settings for every-one while on the move.

Chapter 11

Using Google Voice with the iPhone

*T*he iPhone is the most popular smartphone in the world, with about 40 million sold as of mid-2009 and rising fast. Like the iPod for music players, it usually has the biggest "wow!" factor among mobile phones. And even if your friends have seen their share of iPhones, you can probably still wow them with something cool from the App Store.

However, for Google Voice users, the App store got a little less cool in mid-2009, a few months after Google Voice was announced. Apple turned down the official Google dialer that Google had created and pulled the three existing Google Voice apps from third parties, VoiceCentral, GVdialer, and GV Mobile.

The iPhone is also the leading phone for accessing the Web, with more than half of all mobile Web traffic going through iPhones at this writing. (That's about ten times more than the nearest rival.) Given that Google Voice brings so much power over one's phones to the Web, the iPhone and Google Voice seem a natural fit.

Using Google Voice with an iPhone

The iPhone is an amazing piece of technology on its own, and also the center of an ecosystem of add-on devices and software applications that are making the iPhone itself more and more capable. For an iPhone user, Google Voice can be regarded as possibly the best of the many tools out there of which to advantage.

And iPhone users do indeed take advantage of it. No one is releasing any numbers at this writing, but anecdotally it seems that iPhone may have as strong a lead among Google Voice users as it does on the mobile Web. Web access, a crucial part of using Google Voice, is also perhaps the leading distinguishing feature of the iPhone, so Google Voice and the iPhone are a natural combination.

iPhone sales are closely rivaled by sales of RIM BlackBerry phones, but there's a big difference in how they're used. BlackBerry smartphones are first and foremost business phones, provided by companies to their employees for work purposes in handling both phone calls and e-mail. Many such phones are "locked down" by the carrier or the company to limit their functionality. However, the recently introduced BlackBerry Storm is a touchscreen device that's a full competitor to the iPhone.

The iPhone is a consumer phone first and foremost, though it's gaining increasing traction in business. iPhones are used much more independently, accessorized and customized with applications by their users. Apple's App Store for the iPhone far outpaces any similar offering or rivals.

More conceptually, iPhone users may be in the vanguard among people who do more and more of their computing, as well as a lot of their communicating, through their phones. BlackBerry was the first to stretch the definition of a phone by including robust e-mail capability. However, the iPhone goes it one better by providing a full-fledged Web browser and a wide range of applications through the App Store. Though still evolving, iPhone use is increasingly taking over functions that used to be handled only on the computer.

The iPhone also pioneered one of the distinguishing features now found in Google Voice: visual voicemail, shown in Figure 11-1, which stacks up voicemail messages in a list and was a huge innovation when it appeared with the first iPhone. Instant access to only the message you want, played back with full control takes a good deal of the pain out of voicemail. Being able to forward and merge calls is even cooler.

However, Google Voice outdoes this by not only listing messages separately, and giving you direct access to them, but by providing transcripts as well. Other Google Voice features, such as the ability to redirect calls to various phones, aren't found on the iPhone or on any other phone, though some of them are matched by other (usually paid) services.

The fact that Google Voice is so popular among iPhone users is a bit odd. Google Voice is great for managing several phones, but our impression is that many iPhone users don't use other phones much. They integrate nearly all their calling through their iPhones.

Google Voice is often seen, first and foremost, as a tool to manage multiple phones. It's also great, though, for untangling the spaghetti of personal, personal business, and work calls all arriving at one destination, the iPhone, often all at the same time. Google Voice gives the user control they previously lacked.

The minutes problem and the iPhone

As we mention in Chapter 2, the downside to using Google Voice may be more important for some users. That's the problem of not getting free minutes within a cell phone calling plan when you use Google Voice. For AT&T callers, the plan option that enables this is called Mobile 2 Mobile.

AT&T has been the exclusive service provider for the iPhone in the U.S. since it was launched in 2007. Although these things can change, a major AT&T's service "giveaway" has been free mobile-to-mobile calls among AT&T users nationwide. Not only do you (and the person you're speaking to) not pay, as on any domestic phone call; you don't use minutes on your cell phone calling plan.

Not only did this calling plan feature help close friends and family members who could luck out, or conspire to all be on AT&T to save minutes. The feature also contributed to a certain camaraderie among U.S. iPhone users who were all perforce AT&T customers as well. If you and your friend or family member both used iPhones, and had the option enabled, your mobile-to-mobile calls were completely free.

When you switch to using Google Voice on your iPhone, you and your AT&T-serviced calling partners lose out. You're placing calls to and from a non-AT&T number, your Google Voice number, not directly. Your calls now burn minutes for both parties. By getting in the middle, your Google Voice number has prevented you from getting the freebie.

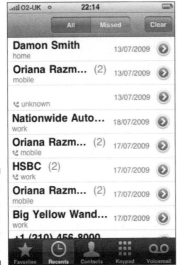

Figure 11-1:
Visual voice
mail is an
iPhone
innovation.

Dialers for the iPhone

When Google Voice was first announced, the iPhone immediately got dialers that let users make calls and get voicemail with less hassle.

A *dialer* is a smartphone application that lets you use your phone just like you'd use the Web interface of Google Voice. Without a dialer, you have to call your Google Voice number, wait for a connection, press 2, then enter the number you're calling.

Dialers take a big step out of the process. They allow you to enter the phone number you're calling and then they dial Google Voice for you. You still have to wait for Google Voice to call you back before the call will connect, but you get the benefit of having outbound calls show as coming from your Google Voice number.

Texts work similarly. You have to go into the dialer application to send a text message to show the originating number as being from Google Voice. This is often less convenient than sending texts directly from the phone, but preserves the Google Voice number as the sending and reply-to number.

In the first few months that Google Voice was available, the iPhone had the best dialers. They were fairly well-integrated with the iPhone, allowing you to use iPhone contacts (which can be synced with several different sources), and with the dialing screen, for example, looking just like the native one on the iPhone.

However, Google has now released new dialers for the BlackBerry and phones based on its own Android phone operating system, but not yet the iPhone. The BlackBerry dialer from Google is about as good as the best current iPhone dialers. The Android dialer, however, takes a big step forward.

The reason is because it's not really a separate dialer. Instead, it allows you to choose how to treat your Google Voice number. The most extreme — and, to many, the most appealing — choice is to use your Google Voice number for all your calls from the phone.

With this option selected, calling and texting from the phone's native screens for these purposes sends out the calls and texts using Google Voice. There's no calling back, unusual screens, or extra steps. The phone operates effectively as a Google Voice handset.

This raises the stakes for the iPhone. The iPhone, of course, has been distributed by AT&T exclusively in the U.S. since its launch. That may mean that both Apple, as the iPhone's manufacturer and AT&T, as its exclusive distributor and service provider in the U.S., have to agree and help in order to provide the same level of integration on the iPhone as on Android phones.

So it's an open question just how integrated Google's upcoming dialer for the iPhone will be. There's then a follow-up open question as to whether other iPhone dialers can match whatever the Google dialer provides or will be, in some ways, restricted.

With this in mind we briefly describe the current state of dialers for the iPhone in the following section. Keep an eye on our blog, getgooglevoice.com, for updates as to anything that occurs after the publication date of this book.

Using a dialer versus using the Web

You certainly can use the GV Mobile site, as described in the previous chapter, to make calls and send texts from your iPhone. You can even use the full Google Voice site, a more practical alternative on the iPhone than on any other major smartphone because of the iPhone's great Web access.

Several problems occur when using either of the sites, though:

- The dialing interface from GV Mobile and the full Google Voice site is clumsy.
- The Inbox is not as nice as the iPhone's visual voicemail.
- The sites are quite slow compared to the built-in iPhone apps for dialing and texting.

An iPhone dialer takes care of all of these problems. Expect your dialer to have:

- ✔ The ability to use a dialing interface, much like the iPhone's, along with access to its contacts and so on.
- ✔ Flexible options as to whether outbound calls, text messages, and replies are shown as coming from the native phone number or your Google Voice number.
- ✔ An iPhone gloss on the interface to call history and the Inbox to make it iPhone-like.
- ✔ Speed; iPhone dialers are much faster than the GV Mobile site or the full Google Voice site.

The upshot is that almost anyone who uses Google Voice from an iPhone will use an app, even if it has a price attached to it. The advantages in speed, usability, and functionality are so great as to make it worthwhile.

However, because Apple has removed dialers from the App Store in mid-2009, only users who got a dialer before then have the option. The other option is to *jailbreak* your iPhone, that is, to disable certain protections that allow Apple to both control and support it. If you do this, you may void your warranty, and you may risk Apple electronically locking your phone. However, you will be able to run apps not approved by Apple.

If you don't have access to a dialer for your iPhone, use the information here and the section on the Google Voice mobile site in the previous chapter to use Google Voice on your iPhone.

Using dialers with iPod Touch

The full Google Voice Web site, the GV Mobile site, and iPhone Google Voice dialers — if you have one or can get one — work on the iPhone and . . . wait for it . . . the iPod Touch as well.

Uh, how do they do that, you wonder?

All of these tools let you set which of your phones to ring when you call out from your iPhone or iPod Touch. When you use this capability on your iPhone, it's a convenience. You would normally take the Google Voice call-back on your iPhone, of course. However, you may want to have the call-back come to another phone that you have registered with Google Voice. That way you avoid using cell phone minutes, leave your cell phone free for other incoming calls or texts, or use a nearby land line handset because it's more comfortable to use.

(Come on, don't tell us you've never sent texts from your cell phone while on a boring landline call. We've done it, too.)

What may be surprising is that you can use the same capability on your iPod Touch. Run a Google Voice dialer on your Touch and set it to ring back to one of your Google Voice-registered phones. You get all the advantages of managing contacts, running GV Mobile (see last chapter) or the full Google Voice Web site on your Touch — which is just as good, for all these purposes, as an iPhone — and use your phones as extensions to Google Voice. Cool, huh?

Finding out what dialers are available

At this writing, three major Google Voice dialers were available on the App Store until mid-2009 and then were pulled. Each has its fans:

- ✔ **VoiceCentral,** shown in Figure 11-2, began back in Grand Central days. It kept legacy support for GrandCentral for users making the transition alongside Google Voice support.

- ✔ **GVdialer** is a multi-phone application that runs on iPhone (until it was pulled), BlackBerry, Windows Mobile, Symbian and Android phones, the widest range of any Google Voice dialer.

- ✔ **GV Mobile,** shown in Figure 11-3 does much the same as the previous dialer, though it's said to do so with more polish.

Which of the Google Voice dialers for the iPhone is best?

It's tough to give a good answer, especially as the applications may be updated, either as apps for jailbroken phones or if they're allowed to return to the App Store. Some people prefer a dialer, like GVdialer, that works the same across several smartphones. Others will like an iPhone-specific application. GrandCentral users who've been using VoiceCentral for years may not want to change in any event, especially as Riverturn, its publishers, have done a good job of keeping it updated.

Now that none of them is available in the App Store, each will no doubt keep its existing users over time. GVdialer will certainly appeal to companies that adopt or support Google Voice and want one app to support across multiple phones. However, we like GV Mobile a bit more so far.

As this is written, we have some reason to hope that Apple will reverse its decision at some point and allow the apps into the App Store again. Perhaps someday there will even be an official Google app, as there is for BlackBerry and Android phones.

In the meantime, the only option available at this writing to most iPhone users is the Google Voice Mobile Web site described in the previous chapter.

Figure 11-2:
Voice-
Central
keeps the
Grand-
Central
flame
burning.

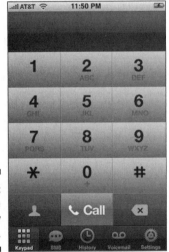

Figure 11-3:
GV Mobile
is very
popular.

The developer of the most popular Google Voice dialer, GV Mobile, has released the app for *jailbroken* iPhones on one of the better-known sites for unofficial iPhone apps. Unfortunately, to use it requires that you jailbreak your iPhone — change its system software in a way that will void its warranty, stop it from getting system software updates, and stop it from being able to use the App Store.

We recommend that you not jailbreak your iPhone just to get GV Mobile. If you've already taken this very big step, though, you may want to take a look at GV Mobile, if you haven't already.

Using Workarounds If You Don't Have a Dialer

If you don't have a dialer, in addition to using the GV mobile site, there are two workarounds you can use to speed dialing your contacts using your Google Voice number.

The first workaround is to create new phone number entries for desired contacts with a special version of their phone number. Use this combination:

- ✔ Your Google Voice number, such as 4085551212. This dials Google Voice for you.

- ✔ The Pause button on the "+*=" keyboard. This pause, which shows up as a comma, gives your Google Voice voice mailbox a chance to answer your call. Use two pauses to make sure the delay is long enough.

- ✔ 2 to tell Google Voice to place a call.

- ✔ The Pause button again, while Google Voice gets ready for the outbound number.

- ✔ The number you're calling, such as 4085553434. This dials your contact's number for you.

- ✔ The pound sign, #. This tells Google Voice definitively that you're done entering the destination number.

- ✔ Check the result. It should look like this: 4085551212,,2,4085553434#. If you use a password for your Google Voice voicemail, put the password and a pause just after your Google Voice number. If your password were 5555, the result would look like this: 4085551212,,5555,2,4085553434#.

- ✔ Add extensions. You may be able to dial a work extension by adding a pause and the extension number before the pound sign at the end.

- ✔ Try the result. You should test at least a few of these numbers to make sure you're doing it right.

- ✔ Replicate it. Go through as many of your contacts as you care to and add a Google Voice-friendly version of their phone number(s). You can cut and paste all the digits in front, but remember to also add the pound sign (#) at the end.

That's it! Sorry for all the extra work, compared to using a dialer. Perhaps the dialer situation will change and make life easier. Until then, though, you can make using Google Voice easy by investing the extra time to do this setup work in advance.

You should also create a contact for dialing Google Voice, which allows you to then dial any number you need to, and a contact for GOOG-411.

There is another way. An online tool has been created that generates Safari bookmarks for quick access to your favorite phone numbers. It takes some work to get started with it, but after the first time, the method is quick and easy. To try it, visit:

```
www.ironicsans.com/gv
```

Is the iPhone the best choice?

The desire for certain features drives people's choice of cell phones. Google Voice is the mother of all features for a cell phone to have. So is the iPhone the best of all possible phones for Google Voice?

Unfortunately, no longer. Not having a dialer is a major impediment to effective usage compared to BlackBerry and Android phones, covered in the next two chapters.

When it comes to using the Google Voice Mobile Web site though — which even dialer users have to do to change certain settings when on the move — the iPhone is a very good choice. It has the largest screen of any mainstream phone out there. That, and the support of gestures on the excellent touch screen, makes Web access easier than on any other mainstream phone. (As shown by the fact that a preponderance of mobile Web site visitors are iPhone users.) So you can handle an awful lot of things on an iPhone that would otherwise have to wait until you had computer access.

The iPhone also has a full keyboard, though it's an on-screen keyboard without mechanical keys. (The best such keyboard ever, according to many users and reviewers.) It also has the App Store, which is a strong and growing "feature" of the iPhone that, to date, no one else can match, even after the dialers controversy. The iPhone also has what is probably the largest community of owners who also use Google Voice, giving you lots of compatriots who can give advice and share tips.

Any currently contented iPhone user will probably not switch away just to get a phone with a dialer for Google Voice. Those looking for a new phone and wanting the very best Google Voice experience as their #1 priority (and who are attracted to the lower prices available from TMobile's service plans) may look to phones running Android ahead of the iPhone before making a final decision.

Chapter 12

Using Google Voice on Android Phones

*G*oogle is involved in a lot of different areas beyond its original focus of Internet search and search-related advertising. One long-awaited venture was a mobile phone operating system called Android.

Android has gradually gained popularity among phone-buyers and software developers alike. The platform reached the key benchmark of 1 million users in mid-2009. This does not sound like many compared to the roughly 40 million each for iPhone and BlackBerry, but it represented a starting point for further growth. Android is widely believed in the tech industry to have fantastic potential for growth.

We predict a proliferation of Android-based phones over the coming years. Because Android is customizable, and because it runs on phones from many different manufacturers, a lot of potential exists for variation in Android phones. Some may be relatively poor hosts for Google Voice, or even relatively poor phones; others may be among the very best for both.

So far, Android users are very active among smartphone users in accessing the Web. They "punch above their weight" compared to Windows Mobile or BlackBerry users. In mid-2009 Android users reached about one-tenth the mobile Web use of the leader, iPhone, despite having a much smaller percentage of the market.

Using Android: A Google Voice Natural

Android's software development kit is made available to anyone who'd like to tinker, and all for free.

Android is inherently well suited to mobile Web usage. iPhone is a natural platform for using the Web on the move; Android is roughly as well suited. Though smaller, it's moving up quickly. A few months after Google Voice was initially released, Google released its own dialers for BlackBerry and Android.

The BlackBerry app was competently designed but not amazing. (See the next chapter.) The Android dialer, however, is a breakthrough. See Chapter 10 for a brief introduction to dialers.

Google's dialer for Android makes the smartphone it's running on act as a handset for the user's Google Voice number. All calls and texts can come to and from the Google Voice number natively; the underlying T-Mobile phone number can be made nearly invisible. (The underlying number can still receive calls and texts, but outgoing calls and texts can all be made to originate from the Google Voice number.)

All this is possible thanks to Google's extensive control over the so-called Google phones. On the technical side, Google "controls the horizontal and the vertical," as Rod Serling used to say when introducing the *Twilight Zone*. Google wrote the operating system, and it's working very closely with its hardware partners, including HTC, Sony, Samsung, Sony Ericsson, Motorola, LG, and other members of the so-called Open Handset Alliance. That means Google can optimize a Google Voice dialer to work with them at a system level. It can even change the Android operating system or the Google Voice offering itself to create a seamless experience for Google Voice users on Android.

On the business side, Google is somewhat fortunate in being a new entrant without large market share or revenues to defend. They can move faster, offer more functionality, and take more risks. There's little but upside for Google and its initial U.S. carrier partner, T-Mobile, in making Android a truly excellent platform for Google Voice. Google and T-Mobile share a need to offer the best possible experience for users and to ramp up their customer base quickly, even if they lose a chance to make a few extra pennies here or there. In the best Internet tradition, they can build up a customer base today and figure out the fine points of building up revenues later.

Android also is probably the player with the most potential to build an application store to rival Apple's wildly successful App Store. Like Apple, Android is relatively easy to develop for. It has an open marketplace — Android Market, shown in Figure 12-1 — and its phones, unlike BlackBerry phones, are far less likely to be "locked down" by a corporation or government agency before being issued to employees. All this is attractive to many developers and should contribute to a growing range of Android Market apps.

The minutes problem and Android phones

As we mentioned in Chapter 2, a downside to using Google Voice is bigger for some people than others. That's the problem of not getting free minutes within a cell phone calling plan when you use Google Voice.

T-Mobile, at this writing the only U.S. carrier to offer Android phones, has a calling plan feature called myFaves. You can specify up to five numbers — T-Mobile numbers or not — to call, or receive calls from, free of any use of your calling plan minutes. Set your Google Voice number as a Fave, and your GV calls won't burn minutes.

However, even T-Mobile, friendly to Google though it is, needs revenue. The ability to use a Google Voice number as a myFaves number may not last forever.

T-Mobile also has unlimited T-Mobile to T-Mobile calling on myFaves plans at $50 a month or more. The number of T-Mobile users is far less than with AT&T or Verizon, so this is unlikely to apply to very many of your calls. Also, with the flexibility of Google Voice for using different phones, and its ability to send and receive texts for free, you may well be able to keep your plan under the limit, meaning you wouldn't get the discount anyway.

All in all, Android phones on T-Mobile are perhaps the least likely to cause you extra expense by missing out on "bennies" from your carrier, and to cause frustration among friends and family who might otherwise have been counting on free calls of their own.

Figure 12-1: The Android Market may soon rank a strong second for apps.

Using Dialers for Android Phones

Android was quick to get the multi-platform GVdialer soon after Google Voice was announced. It seems, though, that other developers knew Google would be creating its own dialer and stayed out of the way.

Smart move. The mobile app — different from the GV Mobile site described in Chapter 10 — is completely integrated with Android phones. (There's still a bit of separation on BlackBerry, as we describe in the next chapter, and it's reasonable to expect there will be on the iPhone as well.)

To get the app, visit:

```
m.google.com/voice
```

Alternatively, go to Android Market and search for "google voice".

The official Google Google Voice app — try saying that three times fast — is shown in Figure 12-2. It's almost 100 percent integrated with Android phones' built-in features:

- ✔ **No log-in:** Google Voice logs in using stored credentials; no need to enter a password to use it.

- ✔ **Choice of when to use the GV number:** You can choose to use the Google Voice number as the "calling from" number none of the time; to use the Google Voice number only for international calls; to check which number to use on every call; or, a choice many will make, to use the Google Voice number all the time.

- ✔ **The default dialer app:** When you call out from Android using your Google Voice number with the new app, calling is quick. You use the default dialer, not a substitute.

- ✔ **No intermediate phone call:** When you call out from Android with the new app, you still use the default dialer. The call goes out to the user just like a call directly from your cell phone; there's no detectable call-back to you from Google Voice.

- ✔ **Call from contacts:** You can place calls using your Google Voice number as the originating number from your contacts list.

- ✔ **Free SMS:** SMS text messages come in and go out through your Google Voice number even if your phone has no SMS service.

- ✔ **Voicemail integration:** Voicemail transcripts are displayed in Android's message list, with no need to visit the GV Mobile Web site.

- ✔ **"Karaoke-style" voicemail playback:** When you're looking at a text transcription and playing back the audio from a voicemail message, each word in the transcription is highlighted as the audio plays back. This makes it much simpler to listen attentively only to the bits that are puzzling in the transcript. (No, your spouse didn't tell you to pick up "garbage" at the store; it was handwash.)

- ✔ **Google Voice as voicemail recipient:** On many handsets, you can set your Google Voice number as the voicemail recipient even for calls to the phone's native number. This is a great trick for moving over to Google Voice completely.

✔ **Background notifications:** Notifications for voicemail and SMS come in even when the app is not active. (Only when you have data coverage, though; carrier-provided notifications come in over the voice network and so are available more of the time.)

✔ **Integrated contacts:** If you use Google for your contacts, changes you make in your native contacts or in Google Voice carry over to the other.

✔ **Call history:** Your call history is displayed in the native Android display.

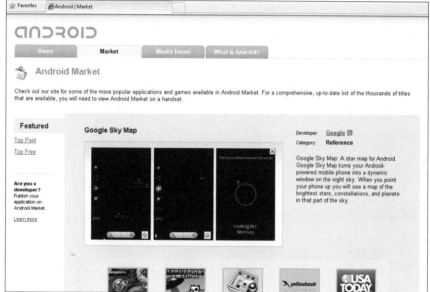

Figure 12-2:
The official
Google
Voice dialer
for Android.

The only visible failures to integrate are in messaging — that is, SMS text messages and MMS multimedia messages:

✔ **Separate SMS:** Instead of coming in through the clean and capable Android SMS application, the app has its own SMS view. (Which does support threaded conversations, thank goodness.)

✔ **Slow SMS:** SMS comes in slower through the app than through carrier-provided SMS.

✔ **No MMS:** As with the GV Mobile site, there's no MMS support. This may be one of those features that gets put off from an initial release and gets done later.

For most of us, the features that have been left out so far aren't deal-breakers — the Android app is a coup for GV users.

With the Google Voice app for Android, you can simply use your Google Voice number from your cell phone full-time, almost completely as if it were the phone's native number. This is a pretty impressive implementation and sets a high bar yet to be matched on other phones.

Braving the Android frontier

Google Voice is the most important cell phone "feature" to come along in a long time. Are phones running Google Android, with the extra integration afforded by the best version of Google's app for Google Voice, the best choice?

Unfortunately, the answer is yes and no. Yes, the integration of Google Voice with Android is truly outstanding. At the time of this writing, Android phones are the only devices that allow you to use your Google Voice number as your native cell phone number. The initial Android phones are very strong offerings, and there are perhaps even better ones to come.

The only minus is that you have to be a bit brave to go on Android today. It has quality applications, but not yet the sheer number and variety of the App Store. You may be the first on your block with an Android phone. The way things seem to be going, though, you probably won't be the last.

If your main concern in a smartphone is that it works optimally with Google Voice, then Android is clearly your best bet. If, like most people, you are weighing a wide range of factors when making a phone choice, Android's Google Voice integration puts it in the mix. If you're already well established in the iPhone or BlackBerry camps, even the strong performance of Google's app for Google Voice is unlikely to pull you away. If you're truly open-minded, there's a very good chance you'll become an Android user soon.

Chapter 13

Using Google Voice on BlackBerry Phones

*L*ong-time users of BlackBerry phones from Research in Motion (RIM) have been through a mania of enthusiasm for the BlackBerry, followed by depression as first the iPhone, and now Android phones have stolen the limelight from BlackBerry.

Now the BlackBerry line is getting more attention as RIM adds new models, winning plaudits for features and styling. BlackBerry phones have a very good Google Voice dialer, from Google itself. While not quite as well-integrated as the Android dialer (see Chapter 12), Google Voice fits into the BlackBerry environment very well, alongside all the other advantages that make a BlackBerry a "must-have" for millions.

BlackBerry: Cool Then, Cool Again

A few years ago, having a BlackBerry was the pinnacle of cool. BlackBerry phones were the only phones that could handle e-mail reliably, so BlackBerry users were that much more in touch than anyone else. Figure 13-1 shows an early BlackBerry model.

Because most BlackBerry phones were issued by corporations and more often to senior or technical people than others, having a BlackBerry implied that you were well-off, powerful, and well-connected. The term *crackberry*, describing the addictive power of always-on e-mail, was declared New Word of the Year in 2006 by Webster's New World College Dictionary.

Figure 13-1:
The original
BlackBerry,
clunky yet
iconic.

Recently, though, Google did its part to undermine the unique appeal of BlackBerry by making Gmail so flexible that it could be used on a cell phone and still stay in sync with Web and desktop access to the same e-mail account. They also made Gmail directly available on cell phones through Gmail applications.

What really took the glow off the BlackBerry, though, was the arrival of the iPhone in 2007. Suddenly there was a mobile device hotter than the BlackBerry, and not only were corporations not issuing it, they didn't even like having them in the building. (An iPhone running the Gmail app is, for instance, a very good way to get around corporate restrictions on the use of Web-based e-mail applications.)

The iPhone's touch screen made the BlackBerry's famous scroll wheel, which is actually a robust little tool, look quaint and limited. Its excellent music player integration embodied coolness and let people combine two devices, phone and iPod, into one.

What really hurt RIM, though, was the way in which, judo-like, Apple made one of RIM's strengths into a weakness. RIM kept a tightly closed shop and discouraged third-party developers from creating applications to run on BlackBerry. Corporate data processing departments loved this restrictive policy, which kept them firmly in control.

Once the iPhone came out, though, every new app that appeared in the iTunes App Store (there were more than 50,000 as of mid-2009) was an indictment of RIM's closed shop.

RIM woke up fast. A slew of new BlackBerry models have drastically updated the "look and feel" of the line to be more consumer-oriented, with high-resolution screens, stereo headphones and social networking apps. There are about 30 million BlackBerry owners as of mid-2009, second to the iPhone's 40 million users.

The BlackBerry Curve, shown in Figure 13-2, is an example of a phone with the best features of BlackBerry — an excellent keyboard, good positioning control via a trackball, BlackBerry's easy-to-use core software — plus a camera and multimedia features and the ability to download and install applications.

Figure 13-2:
BlackBerry
looks good
when
graded on
the Curve.

BlackBerry has quickly opened up to developers and now has its own store, App World, shown in Figure 13-3. App World is, for now, second only to Apple's App Store in number of applications. (Many expect the Android Market to surpass it soon.)

Figure 13-3:
BlackBerry
smartphones
enter a
whole new
(App) World.

Although the number of phones has expanded rapidly, BlackBerry's mainstream phones still tend to have certain things in common:

- ✔ The best-loved integrated keyboards in the business, designed for use with one's thumbs and quite quick for text entry.

- ✔ High-resolution but small screens with the same resolution in pixels as the iPhone — that's 480 x 320 pixels — but half the size physical size, about 3 square inches. (The Storm is the exception, with a screen about 85 percent the size of iPhone's.)

- ✔ No touchscreen support (except for the Storm), but use of a trackball instead.

These features tend to make BlackBerry phones excellent e-mail clients, not only for corporate e-mail, as in the past, but for Gmail and other Webmail services as well. The small screen and lack of touchscreen support conspire together, though, to make BlackBerry smartphones poor mobile Web clients — except the larger-screen, touchscreen Storm. (BlackBerry users tend to visit customized BlackBerry mobile Web pages for news updates, weather, and so on. Time magazine is only one of many publishers who have published BlackBerry-specific sites.)

These advantages and disadvantages tend to make BlackBerry smartphones good for Google Voice, but with different strengths and weaknesses depending on the specific BlackBerry model. BlackBerry smartphones are also good for replying to voicemail via SMS or e-mail, because they take advantage of the generally excellent keyboards that BlackBerry phones boast.

However, lacking the larger screens and nearly complete Google Voice integration of Android phones, and the very large screens and range of Google Voice clients and other apps of the iPhone, the BlackBerry line — except for Storm — has challenges in keeping up with the other major smartphones as a tool for Google Voice. And that's before you consider the skepticism of the large organizations that still issue Blackberry phones by the millions.

If you want to see a well-stated case for what makes a BlackBerry worthwhile, look no further than the essay, Why BlackBerry, on CrackBerry.com:

```
http://crackberry.com/lecture-1-why-blackberry
```

The essay covers all the major points in favor of BlackBerry smartphones, along with some not-so-scientific arguments. (Example, by a female author: "Women with BlackBerrys are HOT.")

Banned in Boston (and New York and Washington and...)

The attitudes of corporations to Google Voice will be hard to predict, as it usually takes them a while to formulate a response to new technology.

One thing we can specify in advance, though: if your work issues you a BlackBerry, or other mobile phone, and tells you not to use Google Voice on it, that's what you should do. If your employer, having provided you with a BlackBerry, tells you more broadly not to use your Google Voice number for work, that's what you should do, too. This applies even more strongly if they issue you a laptop as well.

However, if your job expects you to use personal resources — your own cell phone, your own cell phone service plan, your own computer — for work, they can't really expect to control what tools you use on your own hardware, cell phone service plan and so on to get the job done. You would still need to obey any direct corporate diktat not to give out your Google Voice number as your official work number, put it on your business card etc. It's hard to see, though, how you could be criticized for giving out your Google Voice number on an as-needed basis, as you might have previously given out your personal cell phone number, if that's what it takes to get things done.

Using a Dialer on BlackBerry

The official Google Voice dialer for BlackBerry phones is excellent, second only to the Android version for integration. It's shown in Figure 13-4.

Figure 13-4: The official Google Voice dialer for BlackBerry.

It's a good thing the dialer is strong, because using the GV Mobile or the full Google Voice Web site is not easy with the BlackBerry's limited Web access. In fact, a customized BlackBerry version of both sites is really needed to keep BlackBerry in the running with Android and iPhone as a Google Voice handset.

To get the app, visit:

```
m.google.com/voice
```

The dialer is very good, and just slightly less well-integrated than the Android version. Here are the good points:

✔ **Call from contacts:** You can place calls using your Google Voice number as the originating number from the BlackBerry address book. The Google Voice app must be running for this to work. BlackBerrys support multitasking, so that's not necessarily a big ask.

✔ **Free SMS:** Send SMS text messages to and from your Google Voice number.

✔ **"Karaoke-style" voicemail playback:** As you play back the audio from a voicemail message in the app, if the transcription is displayed at the same time, each word in the transcription is highlighted as the audio plays back. You can focus on the words that are puzzling in the transcript. (Your boss didn't say your pay raise was temporary; she said to commit the amount *to memory*.)

✔ **Background notifications:** Notifications for voicemail and SMS come in even when the app is not active. (Only when you have data coverage, though; carrier-provided notifications come in over the voice network and so are available more of the time.)

The only visible failures to integrate are in the dialer and in SMS text messages and MMS multimedia messages:

✔ **Separate call log:** Voicemail transcripts are displayed in the app's voicemail list, rather than in the BlackBerry's phone interface. This still saves you a trip to the GV Mobile Web site.

✔ **Uses a separate dialer app:** When you call out from a BlackBerry using your Google Voice number with the new app, you have to use a separate dialer, and you get a call-back, both unlike the Android version. The green Phone button can't be made to dial out from your Google Voice number.

✔ **Separate SMS:** Instead of coming in through the clean and capable Android SMS application, the app has its own SMS view. (Which does support threaded conversations, thank goodness.) SMS messages and notifications come into your regular message/SMS folder and the application, which means more cleanup.

✔ **Slow SMS:** SMS comes in slower through the app than through carrier-provided SMS.

✔ **No shortcuts support:** You'll want to reply to SMS text messages from within the Google Voice application, but when you do, BlackBerry shortcuts such as double space for a period at the end of a sentence don't work. After a period, the next letter isn't automatically capitalized. These missing shortcuts are a big deal for BlackBerry users who have these rules hard-wired into their thumbs.

✔ **No MMS:** As with the GV Mobile site, there's no MMS support. This may be one of those features that get put off from an initial release to a later one.

The list of plusses is long enough to make a real difference in using Google Voice. The minuses are significant but, for most of us, not show-stoppers. Work can be done to improve the BlackBerry version of the app up to the same level as on Android, assuming Google wants to do that work.

Going with a BlackBerry phone

It would be hard to argue that BlackBerry smartphones are the best choice for Google Voice. Integration is better on Android. Even if integration improves with future releases of the Google Voice app, the small, non-touch screens and less Web-friendly nature of most BlackBerry smartphones works against their being a first choice for Google Voice.

As with other aspects of BlackBerry smartphones, the Storm and its relatively large, touch-sensitive screen is the exception. If other BlackBerry smartphones go in the same direction as the Storm, they'll be good choices, too.

However, the physical keyboards on most BlackBerrys (again, except the Storm) make them very good for e-mail. If you like to use e-mail to respond to voicemail, you may like using Google Voice on your BlackBerry very much.

Even with today's lineup, as a BlackBerry user, you'll be well-served by Google Voice and the app that Google provides. It's an excellent addition to any BlackBerry user's toolkit. Few BlackBerry users would willingly switch away from RIM, and Google Voice doesn't require you to.

BlackBerry is the right choice today for tens of millions of users, a number that continues to grow steadily. The availability of Google Voice is a plus for BlackBerry users, even though it's a stronger plus for Android users. If you are truly free to make your own choice in the marketplace, though, Google Voice is a stronger plus for Android than for BlackBerry today.

Part IV
Playing Well with Others

In this part . . .

Google Voice works well with other Google Apps offerings and even a third party tool, Gizmo5. You can also use Google Voice in small business and other enterprises. We show you how to get the most out of the Apps suite and more.

Chapter 14

Using Google Voice with Gmail

*G*oogle's product offerings are becoming more numerous, more powerful, and more successful. That's as a group; individual offerings can come and, sometimes suddenly, go. Google Maps will be with us for a long time; Google Lively, Google's virtual reality offering that appeared in mid-2008, did not make the cut.

In this chapter we describe how Google Voice works with Google's successful and ever-more-popular e-mail offering, Gmail, and briefly introduce other important Google products. This orientation to Google's offerings can help you get the most out of Google Voice.

A key change in how you work with your phones using Google Voice is the fact that it sends copies of text messages, voicemail transcriptions, links to voicemails, and phone call recordings to your e-mail Inbox. By moving this, traffic becomes easier to track and manage. You may find yourself replying to a voicemail with an e-mail after you start using Google Voice.

Having this traffic in e-mail, though, also puts new demands on your e-mail Inbox itself. Having "on the go" access to your e-mail Inbox from various locations becomes all the more important.

Gmail is easy to use and flexible, making it a great fit for these demands. We recommend setting up a Gmail account to handle all your Google Voice notifications, so that they don't clog up your regular Inbox. After you start using it, though, you may become a convert and switch over to Gmail for all your e-mailing.

In this chapter, we describe how to use Gmail with Google Voice and briefly touch on Google Voice integration with other Google applications. In the next chapter, we go into depth on other real-time communications applications offered by Google or directly supported by Google Voice: Google Talk, Google Chat, and Gizmo 5.

Exploring What Makes Gmail Cool

Gmail has many attractive features; some in common with other top free e-mail providers, others that distinguish Gmail from the rest:

- ✔ **Easy access:** You can access Gmail and its main competitors (Microsoft Hotmail and Yahoo! Mail) from any Web browser, anywhere in the world, at any time of day or night.

- ✔ **Easy smartphone access:** Gmail has applications for the top smartphones that take maximum advantage of each phone's screen space to produce a crisp, clear display of messages. Figure 14-1 shows Gmail's Blackberry application running on the Blackberry Curve. Android phones and the iPhone are the most fully supported.

- ✔ **Easy dumbphone access:** The Gmail Web page works on any cell phone that can run even a basic Web browser.

- ✔ **Large storage capacity:** Gmail offers more than seven gigabytes of e-mail storage for free and increases this number constantly.

- ✔ **Smart forwarding:** You can set Gmail to forward certain messages to other e-mail accounts, and it's smart enough to know which messages you want to forward and which you don't.

- ✔ **Easy integration with Outlook and Apple Mail:** Google works hard to keep up-to-date instructions available for integrating Gmail with current and past versions of Outlook, Apple Mail, and others. Figure 14-2 shows configuration instructions for several IMAP mail clients.

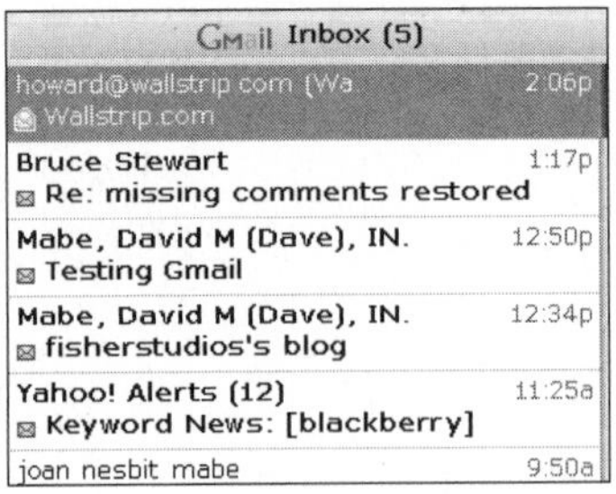

Figure 14-1: Gmail looks good on the Curve.

Gₘail Inbox (5)	
howard@wallstrip.com (Wa	2:06p
Wallstrip.com	
Bruce Stewart	1:17p
Re: missing comments restored	
Mabe, David M (Dave), IN.	12:50p
Testing Gmail	
Mabe, David M (Dave), IN.	12:34p
fisherstudios's blog	
Yahoo! Alerts (12)	11:25a
Keyword News: [blackberry]	
joan nesbit mabe	9:50a

✔ **Easy management of multiple accounts:** You can set up Gmail to import e-mail from other accounts into Gmail and even to reply to it with the other account showing as the sender.

✔ **Easy integration with other Google applications:** After you sign on to your Google account, you get access to more and more capabilities. Google Voice is one of the latest and greatest. Having the same buttons and features across products — right down to keyboard shortcuts — helps keep things simple.

✔ **Google Labs access:** Google's experimental arm, Labs, is always working on cool stuff, and some of it is especially useful for Gmail. For instance, Message translation allows you to translate Gmail messages you receive into other languages. Message translation is potentially useful with voicemail transcriptions, as described later in this chapter.

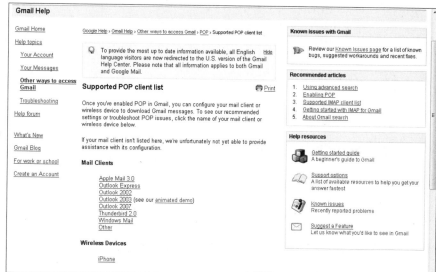

Figure 14-2:
Gmail encourages you to integrate it with your e-mail client.

Gmail is also well-integrated with other Google interactive communications applications, such as Google Chat, as described in Chapter 15.

Gmail has only a few disadvantages. One is that a Gmail address for your e-mail might not be taken as seriously as a "real" company or organizational domain; "gmail.com" might not look as good as "grozcorp.com". Many people, though, ignore this problem, or work around it by running organizational mail through Gmail while using their own domain.

Is Google the new Microsoft?

Years ago, applications such as Lotus 1-2-3, WordPerfect, and Harvard Presentation graphics were leaders in PC software; Microsoft applications were less popular than the bigger players. Since then, Microsoft has made a lot of money by realizing that people might be willing to leave these once-familiar applications for slightly less powerful applications that were more similar to one another. Gathered together with Microsoft Outlook, a breakthrough new application for managing e-mail, Microsoft's Office software package quickly became the industry standard, earning tens of billions of dollars. Office emphasized convenience and standardization just as much as long lists of features.

Now Google is taking advantage of people's desire to share information and to have online tools that work the same to offer its own suite of applications and services. Google Search is the leader and the biggest money-maker, thanks to Google Adwords advertisements. Google Search is a tool nearly everyone who uses a PC or smartphone takes advantage of, the "straw that stirs the drink." It serves as a front door to the entire Internet for many of its users.

Google Voice has the potential to achieve the same kind of success. Google Voice can be the front door to the entire world of voice and, increasingly, online video communications between people. Google Voice may eventually include ads directly, or it may simply contribute useful user information to make possible better targeting of ads in Google Search, Gmail, and elsewhere.

The Google brand is already ranked as the world's most powerful brand in some surveys. With Google Search, Google Voice and supporting services such as Gmail, Google Apps, and others, Google is currently valued by the markets at about half the overall company value of Microsoft, and growing significantly faster. Within a few years, Google may indeed take over the mantle of leading technology giant from Microsoft.

Many people have Gmail accounts and have stuck with them for years. However, you may not want to move over to using Gmail as your main e-mail account if you have another one that you've been using for years.

Another disadvantage to Gmail is that it unalterably uses something called "message threading" to display messages in groups by their subject lines, and that can be confusing. The final disadvantage is that Gmail, like any Webmail package, is sometimes blocked on PCs inside large organizations, as explained in the next section.

Using Gmail for Google Voice

Gmail's features make it a great place in which to receive your Google Voice text message copies, voicemail message notifications, and links to recordings, even if you don't use your Gmail account for anything else.

Gmail is

- ✔ **Free:** Gmail is free, which is pretty amazing, considering that its available storage and features lead the competition in most ways.

- ✔ **Independent:** Gmail is independent of your job, your school, your home ISP and other connections that may change over time.

- ✔ **Cell phone-accessible:** Gmail offers easy access from cell phones, which is great for voice/e-mail interoperability.

- ✔ **Flexible:** Gmail is able to juggle complex demands such as work vs. personal e-mail use.

- ✔ **Adaptable:** Gmail is particularly easy to integrate with other e-mail clients.

- ✔ **Google Apps-compatible:** Gmail is easy to integrate with other Google applications, such as Google Voice and Google Chat.

Search deserves special mention. The powerful capabilities of Google Search are particularly welcome in dealing with the explosion of messages you can expect when your e-mail Inbox is full, not only of e-mail messages but voice-mail messages and SMS text messages as well.

Search depends on specific words, and words are defined by their spelling. It's hard enough to remember specific words that might have occurred in a voicemail message without having to account for the fact that the automatic translation used by Google Voice might have garbled the spelling, but you'll have to work around it. The same applies, for slightly different reasons, to the accidental errors and deliberate compressions that take place in SMS messages composed in txtspk. In both cases, small errors that don't prevent intelligibility may well be enough to prevent searchability.

Large storage, a key feature of Google Voice, may become even more important over time as well. People may end up with decades of voice, SMS, e-mail, and mixed-mode conversations, all stored and searchable, in their Gmail accounts — but only if the space available is big enough. Gmail's 7GB (and growing) should be enough to accommodate just about all users.

To sum up, the barriers to entry for Gmail are low; interoperability and feature count are high. Nothing else that is currently available offers as good a choice for the specific needs of Google Voice users.

Using Gmail inside the firewall

Large organizations have many security precautions in place. The best-known such barrier is the *firewall,* networking software that keeps out many viruses and other malware, but that also prevents some Web sites from working properly. This crippling of Web capabilities is sometime accidental and sometimes purposeful on the part of the organization.

Is Gmail ready for prime time?

Google has put itself in an odd situation. It's busily selling its Google Apps suite to corporations. Yet the core product in the suite, Gmail, still has a "beta" tag on it.

Traditionally, in software development, an "alpha" version was the designation for early-stage version of the software that worked, but might have some planned features missing. Eventually the alpha version matured into a beta version, which was "feature complete" but not fully debugged. After beta came Release 1.0, the first "finished" version of the product. (Though wiser heads often waited for a "dot release", an update often numbered 1.0.1, or something similar, that squashed a few more bugs.)

Google has adopted the strange habit of continuing to designate many of its important products as beta even after it has millions of users for them; for instance, one estimate is that Gmail currently has about 50 million users.

Don't let the beta tag throw you off; it's probably a sign of Google's corporate sense of whimsy, not of the stability of the software. Gmail is more feature-rich and seems to be just as reliable as its main competitors, Microsoft Hotmail and Yahoo! Mail, neither of which is labeled beta. We'll all be a bit relieved, though, when Google gets Gmail to a point where it determines that it doesn't need the beta label anymore.

In particular, large companies are famous for deliberately preventing access to Gmail, Hotmail, Yahoo! Mail, and other important personal applications from corporate PCs. Why do they do it?

The answer boils down to two words: security and productivity. Security because Gmail and its competitors may let in e-mails that a properly maintained corporate e-mail capability would keep out. These e-mails can bring in viruses, worms, and all sorts of other problems.

Gmail and its competitors are also likely to carry some inappropriate content — potentially obscene material, potentially defamatory statements, and so on — that is problematic for the corporation to be hosting, even at arm's length. (Especially when employees forward more or less "humorous" e-mails from Gmail and so on to colleagues over the corporate e-mail system.)

The other, related reason Gmail and its ilk are banned is productivity. It's easy to waste time in an office environment, or to use time productively but in a way that benefits only you, not your employer. Gmail can be a big time sink. So employers keep it out to hog your time themselves.

These steps help the organization maintain its standards, but they create problems as well. It's actually helpful to employees to be able to handle a certain amount of personal business at work, so they can better concentrate on their jobs the rest of the time. Many of us have seen work fax machines being used to transmit mortgage application forms for personal use, for example. Occasional use of organizational facilities of this type is usually allowed.

Having Gmail completely cut off stops this kind of mutually beneficial activity and can often give employees e-mail anxiety, where they rush for any opportunity to get to a PC that isn't locked down to check for a specific message or just whether anything important has come in.

The answer a great many people employ is to use a cell phone to check their e-mail. Gmail really shines, because of its simple text-based mobile interface and light, fast smartphone applications. Using those tools from your phone can help you manage Google Voice notifications, SMS text messages, and transcriptions using Gmail from anywhere, even at work.

Well, almost anywhere. The secure area in the State Department, various spy agencies, and the military prohibit use of even the coolest smartphones. One government employee has the pull to cut through the regulations: Barack Obama fought for and won permission to keep using his Blackberry as President, as shown on the White House blog in Figure 14-3. (Visit `http://blogs.america.gov/obama/2009/01/page/3/` to see the story for yourself.) Staffers can use Blackberries too; during official White House meetings, the devices have to be left in a basket at the door. "Yes we can" indeed! Obama has also been spotted with an iPhone and even a Microsoft Zune player as well.

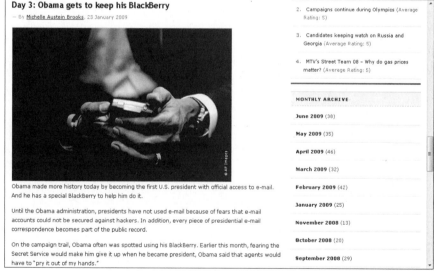

Figure 14-3:
The BlackBerry Baracks the (White) House.

Gmail and the kitchen sync

The most crucial issue in using any e-mail program is synchronization — keeping the message lists straight on different computers.

You can use two approaches. One is to always keep the "live" copy of your e-mail on your PC, which is fast but restrictive and ties the lifespan of your e-mail to the lifespan of your PC. It's about as safe as e-mail gets — certainly safer than phone or Internet cafe. The other is to always keep it on a server, which is flexible and potentially safer but slow and useless when you don't have a connection to a server.

There's also a complex approach, which is to keep the master copy on a server, a local copy on one or more PCs, and other devices for speed, and to synchronize the two as often as practical. This problem is one of the hardest in all computing and one that Google and Gmail tackle head-on.

These last three graphs are more complicated than they need to be. Some people use software that downloads their e-mail from the server where it lives onto their computer, and others just check it using the Web.

There are two standards-based approaches for e-mail synchronization — keeping your Web-based e-mail and clients such as Microsoft Outlook in sync. The older and simpler one is called POP, for Post Office Protocol. Its basic intention is to download e-mail from a server, which acts like a digital post office serving the mailbox on your computer. For security, the POP server can keep a copy, but it isn't intended to reflect all the changes you make on your computer's mailbox, as when you delete or move messages between folders.

The more modern and complicated approach is called IMAP, for Internet Message Access Protocol. IMAP takes on the job of keeping e-mail lists synchronized among a server and the computers and phones that access your e-mail. With IMAP, you can check your e-mail from various devices; you can send new e-mail, delete old messages and so on from any client and the others will reflect the change.

Both of us use it, one (Smith) for synchronization with Outlook on a PC and a Blackberry Curve, the other (Dannen) for synchronization with Apple Mail on two Macintoshes and an iPhone. Each of us also uses e-mail from various Internet cafés and borrowed PCs. We each have piddling gripes, but get along pretty well with these complex e-mail setups.

Touring Gmail for Google Voice

Gmail is relatively easy to sign up for and use, yet it has enough capability that explaining all of it could take up a good part of a book. In fact, it does take up a good part of a book: *Google Apps For Dummies*, by Ryan Teeter and Karl Barksdale (Wiley, 2008), has coverage of Gmail. So please see that book for the details on Gmail and the entire Google Apps suite.

Here we offer a quick tour to help you decide whether to use Gmail and just how much of your e-mail traffic you want to run through it. You may make the same decision as we have: use Gmail for just about all of it!

The Google Voice Inbox

The key to daily use of Google Voice for many people is the Inbox, where you see all your Google Voice e-mail. A typical Inbox — well, the Inbox of one of the authors, which may or may not be typical — is shown in Figure 14-4.

Figure 14-4: Gmail has one of the better-known Inboxes around.

A few items are worth noticing here, some good and some perhaps not so good, depending on your point of view:

- ✔ **No column headings:** Note how there are no column headings over the list of e-mail message headers to designate the sender, topic, and date sent. In a typical Windows application these columns have headings, and you can sort the display by a field by clicking on its heading. But Gmail may have tens of gigabytes of data stored for a user. It's not going to take on responsibility for sorting a display of the message headers for all of it. Being Google, it would rather you search.

- ✔ **Threading:** Gmail presents messages as conversations (Google's term) or threads (what most people call them). Any exchange of messages (dictated by one user clicking reply to another's message), even if it's dozens of messages deep, shows up as a single conversation in the Gmail Inbox. More on threading later. . . .

✔ **Labels:** Outlook, among other e-mail clients, is able to store e-mail in various folders. Not many people have the discipline to use them properly, but one of us had a colleague with five years' worth of e-mails neatly filed — and easily retrievable — in scores of folders. Gmail has mapped its e-mail labels to Outlook's folders to preserve appearances, if not full functionality, between one and the other.

✔ **Ads:** Gmail has low-key text ads, currently positioned at the top of the Inbox or other window. It's weird, at first, to see ads more or less specific to the content of your recent e-mails appearing in Gmail. However, one of us (Smith) has found several useful links here, including one that saved hundreds of dollars in car rental costs on a trip. Most users give these ads, at least in their current form and corresponding low level of obtrusiveness, a pass or even a guarded thumbs up. Others sometimes find them hilariously mismatched to the content of the e-mail.

Of course Gmail's Inbox has additional features, as you might expect. One crucial feature is the ability to quickly start a voice or video chat — see the next chapter — with someone you're corresponding with. It's easy to As Google Voice becomes more widely used, a phone call might be added to the options soon.

The most amazing part, of course, is that it's all free. Of course, "free" really means ad-supported. With Gmail, though, as with watching the Super Bowl, the ads are part of the fun.

If you're part of an organization with 50 users, want more storage per user, and/or want to get rid of the ads, you can pay a per-user charge currently set at $50 per user per year.

For a Top 10 list of Gmail features from Google itself, visit `http://mail.google.com/mail/help/about.html`. The list includes useful links to details about parts of the offering that may be important to you.

Google's designs are usually driven by the results of user interface testing, to such an extent that designers have quit the company in protest. Yet there is one important point where Google has not yielded to sometimes vociferous public opinion: the exclusive use of threads in Gmail.

Most e-mail clients, whether PC-based or server-based, present e-mails one at a time. Some of them, optionally, offer some degree of threading — messages that are replies to each other shown together as a group. No major e-mail client except Gmail presents all e-mail exchanges in threaded form and does not offer an option to show them as individual messages.

The problem with threads is that the time sequence of e-mails is somewhat obscured. Conversations move up or down in your Inbox depending on the timing of the most recent message, but only the new part — the most recent contribution to the exchange — is highlighted, as shown in Figure 14-4. And the new bit can be somewhat buried in the overall exchange. Finding a particular message or attachment, for example, among layers of them can be quite difficult.

Google Voice and the Gmail Inbox

The specifics of how the Gmail Inbox works are especially important for Google Voice users, because the way you manage voice traffic will change once you're using Google Voice. You end up handling a lot of voice traffic by sending an e-mail reply or otherwise taking action in e-mail. Text message copies, Google Voice notifications, voicemail transcriptions, and links to conversation recordings serve as the bridge taking you from *voice world* into *e-mail world*.

Good arguments exist for both Gmail's conversations and the more typical one message at a time approach with regards to the messages that come from Google Voice. Putting more of your life in your Inbox just increases the pressure on your e-mail program to do exactly what you want, exactly when you need it.

There may be a generational gap here. It seems that younger or newer e-mail users "get" the threaded interface well and are happy to benefit from the compression it offers. These users are quick to use search to dig out anything specific that's needed.

Older, experienced users are more likely to recoil in horror from the idea of their carefully crafted, memo-like messages being slipped into a conversational stack like a slice of cheese in a cheeseburger. These users tend to want to sort their e-mails by date — doubly impossible in Gmail — and search the message headers of individual messages to help find the specific thing they're looking for.

Figure 14-5 shows the display of an e-mail in Google Voice within its overall thread. You can see that it's not necessarily easy to get to a specific intermediate message.

Fortunately, there's a workaround that many of us cling to like a floating log after a flood. Gmail works well with Microsoft Outlook, and Outlook displays messages one at a time. Individual messages can be stored in folders, sorted and, yes, searched. Apple users use Apple Mail to get the same effect.

This capability is so important that Google has introduced new software specifically to improve the synchronization between Google mail, address books, and calendars with Outlook. Microsoft, to the shock of many, is working closely with them to help make it work better.

Non-threaded capability is also so important that many users have looked for an online tool that would organize the view of Gmail online into a form more like Outlook's. No such tool has gained enough traction to be widely used as yet.

Google seems happy enough to provide the plumbing and let Microsoft provide the user interface to legacy Outlook users. The company seems to be taking the long view in the belief that it can educate new generations of users who prefer viewing e-mails in its preferred conversational format, while supporting Outlook and Apple Mail to keep legacy users and others from rebelling.

Figure 14-5:
Give cred to the thread.

To view a rather impassioned exchange on the topic of e-mail conversations, visit: www.google.com/support/forum/p/gmail/thread?tid=2878f5 3c699d6f2d&hl=en

First, you see a rather definitive answer from a contributor (not a Google employee) who goes by the user name Subhu: "Conversation Threading is the heart of Gmail. Currently there is no way to turn it off manually."

Click on the link below this Olympian statement to see some of the rather impassioned responses from other users.

Important Gmail features

One of the key features of Gmail is its forwarding flexibility. Part of that is the way it interoperates with other e-mail accounts. Figure 14-6 shows the Accounts and Import features of Gmail.

Gmail enables you to:

✔ **Import e-mail and contacts from Yahoo! Mail, Hotmail, AOL, and other kinds of accounts.** Google is making it easier for more people to move to Gmail.

✔ **Change your name and Reply to addresses.** This feature helps you get your e-mail where you want it. For example, if you use Gmail only for Google Voice notifications, change the Reply-to field so replies go to another e-mail account.

✔ **Receive e-mail into Gmail from other POP3 accounts.** By itself, this feature is again Google making transition from your other account(s) to Gmail easier.

✔ **Change your Send from e-mail address depending on the account it came from.** That's right; if someone sends an e-mail to, say, your Hotmail account, you can have Gmail get it for you. When you reply to it — in Gmail — the reply-to address can be set to your Hotmail address as well. So you can "do" Hotmail without ever opening Hotmail!

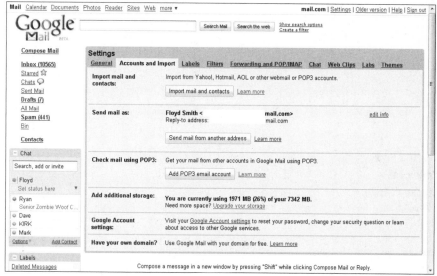

Figure 14-6: Gmail helps you give a good account of yourself.

See the next section for important options relating to how Gmail handles mail coming in from other POP accounts.

The Account and Import features are helpful, and in some cases vital, for working with Google Voice notifications. For instance, you could use your Google Voice number for work, personal use and perhaps even an additional business that you have on the side. Each of these may go through a different e-mail account.

You can use Gmail as a bit player for your Google Voice notifications only; as a peer among other e-mail accounts that you also check; or as one account to bind them all, a master account that spoofs other accounts when needed.

By being so flexible, Gmail is becoming part or all of the e-mail solution for more and more people. You may find it useful for Google Voice at first and perhaps for more of your needs over time.

Forwarding through the fog

Along with dealing directly with your other accounts, as described in the previous section, Gmail can automatically forward e-mail to other accounts — and flexibly deal with its own copy. Figure 14-7 shows the Forwarding and POP/IMAP features of Gmail.

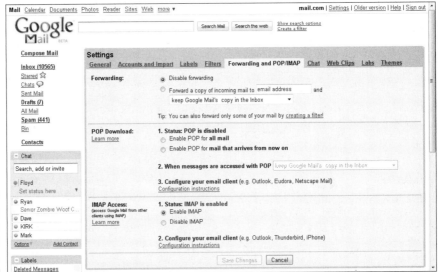

Figure 14-7:
Gmail offers fast, flexible forwarding.

One of the most important features in all of Gmail is contained in two little links, one each in the Forwarding and POP/IMAP Settings area: the two links that say Configuration instructions.

These links take you to instructions on how to configure various e-mail clients to work with Gmail, as mentioned at the beginning of this chapter. Many companies would just tell you "their side" of what to do and leave it up to you to find your e-mail client's documentation and cross-reference the two into a solution.

Google takes on the whole job, explains the steps for the whole process, and helps you actually get things done. These can be very important instructions indeed, a real lifeline when you are moving from one computing environment to another and need to get things working quickly.

The Forwarding and POP/IMAP features allow you to use POP or IMAP so a mail client such as Outlook can pull e-mail from Gmail to your PC. Use POP if you want to support basically one-way traffic to your PC; use IMAP if you want to keep the server and local PC copies synchronized with each other.

Gmail has an All mail folder that can help you avoid big problems. If you have PC trouble or otherwise lose access to your current Inbox, or completely delete an important e-mail, you can always dig it out of your All mail folder.

As with other Gmail features, the forwarding and POP/IMAP features take on particular importance with Google Voice. With these features, you can coordinate just where your notifications are available and whether they stay synchronized between systems.

Translating Transcriptions

Google Labs is the public face of Google Research and Development. Labs Alumni — Google services that have come through the Labs into widespread use — include GOOG-411 (refer to Chapter 7), and Google Docs and Spreadsheets.

You can see all Google Labs' efforts at `labs.google.com`; you can see Gmail-specific ones in the Settings tab of Gmail, as shown in Figure 14-8.

Figure 14-8: Gmail will translate your voicemail transcriptions.

Translating a transcription?

Just how bad is a translation of a transcription likely to be?

A transcription might only be 60 percent accurate on a word-for-word, letter-for-letter basis, but be 90 percent understandable by a skilled reader who understands the context: you!

A machine translation, on the other hand, gets the worse of the odds. Translation has very little chance of correctly translating a word that's even slightly mistranscribed. Worse, machine translation looks at phrases as well; if there's a single mistake in a phrase, that error may make several words in a row difficult to translate correctly.

At best, if the transcription is 70 percent accurate, and the translation is 70 percent accurate, the translation of the transcription will be 49 percent accurate. The math works like this:

```
.70 x .70 = .49 (or, 70% of
   70% is 49%)
```

If you want to use Google Translate with Google Voice voicemail transcriptions, consider editing them. Then you can get the best out of the translation, and the result is likely to be helpful to your audience, though not perfect.

We recommend checking this area regularly to see if there's anything in it that can be particularly helpful. One feature that may be particularly interesting with Google Voice is Message translation. Google Translate is put to work translating your e-mail messages.

This service is potentially powerful when used with voicemail transcriptions. You can have transcriptions translated and then send them on to colleagues or friends who speak other languages.

Of course, the result of an inaccurate machine translation of an inaccurate machine transcription may range from wrong to completely unintelligible. But for long messages, you can use a Google Voice transcript as a starting point for a translation — many times all they require is punctuation to become syntactically correct.

What's hilarious in some contexts may be embarrassing, misleading, or worse in others. Always let recipients know if a translation is likely to be anything less than perfect and consider getting professional help if the translation is at all important.

The voicemail transcription that makes sense when you read it today may not make sense some time down the road. It also may not make the same amount of sense to other people, and it certainly won't translate as well as a "cleaned up" copy would.

So consider using the Note capability, as described in Chapter 8, to add a note to important transcripts you receive. Then copy and paste the transcription into the note and clean up or annotate as necessary. This record will be much more useful to you, and also more useful as input to Google Translate.

Giving Voice to Google Apps

As you start using Google Voice, and perhaps add Gmail to your toolkit, or even move to it completely, you may want to consider using other Google products as well.

Google products are largely linked together and have a more and more consistent interface across core offerings. (Newer and non-core offerings can be idiosyncratic.)

However, there are so many of the darn things that you could recoil from all of them. So here's our quick survey, emphasizing those that are most promising for Google Voice users.

At the top of the screen in its core products, Google lists several offerings it thinks are important or most wants to promote. Those top few, and their applicability to Google Voice, are:

- **Gmail:** Very important to Google Voice.

- **Calendar:** An application for scheduling, greatly helped by Google's collaboration capabilities. Calendar is a good thing to use as you build up your Google Contacts via Google Voice, especially as you evangelize friends, family, and business contacts to become Google Voice users as well.

- **Docs:** Allows collaborative work on word processing, spreadsheet, and presentation-style documents. Not as powerful as the Office applications we're all used to, but much better for sharing. The Docs offering is not particularly applicable to Google Voice.

- **Photos:** A pointer to Picasa, which is both an application (Picasa 3) that runs on your computer and an online site, Picasa Web Albums, for sharing photos online.

- **Reader:** A way to gather updates from your favorite Web sites online. Not particularly applicable to Google Voice, but good for getting interesting information to share.

- **Sites:** Google Sites is a way to create Web sites that incorporate Google Docs and other Google features. This feature may be better suited to intranets and other collaborative sites than to a typical public-facing Web site.

Most of these offerings are also featured under the heading of Google Apps, as shown in Figure 14-9. For personal use, Google Apps is just a container for Google's products. But for organizations (businesses pay one rate, schools, and nonprofits another) Google Apps is much more.

Google Apps allows Google to host e-mail and calendaring for organizations. These offerings are usually integrated with address book management and a domain name, under the title Google Apps for your Domain, to form a fairly complete solution.

Figure 14-9:
Google
offers its
products
as Google
Apps.

If you are among the small but growing number of people who are using Google Apps for your Domain customers, you cannot, at this time, use Google Voice with your Google Apps for your Domain log-in. That means you have to get a personal Google account. Therefore, you may run into some problems Google is currently having with keeping Google Apps for your Domain accounts separate from the personal Google accounts of the same users. Be careful, and talk to your IT team in your organization about how to keep the two separate. (Never signing into both of them from the same machine, nor at the same time, might do it, but that's a lot to ask. You can't sign into two Google ID's on one machine unless you use two browsers, which most people don't do, except for nerds like the authors.)

Searching for stuff

With Gmail's habit of threading conversations, how's a poor person supposed to find their message?

Well, it's Google's mail offering, and Google is all about search. So the answer is, "Seek and ye shall find." Gmail search options are powerful. Experienced Gmail users often search in the Gmail Web client to find messages they can't find in Outlook or Apple Mail.

Start by searching your mail by using the Search box at the top. If that's not enough, click the link, Show search options, next to the Search box at the top of the Gmail window. Search options appear across the top of the window. Alternatively, click Create a filter to route messages by topic, sender, keyword, and more.

Gmail search has many operators that allow you to search specific fields, such as "from:chris" or "subject:book". The same operators work in filters. For a complete list, search Gmail help, or go directly to `http://mail.google.com/support/bin/answer.py?answer=7190`.

Experiment with Gmail search until you get good at it; it's very important for working around Gmail's limitations. One thing it can't work around is misspellings; unlike Google Search, Gmail search doesn't even try to find "sounds like" spellings, similar spellings, or words that share a stem, such as does, doesn't, and don't.

One thing to look out for is that you may have trouble finding a message because it's been wrongly (from your point of view) put in the Spam folder, but Search doesn't look in the Spam folder by default. The only workaround is to use the Search pull-down to choose Spam

as the specific target, or Mail & Spam & Bin together.

Searching through Mail & Spam & Bin is a bit like emptying all your wastepaper bins and file folders onto the floor before starting to look for something; you're likely to have to wade through a lot of junk, but you're more likely to find what you're looking for. Or at least to have the cold comfort of knowing that it probably can't be found.

The ability to mount a search like the one in the figure shows off one of the strengths of Gmail. Its intent is that you take advantage of its huge storage to never delete anything, at least not from your All Mail folder. This allows you to have a deep, ongoing record of all your e-mail; an advantage extended to your phone calls if you use Google Voice and Gmail together.

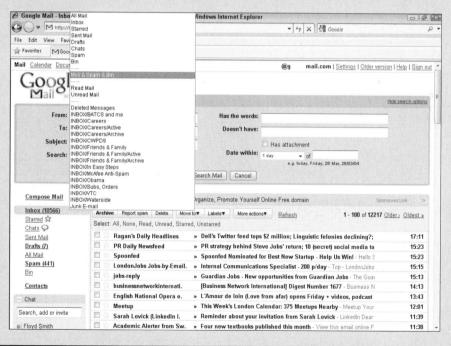

Beyond the products highlighted in the taskbar that shows up across Google applications, Google has many other offerings, as shown in Figure 14-10. Of interest to Google Voice users may be Translate, mentioned earlier as a tool to consider using on Google Voice voicemail transcripts; Google Groups, which are great for sharing files and comments in a group with interests or activities in common; and Alerts, which are particularly good for keeping up on topics you're interested in. (We use it to keep informed about developments with, and comments on, Google Voice while writing this book.)

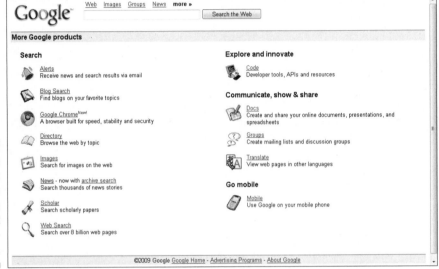

Figure 14-10: Even the More Google products list is not all-inclusive.

Not mentioned on the More Google products page, but also important are Blogger, a very easy to use blogging tool; Google Maps, which is integrated into Google Voice as part of the GOOG-411 offering; and of course YouTube, which has no direct relation to Google Voice but is a whole lot of fun. (And which hosts a lot of useful videos on Google products, including Google Voice.)

Chapter 15

Chatting, Talking, and Using Your Gizmo

Google is the proud owner of 70 percent of the Internet searches done in the U.S., but when you're becoming a giant octopus, your tentacles are bound to get tangled up . . . so it may seem with Google's voice- and conversation-related offerings.

Google has Google Voice, Google voice search, Gmail Chat (also called Google Chat) and Google Talk. It also has tie-ins, in Google Voice, to Gizmo5, a sort of online telephone.

In this chapter, we explain what all these terms mean and help you focus on the ones that will make a difference alongside your use of Google Voice.

Untangling the Spaghetti of Offerings

We have to admit it: each of us has been using Google offerings for years, and we've been focused on Google Voice since the day Google announced it. Yet we *still* get confused among several of Google's offerings that have similar names and closely related — even overlapping — functionality.

The offerings are:

✔ **Google Voice:** The topic of this book; lets you control your existing telephones from a Google-based control panel and more.

- ✔ **Google voice search:** Google voice search was once a separate tool, but it's now integrated into GOOG-411 (see Chapter 8), Google Maps, and the Google Mobile App for smartphones.

- ✔ **GmailChat:** Available only within Gmail, Gmail Chat simply allows you to chat — that is, to send instant messages — to your contacts when they're online. It even supports group chats. You can also use Gmail Chat in third-party clients such as Trillian, iChat (for Mac), and Adium.

- ✔ **Google Talk:** A superset of Gmail Chat, Google Talk requires a separate Windows-only software download and runs in Gmail or in a separate window. It provides text chat, free PC-to-PC voice chat, and even video calls from computers to other computers.

- ✔ **Gizmo5:** Gizmo5 is not a Google product, but you can set up a Gizmo5 client running on a PC as one of your forwarding phones for Google Voice. Refer to Chapter 3. No other non-Google phone product gets this kind of support from within Google Voice.

There's no direct integration between Google Voice and either Google Chat or Google Talk. The more you "go Google," though, in your choice of what tools to use, the more likely you are to find yourself using Google Chat or Google Talk.

How to *under*communicate

All the wonderful communication options described in this book, especially the several complementary ones described in this chapter, can lead to *overcommunication*, the feeling that you can't get away from people who want to interact with you.

A startup, Slydial, has come up with a new way to *under*communicate. Have you ever wanted to leave someone a voicemail without actually talking to them? Call it disingenuous or call it savvy, but you'll probably end up using it.

With Slydial, you call into Slydial, at 267-SLYDIAL (267-759-3425), and then enter the number you want to almost connect with. You listen to a ten-second advertisement, which is your way of paying for the service, then you're connected to the victim's, er, recipient's voicemail. Leave your message and hang up.

Slydial passed the 1 million user mark late in 2008, and the number is sure to increase now that there's a Slydial smartphone application. You can Slydial your contact without dialing the Slydial number or the recipient's number. Just pick 'em and trick 'em.

Now some people much prefer texts, but Google Voice gets around voicemail hell. You might even encourage people to do this to you via your Google Voice number. With Google Voice's voicemail notification and transcription capabilities, you get a version of the message in your e-mail Inbox, along with a link to the voice-mail message. You can respond by e-mail, so you and your "caller" will have successfully conspired to remove any risk of ever actually talking to each other at all.

Using Gmail Chat

Gmail Chat is a simple, instant messaging-type capability built into Gmail, as shown in Figure 15-1. You can easily upgrade to add Google Talk, which adds voice and video capability on either Windows or Macintosh, as we describe in the next section.

The idea behind Gmail Chat is that you're spending a lot of time in Gmail anyway and you easily see which of your contacts are available to chat (a green circle); not available (an empty circle); or available to chat, but with chatting blocked (a red circle with a horizontal dash).

For those with a green circle, you can chat by using text instead of e-mailing. But workplaces, groups of friends, and so on tend to congregate around one solution of this type or another. If Gmail Chat is the solution one or more of your groups begins to congregate around, you may find it useful for more and more of your interactions.

Gmail also saves all the transcripts of your chats. This is great when you need to refer back to a bit of information in a chat, but may be disconcerting when you go searching through your e-mails and find an exchange from a half-forgotten chat instead.

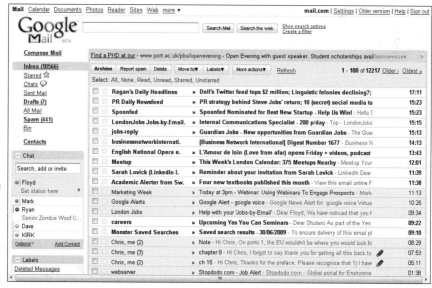

Figure 15-1:
Gmail
extends
itself into
Chat.

What does this have to do with Google Voice, you wonder? Well, Gmail Chat is a convenient halfway point between exchanging e-mails, which can be slow and cumbersome, and having a phone call (or voice chat or video call), which can demand more attention. Google Voice moves a lot of your voice traffic into your e-mail Inbox, so if you use Gmail, as recommended in the last chapter, along with Google Voice, Google Chat becomes a nice additional option to have.

You, gentle reader, will be far from the only person to start using Google Voice in the coming months and years. Many people who start with Google Voice will also adopt Gmail or increase their use of their pre-existing Gmail account. As Google's suite gets increasingly able, you're likely to find that more and more of your friends, acquaintances, and business colleagues are Gmail users and therefore accessible through Gmail Chat.

To invite people into Gmail, and thereby potentially into Gmail Chat as well, click the Invite a friend button in the lower-left corner of the Gmail screen. A list of some of your most frequently contacted contacts appears, as shown in Figure 15-2. Choose the ones you want and type any additional e-mail addresses in the text entry box. You can use, clear, or change the note that Google provides; you may want to mention something about how nice it would be to have the option of using Gmail Chat together. Then click Send Invites to invite them.

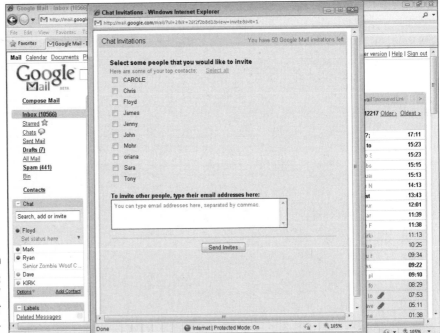

Figure 15-2: Get chattin' with your Contacts.

This chapter is already pretty nerdy, but what the heck: if you really want to get the most out of Gmail, you might think the Google Labs tab in Gmail is the ultimate in nerdiness. Not even close. To really geek out, visit Gtricks at www. gtricks.com. Author Abhishek Mandloi has add-ins to improve Gmail, Gtalk, and more. They may or may not be fully tested and quality controlled, but they're bound to be fun.

You can chat with people who don't have a Google account by adding what Google calls a chatback badge to your blog or other Web page. Visit www. google.com/talk/service/badge/New to get the code. (There's a capital letter in that Google-supplied URL! Don't tell us some Google people don't know UNIX?)

Put the badge in any Web page. The badge shows if you're available and invites people to chat with you. You can even have several separate chats running at once.

You can combine the chatback badge with a Google Voice Call Widget, as we describe in Chapter 8. Then you can offer your Web visitors multiple ways to be in touch with you.

Google Talk

Google Talk adds voice and video communication to Gmail Chat within Gmail. It also runs in a separate window where you can chat, or have a voice call or a video call, as shown in Figure 15-3. (You can only have a group chat, using text not voice or video in Gmail Chat, though.)

Figure 15-3: Google Talk application on the Google Talk home page.

You have to download Google Talk if it's not already set up on your computer. Just click the link, Try video chat, in Gmail, as shown in Figure 15-1. A dialog box opens to allow you to install the needed plug-in.

After you install Google Talk, a camera icon appears next to the names of other Google account users who have Google Talk installed. (Users of non-Windows machines may get the same effect with other software.) You can find details of all this and more in *Google Apps For Dummies* by Ryan Teeter and Karl Barksdale (Wiley, 2008).

Not everyone has the equipment for a voice chat (headphones with a microphone help a lot) or video chat (you need a webcam). Also, different people feel differently about text chat, voice chat, and video chat, just as they do about older, better established forms of communication such as a phone call or stopping by for a — here's the word again — chat.

Is SkypeIn?

We love Google Voice, but we come not to bury Skype but to praise it. Skype is a marvelous invention. Skype brought free international calls over the computer to the world, followed by free video calls. Homes, offices, and Internet cafés around the world are full of people talking to friends, loved ones, and business partners for free over Skype.

SkypeIn and SkypeOut allow you to interact with real phones at very low prices, and mobile support, to enable low-priced calls on the move. The cell phone support usually depends on the availability of a wireless network and is banned by many cell phone service providers, so check before assuming you can use it on your cell phone.

Skype, unlike Google Voice, uses VOIP (Voice over Internet Protocol) technology for most of its work. This sometimes means reduced call quality and even dropouts, but the prices are so low that for most purposes it's worth it.

At this writing, Google Voice has Skype beat on prices by a little bit, and with better call quality.

But Skype works both ways all over the world; in fact, it's less popular in the U.S. than it is in many other countries, perhaps largely because people in these countries travel and work internationally more than most Americans. For the lowdown on Skype, see *Skype For Dummies* by Loren Abdulezer and others (Wiley, 2007).

There's no reason not to continue, or even start, using Skype right alongside Google Voice and the other Google-supported options described in this chapter. In fact, by making you more aware of your many phone calling options, and by making you allergic to paying high prices for any calls at all, using Google Voice may make you more likely to use Skype as well.

Besides saving money, though, there isn't that much in common between Skype and Google Voice; they're similar in purpose but mostly complementary as to which "user scenarios" they support. So there's no harm in using both, and even good reason to do so.

After you're properly equipped, Google Talk increases your options greatly, in ways that some people find marvelous and others find intrusive. You may find yourself, initially, spending as much time establishing equipment adequacy amongst your contacts and sussing out their preferences among means of communication as you do actually conversing with them.

The connection to Google Voice is clear: Google Talk just gives you even more ways to communicate, and always for free, but limited to calls on your PC. International calls on Google Voice use real phones, but cost money. (Not much, but a bit.). With Google's offerings, and the many other ways to communicate being made possible by PCs (see Gizmo5 below), it's a cheaper and easier, as well as a smaller, world.

What's really nice with Google Talk, in addition to low price, is the ease of moving among e-mail, chats, voice, and video calls. For one thing, a phone call can be a massive interruption. Because these PC-based alternatives begin by allowing you to see who's online and who's declared themselves available, you're less likely to disrupt fellow chatters. If you want to give the other person plenty of notice, an online voice or video call can be easily begun with an invitation via chat or e-mail.

Google Talk interoperates with many other chat clients — none that I (Smith) had ever heard of, except iChat on the Mac, but that doesn't mean other clients aren't very important to their developers and users. The current list at the time of writing is shown in Figure 15-4; for an updated version, visit `www.google.com/talk/otherclients.html`.

Welcome to Google Talk

Client Choice with Google Talk

The Google Talk service is built to support industry standards. You can connect to the Google Talk service using Google's own client, as well as many other IM clients developed by third parties. Use the table below to help you choose which client is best for you.

Now, you can also use Google Talk on your BlackBerry. Download Google Talk for BlackBerry devices at http://www.blackberry.com/GoogleTalk.

About Google Talk
What's New
Help Center
For Organizations
Download Google Talk

Additional Resources
Developer Info
Other IM Clients
Google Talk Blog

Client	Windows	OSX	Linux	IM other Google Talk users	Voice calls to other Google Talk users	Cost
Google Talk	✓	✗	✗	✓	✓	Free
Google Talk Gadget	✓	✓	✓	✓	✗	Free
Adium	✗	✓	✗	✓	✗	Free
Pidgin	✓	✓	✓	✓	✗	Free
iChat	✗	✓	✗	✓	✗	Included with OSX
Kopete	✗	✗	✓	✓	✗	Free
Miranda	✓	✗	✗	✓	✗	Free
Psi	✓	✓	✓	✓	✗	Free
Trillian Pro	✓	✗	✗	✓	✗	$25*

*The company that makes Trillian offers a free version of its client, but in order to connect to Google Talk or any other service that supports the Jabber/XMPP protocol, you'll need to purchase Trillian Pro.

Don't see your favorite Jabber/XMPP client on the list? Tell us about it.

Figure 15-4: Make clients serve your computing.

Gizmo5

Gizmo5 is a SIP phone, a virtual phone that runs on a PC, Mac, or Linux box, as well as on dozens of models of cell phones. See the "Just a little SIP" sidebar for a brief explanation of SIP.

A SIP phone is a virtual phone even when it's running on a handset, because all the required phone-specific functionality is running in software. To a SIP phone, any specific hardware is just a replaceable host.

Gizmo5 allows you to make very cheap calls indeed over the Internet. Gizmo5's dependence on the Internet means that you need wireless network access and service provider permission, or at least acquiescence, to use it on a mobile phone.

There are a lot of VOIP and SIP options that Google could have chosen to support rather than Gizmo, whose Web site is shown in Figure 15-5. Why Gizmo5?

We aren't privy to all the reasons, which might include business connections between Google and Gizmo, shared venture capital funding, or even just old school ties. But from an outsider's point of view, Gizmo5 seems relatively mature, and it has a vital tool for Google Voice integration: a hidden, but real, phone number.

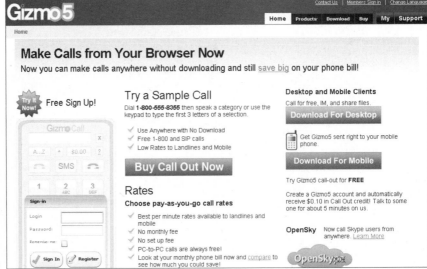

Figure 15-5:
Gizmo is a useful virtual machine.

Just a little SIP

You could spend a lot of time and mental energy learning about SIP, which stands for Session Initiation Protocol. It's used for creating and ending voice and video calls over Internet Protocol. We admit to not fully understanding the diagram in the figure, for instance. If you need to understand it, start by visiting Wikipedia and looking up Session Initiation Protocol.

We do know what a SIP phone is, though. It's a telephone, whether real or virtual, that runs over IP (Internet Protocol). If anyone asks you what Gizmo5 is, just tell them it's a virtual Session Initiation Protocol phone running over IP. Then, while they're scratching their heads trying to figure out what you said, you can make your escape before they ask you to explain it.With Gizmo5's phone number you can use it as a virtual, but very useful, forwarding phone from Google Voice. You can use your Gizmo5 SIP phone right alongside your cell phone, home phone and so on.

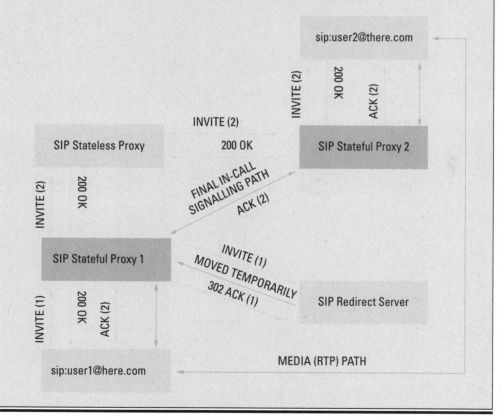

To find your Gizmo SIP number, just sign up for Gizmo5, beginning on the home page. Then visit `my.gizmo5.com`. Your Gizmo5 SIP number is displayed just below your name. At this writing, Gizmo SIP numbers start with 747 — the area code for the San Fernando Valley area of Los Angeles, CA in case you're interested. (We are, like, totally)

You can use Gizmo 5 and Google Voice to make free calls from the Web that don't even use minutes from a cell phone plan. With an SIP phone (see the sidebar, "Just a little SIP"), you can do the same thing while on the move. For details, see the Gizmo 5 Web site at `www.gizmo5.com`, or this article from the excellent LifeHacker site:

```
http://lifehacker.com/5323632/make-free-outgoing-calls-
            with-google-voice--gizmo5
```

Chapter 16

Using Google Voice for Business

*G*oogle Voice can offer a great deal of savings and capability to businesses and organizations. But because Google Voice is a consumer-based tool, it doesn't have all the things a business needs to make full use of it.

Yet Google Voice is too capable for business to ignore. It offers too much in efficiency, too much in cost savings, and will be taken up by too many employees and competitors for business not to try to make use of it. How a business might best do that is the subject of this chapter.

Using Search in Organizations

Google Search has been one of the secrets of making the Web really useful in organizations. As the Web has become more useful, organizations and individuals have invested more time, effort and money in their Web sites and related services such as blogs. As they have done so, there's been more and more to find, making search ever more important. Google has largely kept up with the challenge.

In larger organizations, in fact, Google Search presents a big comparative challenge. Large organizations typically have very large amounts of data they keep internally, accessible via the company intranet. The challenge that Google Search presents is that it's too good; employees in large organizations constantly complain about their inability to find things on intranets.

A business or an organization?

We're abusing the term *business* here. Most of what we're describing applies not only to businesses but to all organizations, including governments, non-profit organizations, and schools. However, each of these has its own specific concerns in addition to the usual concerns of a business.

So we're using the term business here in the way many others do: to describe actual for-profit businesses as well as the business-type concerns that other organizations have. What we don't account for is the specific concerns of each type of non-business organization, because those concerns can be quite complex and, to an outsider, quite arbitrary. Sometimes, we can say from experience, they seem arbitrary to the insiders as well!

The Nielsen Norman Group is among the leaders in promoting high standards for intranet design. Their Intranet Design Annual, shown in Figure 16-1, highlights ten intranets they name as the "best" each year. This report is particularly valuable because the key aspect of intranets is that you usually can't easily get a look at anyone else's.

Now a situation similar to that with Google Search may unfold with Google Voice. Consumers and small businesses can take full advantage of Google Voice to save money and to provide convenience for all concerned, as we'll describe below. Bigger businesses won't be able to use it much or even at all, as it doesn't match their concerns for security, reliability, and control.

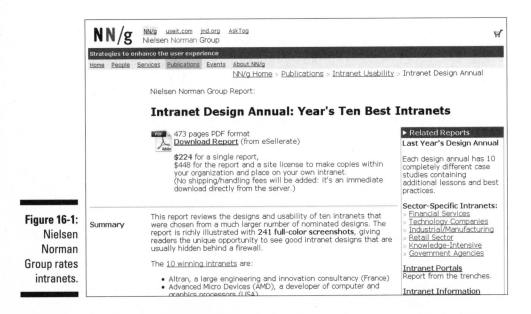

Figure 16-1:
Nielsen
Norman
Group rates
intranets.

We begin by describing how Google Voice works from an employee's point of view, the most important perspective of all. We then show you how to get the most possible out of Google Voice in smaller and larger companies, and why the end result may leave people in large organizations unsatisfied.

Whatever your role in business, it's good to read all three parts, so you can best look for opportunities to get the most out of Google Voice and offerings from other vendors.

Google Voice for Employees

For an employee, Google Voice is wonderful. Used properly, it can help you get key messages from home without disruption. Your cell phone behaves better too, causing fewer unneeded interruptions, with all manner of controls and notifications to put you in charge.

With Google Voice, you can do a much better job of not having personal calls ring your cell phone during the work day; just assign various callers to voicemail. If you use Groups properly, you can do this with just a few clicks.

Even though you are blocking many or all calls, you can still get back to people relatively quickly by using the SMS text message forwarding, e-mailed voicemail notifications, and voicemail transcriptions that Google Voice provides. And these tools keep you out of "voicemail hell" much of the time, avoiding the situation where you miss a crucial business message that's hidden between long, "how ya doin'" messages from friends and family.

Voice mail is becoming a topic of national and international discussion. Publications such as the *New York Times* have discussed its failings at length. People get so many messages they can't deal with them all, and voice mail messages are the hardest to deal with, because messages often have to be listened to in the order received and because listening, unlike reading, can't easily be sped up.

Having Google Voice notifications come to your personal e-mail account, such as a Gmail account, is convenient. Some employers frown on, or even actively ban, use of personal e-mail services such as Gmail at work. You can check Gmail on a cell phone or set Gmail to forward messages to your work e-mail during the workday.

Gmail's flexibility makes it particularly good for routing messages from Google Voice. A simple way to do this is to use the Gmail option that forwards a copy of messages to your work, but also keeps a copy for Gmail. (See Figure 16-2.) That way you can deal with the work copy as a disconnected notification that you can delete if it doesn't require immediate action, without prejudice to your ability to later reply to it, search for it, store it, or otherwise do as you want with it in your Gmail account.

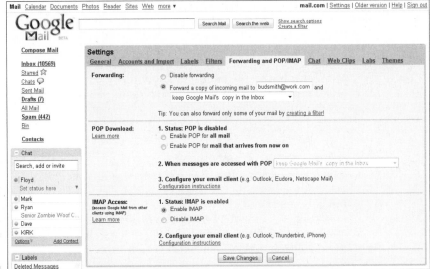

Figure 16-2:
Ping your
work e-mail
with Gmail
messages if
you have to.

It does take some self-discipline to manage your personal life successfully during the workday using Google Voice. It further pierces the veil many of us try to keep between our work and our personal lives. Try to use Google Voice to help you be aware of any emergencies or important opportunities, while deferring as much as possible of the other stuff until your own time.

The Do Not Disturb feature, found on the General tab of the Settings menu of the Google Voice Web site, is a good one to use at work. Use it to give yourself a real break from the phone during a meeting or at lunchtime. This setting sends all your Google Voice calls to voicemail. You still see voicemail notifications and SMS text messages in your e-mail Inbox, so you won't be too far out of reach — just far enough to focus on people, get time to yourself, or devote uninterrupted chunks of time to getting work done. The Call Presentation and Call Screening features can be good ones to turn on during the workday as well. All of this may create some fun for couples and families. Couples may have to negotiate whose Google Voice account gets used as the home number. If a spouse, partner, or children, especially older children, are involved, you may also have to get quite good at routing callers who are trying to get to the home phone to actually ring that phone when someone other than the Google Voice account holder is at home.

Using Google Voice features at work

Previous chapters in this book have covered setting up Google Voice (Part I) and using its features (Part II) pretty thoroughly, so hopefully you've gotten to use it by this point. But how do its features apply especially at work?

Here's a quick magnificent seven list of Google Voice features that make a difference at work:

✔ **Free U.S. calls, cheap international calls, and impromptu conference calls.** Voice can save your company money and save you the hassle of filing an expense report for calls you make. It can also keep you from having to come into the office at odd hours to make international calls just for the ability to conference or put the call on the company tab. Google Voice generates a very small bill and has its own conferencing capability.

✔ **Call screening, ListenIn, and blocked calls.** Call screening and ListenIn, which is referred to as Call Presentation in Google Voice settings, ask callers to say their names if they're calling from a number that's unknown or not in your contacts, and allow you to listen in on any voice mail message as callers are leaving it, so that you can jump into the call if you like. Turn these features on at work for most or all of your personal callers; they will save you tons of time and allow you to stay focused.

✔ **SMS text message forwarding, voicemail notifications, and transcriptions; call recording.** These features let you stay on top of your voice messages and recordings from your e-mail Inbox. You avoid the interruption of a phone call but still get important messages in a timely fashion. And you can forward or embed messages, notifications, and recordings for others to respond to or use for reference.

When forwarding or embedding messages, always protect the caller's privacy regarding anything confidential such as the caller's phone number.

✔ **Phone switching.** On incoming calls, you can switch a call from one of your forwarding phones to another, just by pressing * during the call. All your forwarding phones then ring (which might cause a bit of consternation on the home front if your home phone rings briefly, then goes silent again). This is great if a call comes in on your cell phone at work and reception is iffy; you can transfer the call to your desk phone, as long as it's not an extension.

✔ **Customized greetings.** You can personalize greetings to convey the right businesslike and/or friendly tone for work and personal calls. But you can also convey information, sometimes reducing the need for a "live" phone call.

If you're on your honeymoon, for example, you can use a customized greeting to tell business callers "I'll be on personal leave during July. Please contact. . . ." On the other hand, you can create a different message daily for friends to keep them up to date: "Honeymoon, Day 1: Wow!" Both dissuade people from ringing through to bother you, but in very different ways.

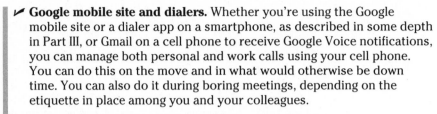

✔ **Google mobile site and dialers.** Whether you're using the Google mobile site or a dialer app on a smartphone, as described in some depth in Part III, or Gmail on a cell phone to receive Google Voice notifications, you can manage both personal and work calls using your cell phone. You can do this on the move and in what would otherwise be down time. You can also do it during boring meetings, depending on the etiquette in place among you and your colleagues.

✔ **Managing callers by group.** The ability to use Google Voice to manage callers by group can be a great time saver, and work is where saving time often takes precedence over any other concern. So taking the time to set up caller groups properly can be a real bonus at work. (See Chapter 5 for details on setting up caller groups.)

Determining what doesn't work so well

Google Voice at work doesn't always work so well. Here are the most important, in our book:

✔ **What number to give?** Should you give your Google Voice number out as a work number? Having carefully considered this, we can definitively answer: it depends. See the next two sections for more.

✔ **What about traveling?** A Google Voice number does not forward calls to phones that travel outside the country, which basically means that the receiving capability of your cell phone — half of what defines a telephone — stops working via your Google Voice number. Your boss or clients, for one, probably will not like this. You can call people, by making a long-distance call back to your Google Voice number in the U.S., but you can't directly receive calls. This is often a blessing but in some cases a real problem; see Chapter 7 for the future prognosis and workarounds.

✔ **Extension phones.** Google Voice doesn't work with extensions. It may or may not work if you have your own dedicated number, but one that's routed through an office phone system; try it to find out. You may end up needing to request a direct line to your desk, as people used to have to do for fax machine or Internet access at work.

✔ **Mixed messages.** What feels to you like control, such as sending some people straight to voicemail or, in particular, using the ListenIn feature, can feel to others like rudeness. Follow the Golden Rule — do unto others as you would have them do unto you.

✔ **Missed signals.** All the options Google Voice gives you can make it possible to miss a truly important call. In the early days especially, be generous about letting calls through and picking up calls to avoid mistakes.

✔ **Geeking out.** If others see you spending a lot of time managing Google Voice and don't know about or understand the benefits you and your company are getting from it, it's easy for them to question the usefulness of Google Voice, the usefulness of you, or both. This is a case where the other Golden Rule applies: them that have the gold make the rules. Be careful.

✔ **Who calls whom?** Conferencing, recording, and call switching to another phone all work only on calls coming in to you. Free national calls and very low international rates only apply on calls you place. When you make phone appointments, consider the logistics of who should call who.

✔ **Managing home while away.** Like e-mail and chain messages, GV might be restricted at your workplace.

Using Google Voice at work versus for work

Unless your organization expressly forbids it, you can and should use Google Voice at work. Used properly, it makes it easier to deal with a few urgent things from the rest of your life while at work, protecting the rest of your time and focus for doing the job.

Banned? Seriously?

You might have trouble imagining an organization banning Google Voice use at work, but we'll be surprised if it doesn't happen in at least a few. We've both worked in large corporations that banned Gmail, Hotmail, YouTube, Skype, most instant messaging, and much more. To add insult to injury, they forced employees to use Lotus Notes as well. (A bit of a joke there, as many people hate Notes, a productivity package that went through a stretch of about a decade with minimal updating. Some others reportedly love it.)

In this organization, as in many others, PCs were locked down; users were not allowed to install any additional software, but had to make a request to the IT department, which might or might not carry it out. Even IT employees weren't above the letter of the law.

This organization also gave cell phones out to most employees — BlackBerry phones, as is usually the case where security is a concern. These were "locked down" as well; employees could visit the Google mobile site, for example, but not install a dialer. Webmail was banned on the BlackBerry phones as well. Most employees brought a personal cell phone to stay in touch personally.

But what about using Google Voice *for* work? This boils down to two questions: Should you use Google Voice to make work calls where it makes sense, such as cheap international calls and cheap and convenient conference calls? And, the really important question from an organization's point of view: Should you give out your Google Voice number for work purposes?

These seemingly simple questions fall into a category called governance, in which organizations try to operate according to carefully reviewed, internally agreed-on rules, despite the messy complexity of the real world. Corporate governance is a complicated but important topic that will have to stretch to accommodate Google Voice and similar offerings that may come out in the future.

Calling out on Google Voice can save your company a lot of money, and you a lot of hassle, as described above. But it also means people you call may see or capture your Google Voice number for contacting you in the future, which organizations that understand the issue probably don't want.

Many organizations won't worry too much about this, but other organizations will "just say no" and ask employees not to use Google Voice numbers for work at all.

With Google Voice having just been launched, it may take some organizations a while go come up with a policy covering it. If this is the case at your place of employment, and if the organization tends to be strict on these issues, we recommend that you do use Google Voice to save all involved money on outbound calls and occasionally for casual conference calls. But you should probably avoid having a Google Voice number printed on your business card, placed in official company directories, or otherwise used officially, unless your organization also allows personal cell phone numbers to be used in this way.

The bottom line is that many reasons exist for both your employer and you to embrace your use of Google Voice for work purposes, but some employers may ban it to at least some extent. If the employer provides you a cell phone and cell service, this is reasonable, if harsh; if they don't, it seems unreasonable, but it's not worth getting fired over.

If your company is usually open to new technologies, it will probably evaluate Google Voice and make an informed policy decision that you can live with. If it tends to quash new technologies, well, you might want to keep your Google Voice account a secret so they don't hassle you.

Competing for telecommunication dollars

What's the future of Google Voice? Will this thing be around forever, or at least for a very long time?

Google Voice is one of the most important offerings ever from one of the most important technology companies around. You shouldn't worry about investing time and effort in getting a Google Voice number and putting it to use.

You also have good reason to hope that Google Voice will not only survive, but thrive. Google owns the Android operating system for phones, and they have deals with major resellers such as Samsung and HTC. They have also purchased billions of dollars in wireless spectrum rights.

The hope for any Google Voice user (who isn't also a telecoms executive) is that Google will more or less become a telecoms company, a one-number clearing house for home, cell, and even business phones, tied into e-mail, chat, video, e-commerce, and more. And that they'll offer all this for a tiny fraction of the prices people pay now.

An effort like this will make the existing telecoms providers raise their games considerably, so that everyone, Google Voice user or not, benefits greatly. You are, by using Google Voice today, helping make a future like this one possible.

Using Google Voice for Small Business

If you're a small businessperson, a contractor, or entrepreneur, using Google Voice is a no-brainer. Google Voice's features are ideally suited for helping you manage your bustling work and social life, and can help you save money on your phone bill.

Google Voice is so advantageous for individually-based businesses that you may want to consider moving to it even before inbound phone number portability is supported. (That is, before you can transfer your cell phone or business number to Google Voice.) It's a hassle to get everyone to change what number they call you on, but you only have to do it once, and you can benefit from the cost savings and features right away.

Instead of worrying about what number to call you on and when, your friends, family, and business contacts will be able to call you on one number, and for you to be able to manage the call in a way that works for both them and you.

Corporate employees may have another reason for *entrepreneur envy*; people in locked-down environments who are more or less prohibited from using Google Voice will wish they were you.

What if you have several employees and find yourself incurring significant phone bills, including running a small multiline phone system? You have two alternatives here. You can move to a completely Google Voice-controlled system, although the limit of six forwarding numbers can quickly chafe if you have more than two employees total.

If your business phone number has gained any currency at all with current and potential customers, employees, and others, consider waiting for inbound phone number portability before using that number for Google Voice. In this way you can keep your valuable phone number while gaining the features of Google Voice.

Another concern before forwarding your current number to Google Voice is to see how your current provider, or competitors, will support the need for another phone number to replace the one that you transfer for use by Google Voice.

Ooma, a provider of inexpensive VOIP-based phone systems for small business, was the first to announce a Google Voice compatible system; the announcement is shown in Figure 16-3. This system has the effect of porting your existing phone number to Google Voice without your having to actually do so.

When users of the ooma system dial out, the call appears to be coming from your usual phone number, which gets all the benefits of Google Voice. The system includes landline handsets that send and receive SMS text messages. Ooma seems to have achieved a breakthrough, although they're likely to have a lot of competition for your business in the months and years to come.

Figure 16-3:
Ooma adds
oomph to
Google
Voice.

Short of switching to ooma, you can use an alternative approach as an interim move while waiting for more options to appear, or possibly as a permanent approach. If you're a small company with more than one or two employees and an investment in a widely used phone number and a phone system, you may want to consider integrated use of your current phone setup and Google Voice.

In this approach, the phone system and the old phone number remain. That gives a consistent experience for everyone you deal with. But you still use Google Voice by encouraging, or even requiring, your employees to use Google Voice where its capabilities are beneficial.

Every employee will be able to be reached by either the office number or Google Voice. Basically you're formalizing and optimizing the use of cell phones by employees by incorporating Google Voice into the overall solution. Encourage employees to make international calls using Google Voice, and to provide their Google Voice number for incoming calls as well.

Using Google Voice has a few immediate advantages. It provides all employees with free national calling, which you may have already, and very cheap international calling, which you probably don't have. It supports casual conference calls and recording of both conference calls and important one-on-one calls.

And it puts your employees in control, while keeping the official phone number in the mix.

There are half a dozen steps you can consider that will help you get the most out of a mixed approach with a main number at the core and Google Voice numbers for employees:

1. **Write it down.** Write down how you want people to use the office phone number and Google Voice. Circulate the draft for review and gather input. The result is an improved solution that everyone can live with.

2. **Provide training.** Organize classes on Google Voice and make sure everyone attends, just as you would with a new phone system. People will complain, but this is too important to leave to trial and error.

3. **Consider providing cell phones.** You may want to provide cell phones — in particular, smart phones — to many or even all your employees. The cost will be far less with Google Voice handling formerly expensive international calls, and with a smart phone in particular, your employees will now have an easy way to keep on top of Google Voice phone calls and e-mailed notifications.

If an employer-provided cell phone threatens to overload your employees with one device too many, show them how to forward their personal cell phone number to the phone you're providing. This keeps them "in the loop" with their personal lives and save them money.

4. **Consider including PC-based calling.** Google Talk, Skype, and Gizmo5 (see Chapter 15), support calls without tying up office phone lines or burning cell phone minutes.

5. **Cut out expensive calls.** Keep a close eye on phone bills to make sure that expensive international calls from personal cell phones, home phones, and the office phone aren't made anymore, and that inexpensive Google Voice calling is used instead.

6. **Traveling on business with Google Voice.** When you go abroad, Google Voice will not be able to ring your cell phone, even if you have enabled worldwide service with your carrier. If you're okay with sending all your calls to voicemail, then make sure you turn on e-mail notifications, so you can keep tabs on your messages from your computer or smartphone. (Beware of data roaming charges abroad; they're steep.) If you don't want to send all incoming calls routed through Google Voice to voice mail, have Google Voice point all calls to a domestic landline back home. Then call the phone company, and have your landline forwarded to your true cell phone number. Problem solved! Just remember to turn off your landline forwarding when you get home.

This approach has limitations, some of which you, with your own phone management to worry about, may feel keenly. A big concern is that only one Google Voice number can claim the main office number as a forwarding number for Google Voice. In most cases, it's likely to be your Google Voice account that "claims" the main office number, preventing anyone else from doing so. (Sometimes it's good to be king, or queen!)

 You can use workaround for this problem that's a bit hidden, but that almost everyone will find useful sometimes. It's called temporary call forwarding and is described in Chapter 9. The Google Voice Help screen for temporary call forwarding is shown in Figure 16-4; you can visit it at `www.google.com/support/voice/bin/answer.py?hl=en&answer=115084`.

To use temporary call forwarding, call into your Google Voice number's voice mail. Press 4 to access the main settings menu, then 4 again for temporary settings. Press 2 to set a temporary number and enter the number.

If you're working in a small business setting and several of your company's employees are abroad, they can use temporary forwarding to forward their Google Voice numbers to the main office line. The person attending the main phone can screen calls, handle routine requests, and put through anything truly urgent.

If you're running a small business, you may want to have your employees keep their contacts in a centralized dossier, to prevent the loss of a customer should an employee leave. Doing this is easy with Google Sync, which wirelessly backs up an employee's contacts from their mobile phone or PC to their Google contacts. This puts the same contacts on their mobile phones as it does in their Google applications like Gmail or Google Voice. Then you can quickly move to maintain relationships when an employee leaves, whether there's a competitive concern or not.

The philosophy of work

Academics who study management largely agree that management in large organizations is primarily about two issues, referred to as functional simplification and closure. This can be translated as two exercises: Boiling complex situations down to simple questions, preferably with a "yes or no" answer; and agreeing on and enforcing simple answers to these questions.

Functional simplification and closure, considered together, form a complex process. Lots of things that large organizations do that seem incomprehensible or even stupid from outside suddenly make sense if you study the process by which decisions are reached.

Most of us like people who are optimistic and inclusive. Organizations are pessimistic and exclusive; the organization is defined as much by what it keeps out as by what it lets in. "No" is a very comfortable answer indeed for a senior IT manager.

The use of Web-based e-mail at work is a good example. Large organizations hate security breaches. Using functional simplification, an organization quickly determines that Web-based e-mail is a ready source of security breaches. So closure is easy: no Web-based e-mail at work. Notice that the relative merits of productivity, individual freedom and attractiveness as an employer never got a look in: the functionally simple question was, does this practice cause security concerns?; closure was easily provided by the answer: no Webmail.

Similar concerns arise with Google Voice. Google Voice can be banned in an organization, to one degree or another, before its benefits are even considered. "If you don't understand it, ban it" might be a simple way of describing the reason in many cases.

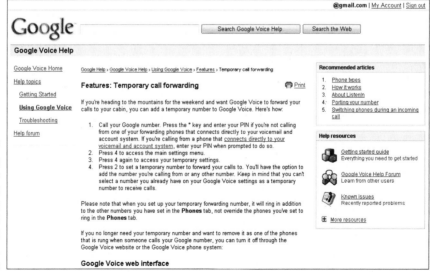

Figure 16-4: Temporary call forwarding is good for small business.

Google Voice provides small businesses with an opportunity to take advantage of their ability to move quickly and immediately to start saving time, money, and effort with Google Voice. To get the most out of it requires a bit of structure, as described above, but the rewards are significant.

Using Google Voice in the Enterprise

If you work in a large organization that has to decide how to handle it, you may find that Google Voice is hard for very large organizations to swallow. It's not just us saying this. Telecom TV, a telecommunications-focused Web site, hosted an article about Google Voice soon after it was announced. The headline, shown in Figure 16-5, says it all, albeit with a touch of hyperbole: "The killer weakness with Google Voice: Enterprises will never go for it."

Figure 16-5:
Never is a
long time.

In some respects, that's true; people in IT tend to be suspicious of Google's free services and don't like consumer tools of any sort coming into their closed shops.

The article's headline is an overstatement in three ways, though:

✓ **Enterprise problems are not a killer weakness.** Even if enterprises never go for Google Voice, that's only a killer weakness in the enterprise. Google Voice can become very successful, even if it's only a winner among consumers and in small and medium-sized businesses.

✔ **Never is a long time.** Google Voice offers truly impressive cost savings and great features that may be hard for others to duplicate. It can be made more enterprise-friendly, though Google has not shown much natural ability to do this with its other offerings. (Google Mail still being in beta five years after launch is the, well, killer example.)

✔ **Google can win by proxy.** Google can license key features to enterprise-friendly competitors, profiting from "competing" products. Google can also partner with or buy other companies to help it get in the door. If not, it can just force the entire telecoms establishment to spend much of its time and energy trying to catch up in the enterprise while Google captures most of the other business.

We describe most of the concerns relating to Google Voice in the enterprise in the beginning of this chapter, from the perspective of the employee. Because Google is a tool for consumers, that's the best way to look at it.

Based on this analysis and a bit of additional thinking, we can make a brief set of overarching recommendations for enterprises to begin dealing with Google Voice:

✔ **Develop expertise.** You should have at least a small group of Google Voice users inside your organization who you can tap into to understand its plusses and minuses, both in general and as they apply to your company. This expertise is crucial, because many of your employees are likely to become accomplished Google Voice users, and will expect you to hold up your end of a conversation about it, from features to implications in your organization. A serious evaluation of Google Voice will stand you in good stead all around.

✔ **Jawbone your suppliers on price.** Google's very low prices for international calls, shown in Table 7-2, are the new benchmark for what any organization should be paying. Note that these prices include calls from cell phones and are in some cases a tenth what other suppliers charge. Get your current suppliers and their competitors in and demand convergence with the new "Google price" within months at best, a year or two at worst. If a supplier tries to tell you why they can't do it, give them a one-word answer: "Next."

✔ **Jawbone your suppliers on features.** Enterprise customers are hardly going to be in a hurry to get in touch with a new supplier like ooma, featured in the discussion on small business above. But Alcatel-Lucent is a reputable name in big-company telecoms, and they unveiled an answer to Google Voice in March 2009 at the CTIA trade show for wireless telephony, shortly after Google Voice was announced. A Web portal for management and conversion of voicemail to text were shown; a Web phone was promised. (See the diagram in Figure 16-6 to see the place of Rich Communications Manager in the enterprise.) Products based on this offering from carriers are expected soon.

✔ **Set a direction.** "If you don't know where you're going, any road will take you there," said the white rabbit in Alice in Wonderland. Decide how you see your employees' personal and work phone usage working in the future.

✔ **Develop a policy.** Develop a policy for Google Voice use in your organization. One sensible policy for many enterprise organizations would be as follows: allow people to forward Google Voice notifications to their work e-mail address; allow (or, optionally, encourage) people to use Google Voice to make international calls when not in the office; but don't allow Google Voice numbers or personal cell phone numbers to be included on business cards or in company directories. (If you allow it for personal cell phones, you should allow it for Google Voice.)

✔ **Sell the policy.** "Because I said so" is not a very good answer to give today's employees, especially the younger ones, many of whom have a particular concern about work-life balance and will rightly see Google Voice as a powerful tool for improving it. Reach out to active Google Voice users; get their input and explain your policy — even modify it, if appropriate — until everyone's comfortable, if not necessarily in agreement, with it.

Don't be mistaken; at least some of your employees will see adopting Google Voice as a necessity. Some will be fans of Google in general, others just very impressed with what Google Voice does for them. They're not likely to be very impressed, in turn, by anything less than a carefully thought through and well-communicated, yet rapid, response to Google Voice.

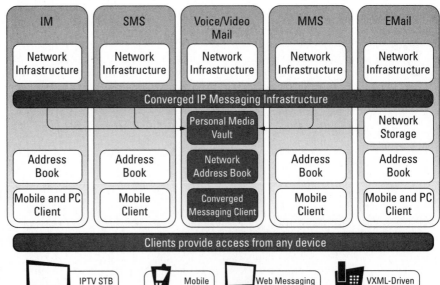

Figure 16-6: Rich Communications Manager fits right in.

Aiming to be enterprise-ready

Google has done very well to become perhaps the top brand and one of the most highly valued companies on Earth without gaining the confidence of large businesses. Will this ever change?

One would have to guess that it won't change soon. Google's approach is to put everything into algorithms and to run those algorithms on vast, cheap server farms. Google is happy to pay — some would say, to pay over the odds — for talented people to invent, program, run, and, to a certain extent, market these products. But the company avoids paying for lots of people in sales and support.

Big business needs handholding, care, and customization; all the things that Google doesn't do. It's a bit like asking McDonald's to create Michelin-starred food; it's not what they do.

Even Google's style, which endears it to many customers, is off-putting to big business. Big business doesn't want a company's logo to change every day; for products to be introduced and withdrawn in dizzying succession; and, worst of all, for products to run for years with a beta designation and never be properly launched, nor to bear version numbers and other identifiers needed for management control.

Google aims its products at employees rather than employers. Using Google Voice in the enterprise requires a series of workarounds and compromises, and will do so for quite a while. Eventually, Google and its competitors will tame Google's innovations and offer them in a form the enterprise can more easily accept and deploy internally.

If you do come up with a creative, yet solidly grounded approach, though, Google Voice has opened the door to a much less expensive and much more effective use of telephones in the future, whether your organization specifically adopts Google Voice or not.

Part V
The Part of Tens

PERSONAL TECH UPDATE:
THE CELL PHONE/PDA TOUPEE WITH
DISCREET VIBRATING PAGER FUNCTION

©RICHTENNANT

"Will you excuse me? I'd better take this."

In this part . . .

You want to get the most out of Google Voice. You're in a hurry. Could there be some quick tips to help? Here they are!

Chapter 17

Ten Points of Netiquette for Google Voice

In This Chapter

▶ Letting people know the benefits of Google Voice

▶ Being gentle when replying to a call by e-mail

▶ Getting permission before circulating recordings

▶ Knowing when not to use Google Voice

*N*etiquette, etiquette for the Internet, became a popular topic in the 1990s as millions of people used e-mail and online message boards for the first time.

When you're playing with a new Web tool, expressing yourself too directly is very easy to do. For example, you might use all caps for emphasis, even though, to others, this comes across as impolite shouting.

Netiquette isn't just for the benefit of others. We all want to be effective in communication. Communicating in a way that feels good to you but is off-putting to the recipient isn't really effective.

Google Voice has its own evolving etiquette, a mix of netiquette, phone etiquette, and specific rules that relate to Google Voice's own specific functions. We offer our own guide here; use it as a starting point for developing your own approach to using Google Voice effectively.

Don't Announce It's Google Voice

The term Google Voice sounds quite robotic and even, for those who don't know it well, a little scary. So tell people that you have a new number or that it's your work number. Tell them that this number is the best way to reach you. (It will be, but only if and when you want to speak to them.) Don't bother announcing to everyone the nuances of the system; if you do, they might stick to your old number out of confusion.

Tighten the Noose Gradually

Much of the power of Google Voice is to restrict people's ability to contact you. The temptation, when you first start using Google Voice, is to greatly restrict the number of calls you get right off the bat.

However, a tight regime will probably be obvious to people who are trying to call you, especially people who are used to being able to reach you directly. It will seem quite simple to them: they're used to having two or three numbers to try for you and reaching you perhaps half the time. Then, one day, you ask them only to call you on a new, Google Voice number.

Perhaps they do and from that moment on, never reach you directly again. To them, Google Voice has caused frustration and inconvenience. It might even cause them embarrassment, as they realize all the trouble you have gone to to cut yourself off from their calls.

You may eventually realize that you've become too hard to reach and start letting more calls through. The damage may have already been done, though.

To avoid needless frustration to your callers, tighten Google Voice's settings gradually. Don't screen calls right away; making people announce themselves can feel hostile. Build up your contacts first so that few people are subject to screening if and when you do impose it.

Sell the Switch

When you switch to Google Voice, people may ask you why you switched. Answer people in terms of the benefits to *them*. The benefits to you might be neutral or even off-putting to others — deferring calls and reducing your time on the phone, for instance. The benefits to both sides include the fact that one incoming call can ring several of your numbers, giving them a better chance of reaching you. You don't have to tell them you got Google Voice to screen calls.

Minimize Cell Use during Meetings

Whether to use your cell phone to send and receive text and e-mail messages during meetings is an active topic of discussion. The answer seems to be different for people depending on their age: younger people tend to see it as acceptable in more situations than older ones.

Google Voice makes the temptation to use your cell phone during meetings even greater. Without Google Voice, phone calls that come in during meetings can create a crisis: you have to ignore the call or take it. If you take the call, you interrupt the meeting, so you tend to ignore calls.

With Google Voice, the phone call may ring through or be blocked, depending on the settings applying to the caller's phone number. The bigger difference, though, is that you'll soon receive a notification and, if a voicemail message was left, a transcript.

This gives you an opportunity to see approximately what was said and to respond by text, e-mail or, if the message seems important and urgent enough, by leaving the meeting to return the call.

Some meetings today begin with a request to turn cell phones off or to silence. With Google Voice, you can be tempted to spend several minutes changing settings instead.

Our recommendation is simple enough: when in Rome, do as the Romans do. Don't use your cell if others aren't using theirs. If there's a possibility of a call or message you absolutely can't miss, use Google Voice to modify your settings to let only that call through.

Plan Calls around Google Voice

Plan calls around Google Voice. For example, if you want to record a call, plan for the call to begin with the other person calling you. The same applies if you want to use Google Voice to support a conference call. That way you don't have to interrupt a meeting that began with you calling out to have the other party or parties call you.

Turn Off Phone Screening for Phone Meetings

Make sure that phone screening is turned off for scheduled meetings. A call for a meeting may come from a previously unknown number, so turn phone screening off for all callers before the meeting. That way the person you have invited to contact you won't have to announce themselves in order to do it.

Move Calls from Skype to Google Voice

When arranging calls, especially international calls, you may encounter people who prefer to use Skype, because it's long been the best way to carry out such calls at low cost. You will, however, want to use your Google Voice number to get the other person familiar with using your GV number, to take advantage of call recording and conferencing, and so on.

Among the reasons for moving to Google Voice that are the most convincing to others, and that you should therefore use, are that the Google Voice call is less likely to suffer drop-outs, and voice quality is likely to be better. (This is true because Google Voice is not voice over IP, which tends to suffer such problems. If you want to get technical, it's a *switching layer* over regular telephone service.)

 Don't put down Skype as you urge people to use Google Voice for calls. There's no reason to offend people who have probably received great benefit from Skype. And don't forget that, when you travel overseas and your Google Voice number stops working, you'll probably be using Skype yourself.

Smooth the Transition to E-Mail

You may find yourself using Google Voice to reply to an incoming phone call via e-mail. Smooth the transition by being explicit about the change. Begin your e-mail with words somewhat like these: "I got your voicemail, and here's what I think. . . ." This kind of introduction acknowledges how you were contacted and tacitly moves the discussion forward in the different medium.

Get Permission for Recordings

Most people aren't used to having their calls recorded, nor to having those recordings make their way around a workgroup, a company — or the world.

Ask for permission before making a recording, before distributing it by e-mail to a small group, and before making it available, by e-mail or on the Web, to a larger group. If the material is at all sensitive, ask by e-mail, so you have a record of the participants' agreement (or, if there's no response, of their failure to object). Provide a link to the version you plan to publicize, and consider making a transcript so participants can quickly scan the content rather than having to listen to all of it.

Know When Not to Use Google Voice

Google Voice is not always the answer. Trying to connect with someone at a crowded conference, you may want to communicate cell to cell for quicker reception of texts, for example. Google Voice is convenient, but a little cumbersome when you're in a hurry, so those "where are you?" calls with close contacts may be better handled directly.

Chapter 18

Ten Online Resources
for Google Voice

Sometimes the obvious thing isn't easy, and sometimes the easy thing isn't obvious.

However, finding ten worthwhile online resources for Google Voice is both easy and, obviously, a good thing for us to provide. Google Voice is fast, changing, and deep; there is always news and always more to know about the parts of Google Voice you thought you were familiar with.

You may want to bookmark all of these resources plus, perhaps, another ten or so for using Google Voice and other time- and money-saving resources on your specific type of cell phone. With that kind of line-up, you'll be well-informed and always learning new things to get the most out of Google Voice and your phones.

Without further ado, here we provide ten must-have online resources for Google Voice. Cleverly, or perhaps cruelly, the tenth one opens the door to dozens more resources that you may wish to keep an eye on as well.

gvDaily.com

Google Voice Daily (gvDaily, for short) is the Google Voice blog edited by one of the authors of this book, Bud Smith. Google Voice Daily is the first regularly published blog devoted exclusively to Google Voice. Its intent is to keep you up to date on news items and announcements for Google Voice, what they mean and how to use them. Google Voice Daily will also include extensions to the book to cover new features that come out after our publication date.

The blog includes a section, "get Google Voice," which is not just an encouragement to actually get a Google Voice phone number and start using it. The section's name is also an encouragement to really understand Google Voice, to "get" it in the sense of understanding it, of grokking it, to use an old science fiction term (from Robert Heinlein's *Stranger in a Strange Land*). You could also say in the sense of taking the red pill, to use a newer one (from *The Matrix*). Now we'll toddle off to dream of a few electric sheep.

Google Voice Online Support

It may seem strange to say in a book about Google Voice, but we found the online support for Google Voice to be quite useful. The clean and attractive interface of Google Voice seems to be matched by an easy-to-use online help system.

However, it's good to be clear about what the online support does. It offers a brief take on what Google Voice does. It doesn't tackle how to do more complex tasks or why things are done the way they are.

We found ourselves having to go to a variety of resources, including extensive experimentation over years of experience and asking questions directly of the Google Voice development team, to get into the underlying details.

The online help also lacks a big picture perspective. You won't find much there about how the top level of Google Voice settings interacts with group-level settings, then with settings per contact, and how all that interacts with the Google Voice Mobile site.

Google Voice Support Site

It's useful to get into Google Voice support by clicking Help from a given screen within the Google Voice Web site, but to get a broader view you may want to go directly to the Google Voice support site. The Web address is:

```
www.google.com/support/voice
```

From here you can search specifically within Google Voice online support and link from one topic to another.

If you're in a hurry and want a quick answer without going into the Google Voice Web site in general or the Google Voice support site in particular, try using regular Google Search, but add the following to the search:

```
site:google.com
```

This restricts your answers to those from the google.com Web site. You find most of the hits come from the Google Voice support site.

Official Google Voice Blog

If you've taken the trouble to start using Google Voice and to acquire this book, you're off to a good start in developing expertise with Google Voice. An important step in maintaining your expertise is to follow the official Google Voice blog. (You can also do this indirectly by using a Google Alert, as described in resource 10 below.)

You can visit the official Google Voice blog via a link from the support site, above, or by visiting:

```
http://googlevoiceblog.blogspot.com/
```

After you arrive at the blog, you can read past entries and use one of the buttons to subscribe to the site. It won't overwhelm you; in the first four months after Google Voice was announced, a very busy time in the product's history, there were only ten entries. All the more reason why you may feel the need to know soon on those rare occasions when a posting actually is made to the blog.

Craig Walker on Twitter

Craig Walker is one of the key founders of GrandCentral, precursor to Google Voice. He's now Group Product Manager for the Real Time Communications group at Google, an area of the company that includes Google Voice.

You may be an active Twitter user or wonder what all the fuss is about. Now you have a(nother?) reason to use it. Craig Walker keeps up an active presence on Twitter as cwalker123; follow him on Twitter to keep up with news and various events around Google Voice, everything from major product announcements to reviews to tech support issues.

YouTube

Google is making increasing use of video to demonstrate and support its products, and Google Voice is very much part of this. Google products are also popular subjects of videos others make. There isn't, unfortunately, an official Google Voice YouTube channel, as there are for some other products. However, you can learn a lot by searching on the term Google Voice in YouTube.

To see all official Google videos, visit:

www.youtube.com/user/google?blend=1&ob=4

Search within the official Google videos area to find all official Google Voice videos.

Lifehacker

Lifehacker is a very good how-to site for a wide variety of tech and non-tech issues. (Of six recent featured articles, five were about technology; the sixth was "Make Reverse-Engineered Kentucky Fried Chicken at Home.") Lifehacker has been very much on top of Google Voice and provides great tips and tricks on how to use it. This site is a great online complement to this book. Visit Lifehacker and look up Google Voice; you're bound to find something interesting.

TechCrunch

TechCrunch is a great source for tech news and views and has been a consistent, "fastest with the mostest" resource for Google Voice. TechCrunch articles also get a lot of comments, some quite interesting and useful.

Visit TechCrunch at:

www.techcrunch.com

GigaOm

Facts and opinions from blogger Om Malik, formerly senior writer at Business 2.0. He covers the Web, broadband access, infrastructure, mobile and voice communications, so Google Voice comes up in his posts a lot. You won't always agree, but your thinking will always be stimulated.

Google Alerts

Just as Google Voice has been called "one number to ring them all," Google Alerts can be one source to get all the updates in the resources listed above and many, many more. Google Alerts cover news, the Web, blogs and more.

To get started, go to the Google Alerts Web site:

www.google.com/alerts

Set up an alert for Google Voice. Ours is set for once a day and keeps us thoroughly up to date on Google Voice.

Chapter 19

Ten Key Google Voice Features for Business

*I*n mid-2009, the city of Los Angeles announced that it was considering using Google Apps for many of its core computing needs.

This announcement represented a watershed in the use of hosted applications in general and Google tools in particular. In the past, organizations could be seen as irresponsible if they adopted a Google-hosted solution, due to concerns about privacy and security.

With Los Angeles' move, an organization could now equally be seen as irresponsible for wasting taxpayer, shareholder, donor or other money on traditional approaches that demand extensive in-house IT resources.

And it's not just money. Managing IT takes up huge amounts of management time and attention. Yet few companies or other organizations are going to gain real competitive advantage or other breakthroughs in carrying out their core missions by delivering basic IT services better than their peer group.

With Los Angeles' move, Google took a big step toward making this an accepted viewpoint. If Los Angeles can get a substantial part of its needs met through Google-based services, few organizations can dismiss such solutions offhand.

Organizations now need to consider Google-based and competing solutions in all areas of data processing and, yes, telecommunications.

Google Voice is a point solution that can work with existing systems, and it offers tremendous savings in cost and greatly increased convenience.

Following are ten advantages of using Google Voice in business that every organization should consider in deciding whether and how to adopt it.

Cheaper Calls

Business can't ignore the reduced cost of calls on Google Voice. It's worth taking a sampling of domestic and international calls and comparing what they actually cost your business with what the costs would have been using Google Voice.

Some related costs are worth paying attention to as well. With a work-supplied Google Voice number, employees will be more likely to make and receive calls when and where needed, rather than avoiding a big cost for the company or an embarrassingly large expense submission. The phone does more of what companies are paying for when they take on the expense of buying and maintaining them.

Free Conference Calls

Many calls would benefit from having another person or two included, but it can be quite difficult and expensive to set up conference calls. Google Voice makes casual conferencing easy and free.

Businesses can look at both the savings on conferencing costs and the business benefits of more conference calls being made because doing so becomes easy and free. This means more collaboration with no additional costs, including not only conferencing costs but also travel costs.

Free Call Recording and Sharing

Better record keeping is important for businesses, and so is greater collaboration. Having the ability to record calls for free improves record-keeping, and the calls can then be shared, improving collaboration.

E-Mail Notifications and Transcripts

Many company employees spend a good deal of time scanning their smartphones and PCs for incoming e-mails and dealing with them, yet dread the voicemail queue that can accumulate after a single meeting, let alone a day away from the office.

Google Voice sends notifications, with attached transcripts and links to the call, by e-mail. This allows e-mail scanning to do double duty, alerting employees to important voice mail messages as well as important e-mail messages. Voice messages get handled more quickly, improving responsiveness to colleagues and customers, yet also more easily, making employees who receive calls more productive.

Free Text Messaging with Records

Google Voice puts the text message Inbox on the computer, integrated with the voicemail Inbox. This improves record keeping and the ability to respond to text messages flexibly, including forwarding them easily to multiple people, and with one eye on relevant e-mails or other information where needed.

Contacts Integration

Google Voice makes it easy to integrate contacts using Google contacts or spreadsheet files. This makes it easier to create and maintain shared lists of contacts within a company, eliminating a major hassle for all employees.

One Number to Ring Them All

Everyone who's ever worked in business has probably had the experience of getting a call on their mobile phone, ignoring it, only to have the same person call second later on their office phone (or vice versa). Persistent callers may go on to try receptionists, secretaries, colleagues, even someone's boss to try to reach them.

Google Voice's "one number to ring them all" feature is not only convenient for recipients; callers only have one number, so know that the person will get their message and respond as fast as they're able.

Variable Greetings

Employees can treat callers better with variable greetings. A greeting can even be used to convey crucial information, such as when the person will become free and be able to respond — again, improving responsiveness while reducing anxiety for all confirmed.

Switchboard Functionality

We've all been in the position of answering the phone quickly because we're waiting for one particular call, and being disappointed — perhaps again and again. The ability of a Google Voice user to put calls where they need to go is a big advantage for business. Personal and business calls can be managed closely — put off when needed, allowed through where they're urgent. The ability to know that a critical call can be allowed through — with the non-critical ones fended off — actually increases people's ability to concentrate on business in the meantime.

Cell Phone Apps and Mobile Site

Companies make big investments in cell phones for employees. Often, much of the purpose is to allow on-the-go e-mail access through the same hardware and connections as phone calls. Google Voice's apps (for BlackBerry and Android) and mobile site (for iPhone and other phones) take this integration to another level, making employees that much more efficient.

Index

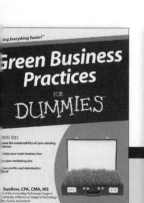

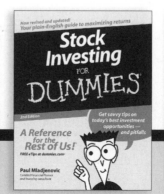

Internet

Blogging For Dummies,
2nd Edition
978-0-470-23017-6

eBay For Dummies,
6th Edition
978-0-470-49741-8

Facebook For Dummies
978-0-470-26273-3

Google Blogger
For Dummies
978-0-470-40742-4

Web Marketing
For Dummies,
2nd Edition
978-0-470-37181-7

WordPress For Dummies,
2nd Edition
978-0-470-40296-2

Language & Foreign Language

French For Dummies
978-0-7645-5193-2

Italian Phrases
For Dummies
978-0-7645-7203-6

Spanish For Dummies
978-0-7645-5194-9

Spanish For Dummies,
Audio Set
978-0-470-09585-0

Macintosh

Mac OS X Snow Leopard
For Dummies
978-0-470-43543-4

Math & Science

Algebra I For Dummies
978-0-7645-5325-7

Biology For Dummies
978-0-7645-5326-4

Calculus For Dummies
978-0-7645-2498-1

Chemistry For Dummies
978-0-7645-5430-8

Microsoft Office

Excel 2007 For Dummies
978-0-470-03737-9

Office 2007 All-in-One
Desk Reference
For Dummies
978-0-471-78279-7

Music

Guitar For Dummies,
2nd Edition
978-0-7645-9904-0

iPod & iTunes
For Dummies,
6th Edition
978-0-470-39062-7

Piano Exercises
For Dummies
978-0-470-38765-8

Parenting & Education

Parenting For Dummies,
2nd Edition
978-0-7645-5418-6

Type 1 Diabetes
For Dummies
978-0-470-17811-9

Pets

Cats For Dummies,
2nd Edition
978-0-7645-5275-5

Dog Training For Dummies,
2nd Edition
978-0-7645-8418-3

Puppies For Dummies,
2nd Edition
978-0-470-03717-1

Religion & Inspiration

The Bible For Dummies
978-0-7645-5296-0

Catholicism For Dummies
978-0-7645-5391-2

Women in the Bible
For Dummies
978-0-7645-8475-6

Self-Help & Relationship

Anger Management
For Dummies
978-0-470-03715-7

Overcoming Anxiety
For Dummies
978-0-7645-5447-6

Sports

Baseball For Dummies,
3rd Edition
978-0-7645-7537-2

Basketball For Dummies,
2nd Edition
978-0-7645-5248-9

Golf For Dummies,
3rd Edition
978-0-471-76871-5

Web Development

Web Design All-in-One
For Dummies
978-0-470-41796-6

Windows Vista

Windows Vista
For Dummies
978-0-471-75421-3